ONE DAY INTERNATIONAL CAREER

To end of 2003–04 season

Source: Cricinfo

W0038111

Name	Mat	I	NO	Runs	HS	Ave	SR	100	50	Ct	St	Team
SR Tendulkar	333	324	31	13134	186*	44.82	86.53	37	66	100	–	IND
Inzamam-ul-Haq	312	292	42	9796	137*	39.18	73.19	10	68	94	–	PAK
M Azharuddin	334	308	54	9378	153*	36.92	73.99	7	58	156	–	IND
SC Ganguly	249	241	20	9309	183	42.12	74.94	22	53	86	–	IND
PA de Silva	308	296	30	9284	145	34.90	81.13	11	64	95	–	SL
ST Jayasuriya	313	305	13	9248	189	31.67	88.86	16	55	103	–	SL
Saeed Anwar	247	244	19	8823	194	39.21	80.66	20	43	42	–	PAK
DL Haynes	238	237	28	8648	152*	41.37	63.09	17	57	59	–	WI
BC Lara	229	224	24	8533	169	42.66	79.17	18	53	97	–	WI
ME Waugh	244	236	20	8500	173	39.35	76.83	18	50	108	–	AUS
SR Waugh	325	288	58	7569	120*	2.90	75.91	3	45	111	–	AUS
A Ranatunga	269	255	47	7456	131*	35.84	77.91	4	49	63	–	SL
Javed Miandad	233	218	41	7381	119*	41.70	66.99	8	50	71	2	PAK
R Dravid	229	210	26	7251	153	39.40	69.18	8	51	134	12	IND
Saleem Malik	283	256	38	7170	102	32.88	76.41	5	47	81	–	PAK
RT Ponting	198	194	25	7154	145	42.33	77.60	15	40	79	–	AUS
JH Kallis	196	187	35	6978	139	45.90	71.18	12	47	83	–	RSA
MG Bevan	232	196	67	6912	108*	53.58	74.16	6	46	69	–	AUS
G Kirsten	185	185	19	6798	188*	40.95	72.04	13	45	61	1	RSA
A Flower	213	208	16	6786	145	35.34	74.60	4	55	141	32	ZIM
IVA Richards	187	167	24	6721	189*	47.00	90.20	11	45	100	–	WI
MS Atapattu	206	203	24	6637	132*	37.07	66.88	10	45	55	–	SL
Ijaz Ahmed	250	232	29	6564	139*	32.33	80.30	10	37	90	–	PAK
GW Flower	219	212	18	6536	142*	33.69	67.54	6	40	86	–	ZIM
AR Border	273	252	39	6524	127*	30.62	71.40	3	39	127	–	AUS

	O	M	R	W	Ave	BBI	4w	5w	SR	Econ
Bowling	1480.3	56	6761	195	34.67	4–33	3	0	45.5	4.56

FIRST-CLASS CAREER

	M	I	NO	Runs	HS	Ave	100	50	Ct	St
Batting & Fielding	356	551	88	24052	216*	51.94	79	97	273	0

	O	M	R	W	Ave	BBI	5	10	SR	Econ
Bowling	2904.4	690	8155	249	32.75	6–51	5	0	69.9	2.80

'ONE WHO WILL'

THE SEARCH FOR
STEVE WAUGH

It had been a long hard tour. A brief press conference for the Sydney members of the touring party was ending when someone said, 'I suppose you blokes will be playing grade on Saturday.' It was meant to be a joke, there was a mutter of dissent, but then a quiet voice said, 'I know one who will.' It was Steve Waugh.

'ONE WHO WILL'

THE SEARCH FOR
STEVE WAUGH

Jack Egan

ALLEN&UNWIN

First published in Australia in 2004

Allen & Unwin
83 Alexander Street
Crows Nest NSW 2065
Australia
Phone: (61 2) 8425 0100
Fax: (61 2) 9906 2218
Email: info@allenandunwin.com
Web: www.allenandunwin.com

National Library of Australia
Cataloguing-in-Publication entry:
Egan, Jack.
One who will: the search for Steve Waugh.

Bibliography.
Includes index.
ISBN 1 74114 386 1.

1. Waugh, Steve, 1965– . 2. Cricket captains—Australia—
Biography. 3. Cricket players—Australia—Biography. I.
Title.

796.358092

Typeset in 11.5/15 Garamond by Midland Typesetters, Maryborough, Victoria
Printed by Griffin Press, Netley, South Australia

10 9 8 7 6 5 4 3 2

CONTENTS

BANKSTOWN

Saturday 27 September 2003

The Friday was hot and still, a September prelude to summer, a perfect day for cricket. Overnight the southerly came through and on Saturday morning it was blustery and cool at Bankstown Oval, but the small crowd—60 or 70—was out of the wind in the main stand. The ground was green and trim, the Stephen and Mark Waugh Pavilion immaculate with its cream and green paint and its matching Dion Bourne Scoreboard, named for the twins' uncle. Dion Bourne, Bev Waugh's brother, played cricket for Bankstown for twenty years and scored a record 9131 runs for the club, most of them in first grade. He captained first grade for seven years, was treasurer of the club for nineteen years and eventually became a State selector. He was known to all as 'Lunch', possibly because of a milk advertisement from the 1960s with the slogan 'Crack a bottle with lunch'.

The Oval has a picket fence, painted cream to match the pavilions, and advertisements are spaced around it for Schweppes, Bankstown City Credit Union, Revesby Workers' Club, Bankstown Sports Club, Toyota, and local solicitors Macree Scully Karras.

The game—a one-dayer to open the Sydney grade season—started at 9.30. I arrived at 9.35 to find Bankstown 1 for 1, the Waugh twins at the crease. Wests' opening bowler was Daniel McLauchlan, said to be as quick as anyone in Sydney grade. His partner Colin Barry is not as quick, but Wests' coach Neil D'Costa says he can bowl to a plan and can move the ball off the seam. 'We weren't going to give them anything on their legs,' D'Costa said, and the plan was to make them go for their shots on the off and hope to get one 'off the edge or through the gate'.

Wests' uniform for one-day games is black pants and a white top with a wide horizontal black stripe. Bankstown wear blue pants with a vertical blue and white striped top with a red Toyota logo on the back.

It's hard to tell the Waugh brothers apart in their helmets, but when they move, the difference is evident. Mark looks relaxed and assured, as ever, middling the ball and at one stage feigning a charge, then, when Barry drops short, caressing it through cover off the back foot. Steve is more purposeful and looks a bit scratchy, but he is patient, content with singles and some sharp running between wickets, and when the loose ball comes along, his shot-making is not lacking in style.

They confer briefly at the end of each over.

Old-timers in pairs dot the picket fence. Lennie Pascoe strolls around the oval in animated discussion; he has put on some weight,

Steve Waugh bowled by Colin Barry for 8. Bankstown v Western Suburbs, Bankstown Oval, September 2003. (*Jack Egan*)

but looks very fit, a little more solid then when in his prime, but no less menacing.

After about half an hour the wind dropped and the sun came out. McLauchlan over-pitched and Steve drove him straight back down the ground with brutal efficiency. He was starting to look settled when he tried to drive at Barry and his off stump was knocked out.

Two for 19 as the world's most experienced cricketer trudged off towards the pavilion bearing his name. A couple of overs later Mark edged a good length ball from McLauchlan and was caught at first slip. Three for 19; surprising, but as an old-timer from Wests said, Steve is going to go through a summer of international cricket and he won't play against fast bowling that's a lot better than he faced today.

What Wests' captain Michael Clarke thought about this would have been interesting. Aged 22, with a shock of blond hair, Clarke is generally thought to be the next big thing in Australian cricket. In his two one-day internationals to date Clarke had made 37 not out against England and 75 not out against the West Indies. With players like him and the talented Simon Katich around, there are some who think that Steve Waugh, who came into the Australian team in 1985 at the age of twenty, would be doing the right thing if he retired and made a place for a younger player.

As I left at about 10.15 to go and look at the house where Stephen and Mark Waugh grew up, ten minutes away in Picnic Point Road, Panania, others were leaving too, but people were still arriving in dribs and drabs.

Three skinny kids with an old bat and ball come through the gate. They stop, look briefly at the game, then at the scoreboard, then one of them says, 'Aw shit.'

2

SCARED AND SHY

Waugh's Test debut

Steve Waugh played in 168 Test matches. His final Test, played in Sydney against India in January 2004, was the 1680th Test match played since the game in Melbourne in March 1877 which is now classified as Test number 1; Waugh had played in exactly 10 per cent of all Tests ever played to the date of his retirement. His last one-day international, played in Perth against South Africa in February 2002, was number 1802. He had played in 325 or 18 per cent of all the ODIs played to that date.

Waugh played his first Test at the Melbourne Cricket Ground, starting on Boxing Day 1985, the second Test of the series against an Indian team which included some of the great names of Indian cricket: Sunil Gavaskar, Mohinder Amarnath, Ravi Shastri, Kapil Dev. He made 13 in 32 minutes with two fours, before being caught by Kapil Dev at point off the young Indian leg spinner Laxman Sivaramakrishnan. In the second innings he scored five runs in half an hour before being bowled by Shastri.

Australia made 262, Greg Matthews not out 100, then India replied with 445, Bruce Reid 4 for 100 from 38 overs, the best of the bowlers, with Gilbert, Matthews and Waugh taking two wickets each. Waugh's first Test wicket was Shastri, caught behind by Wayne Phillips for 49. The Test was drawn with honours fairly even.

The next Test was played in Sydney, India declared at 4 for 600, and Australia (396 and 6 for 119) only just managed to avoid a

Steve Waugh, in his first Test, facing Ravi Shastri. Melbourne, December 1985.

Caught Kapil Dev, bowled Sivaramakrishnan for 13.

Australia v India, second Test, Melbourne Cricket Ground, December 26–30, 1985

Result: Match drawn

AUSTRALIA

+WB Phillips b Yadav	7	(7) c Srikkanth b Yadav	13
DC Boon lbw b Shastri	14	c & b Kapil Dev	19
GR Marsh c Sivaramakrishnan b Yadav	30	(1) c Sivaramakrishnan b Shastri	19
*AR Border c & b Sivaramakrishnan	11	(3) st Kirmani b Yadav	163
DW Hookes b Shastri	42	(4) c Srikkanth b Shastri	0
SR Waugh c Kapil Dev b Sivarama	13	(5) b Shastri	5
GRJ Matthews not out	100	(6) c Azharuddin b Sivarama	16
RJ Bright b Shastri	28	lbw b Kapil Dev	20
CJ McDermott c Kapil Dev b Shastri	1	c & b Shastri	2
BA Reid c Srikkanth b Kapil Dev	1	c Sivaramakrishnan b Yadav	13
DR Gilbert c Kirmani b Yadav	4	not out	10
Extras	11		28
Total	262		308

FoW 22 26 41 90 109 127 193 195 216 262   32 54 54 84 126 161 202 205 231 308

Bowling	O	M	R	W	O	M	R	W
Kapil Dev	23	6	38	1	22	7	53	2
Binny	3	0	11	0				
Shastri	37	13	87	4	47	13	92	4
Yadav	27.5	10	64	3	38.5	15	84	3
Sivarama	13	2	51	2	13	1	43	1
Amarnath					3	0	9	0

INDIA

SM Gavaskar b Gilbert	6	b Reid	8
K Srikkanth lbw b Gilbert	86	c Bright b Reid	38
M Amarnath c Phillips b Reid	45	not out	3
DB Vengsarkar c & b Matthews	75	not out	1
M Azharuddin b Matthews	37		
RJ Shastri c Phillips b Waugh	49		
*N Kapil Dev c Hookes b Reid	55		
RMH Binny c Matthews b Reid	0		
+SMH Kirmani c Phillips b Waugh	35		
L Sivarama c Phillips b Reid	15		
NS Yadav not out	6		
Extras	36		9
Total	445		2 for 59

FoW 15 116 172 246 291 370 372 420 425 445   39 57

Bowling	O	M	R	W	O	M	R	W
McDermott	15	5	52	0	6	1	17	0
Gilbert	22	1	81	2	4	0	9	0
Reid	38.2	11	100	4	8	1	23	2
Bright	31	8	76	0	7	4	5	0
Matthews	31	7	81	2				
Waugh	11	5	36	2				

comprehensive defeat. Waugh's contribution was 8 in the first innings, a duck in the second and 0 for 33 from 7 overs.

It was hard times for Australian cricket, with sixteen players, including John Dyson, Steve Smith, Trevor Hohns, Steve Rixon, Terry Alderman and Carl Rackemann, banned for taking part in the rebel tour to South Africa.

Twenty years old at the time, Waugh himself has said, 'Looking back I probably wasn't prepared . . . at the time I didn't think I was quite ready. I was probably a little bit scared and surprised . . . I would have been a lot shyer than most guys at that time. I found it tough.'

Australian cricket was at a low ebb. Early in the summer the team had lost a series against New Zealand, played in Australia, two Tests to one and in the English summer of 1985 they lost a six-Test Ashes series 3–1. Following the series against India, they played three more Tests in New Zealand, losing one with two Tests drawn. In the second Test, Waugh played his first Test innings of consequence, coming in at 5/74 and partnering Allan Border in a 177-run stand, before being lbw for 74 to Richard Hadlee, who took his 300th wicket during the series.

It was after the third Test of this series, when Bracewell took 6 for 32 and Australia collapsed for 103, that Allan Border publicly criticised the team and talked of quitting. Border, who had played with the Chappells, Lillee and Marsh in the days when Australia was winning, found it hard to communicate with some of the younger players. David Boon (who is generally unstinting in his praise of Allan Border) wrote: 'Some of the blokes in our team found it hard to approach him . . . some of them thought the only way to speak to him was in the bar after the day's play, which was an environment they weren't used to and maybe didn't enjoy'.

There had been an improvement in the financial arrangements for the players, including win bonuses, but as Richie Benaud pointed out, there was no guarantee that the players would be able to collect them. Benaud also noted that New Zealand's success was a result of careful planning with the appointment of Glenn Turner, former New Zealand Test batsman, as assistant manager and cricket manager . . . Turner was an astute cricketer when in the New Zealand team. He has never made any secret of his competitive nature where Australians are concerned, and the New Zealand Cricket Council had to break with tradition in making the appointment. The New Zealanders arrived in Australia to find the local team not exactly in disarray, but certainly not at peace with the world.

The appointment of Bob Simpson as Australian coach before the tour to New Zealand had been an attempt to redress this situation.

Waugh's first five Tests had produced four draws and a loss. He had nine innings for scores of 13, 5, 8, 0, 11, 74, 1, 1 and 0. His bowling was slightly more productive, with one haul of 4 for 56 against New Zealand and overall figures of 7 wickets for 152.

During the series in New Zealand, Richard Hadlee was dismissive of one-day cricket, saying, 'It's a terrible concept and we play it only as a service.'

Unlike a number of top players, Steve Waugh has never been critical of the shorter game, accepting that it was a valid and vital part of the international game, and saying that he enjoyed it.

Perhaps one reason for this is that early in his career, when his performances in Tests were less than had been expected, he had a steady stream of success in one-day internationals. In the summer of 1985–86, when their Test record had been so dismal, the Australians won the three-cornered World Series contest with India and New Zealand. Waugh made several useful contributions with the bat, top-scoring twice, and, importantly, Border found that he could bring him on to bowl in a tight situation and rely on him not to give anything away.

3

MODERN CRICKET

Influence and myth

One of the myths of modern cricket is that the great teams of recent years—Ian Chappell's Australian team in the 1970s, the West Indies sides of the 1980s and Australia again under Mark Taylor and Steve Waugh—brought a new level of professionalism and commitment to the game.

This is not a new idea, however. In fact, it can be said to date back as far as W.G. Grace who, incidentally, was paid £3000 plus expenses to tour Australia with the English team in 1891–92. In *They Made Cricket*, G.D. Martineau wrote 'modern cricket, the infinite art, comprehensible only to a devoted minority, is really the work of "The Champion"'. Born in 1848, Grace played first class cricket from the mid-1860s until 1906.

For the devoted minority of my generation, cricket was rein-vented by the West Indies teams of the 1950s and 1960s. As Jack Fingleton, journalist and Test opening batsman of the 1930s, said, 'the orginal purpose of the game had been perverted by several generations of "total cricket", in the evolution of which my own Australia must certainly accept her full share of responsibility'.

Tests between Australia and England had become wars of attri-tion, culminating in the first Test against England in 1958–59, played in Brisbane, where on a reasonable wicket in fine weather, 61 overs were bowled on the first day, during which England were all out for 134 and Australia made 8 without loss. And it got worse—the second, third and fourth days produced 148 runs, 122 runs and 106 runs respectively and Trevor Bailey took 7 hours and 38 minutes, and 427 balls, to compile 58 in England's second innings.

Into this void of entertainment strode Frank Worrell's West Indies side in 1960–61, and it's another myth that the game they played was born of a carefree outlook on life and a cavalier attitude to cricket.

My favourite cricket book is C.L.R. James's *Beyond a Boundary*, first published in 1963. James was a novelist and social historian who lived much of his life in England and America, but was born in Trinidad and brought up not far from Port of Spain in a house with a view of the local cricket ground where, as he wrote, 'an umpire could have stood at the bedroom window'. If Neville Cardus makes you feel like a spectator at the game, James makes you feel as if you are a participant. Playing for Maple, which James describes as Trinidad's 'club of the brown-skinned middle class' against Shannon, 'the club of the black lower-middle class'—but also the club against which the cricket of all the other clubs was judged and the club of the legendary St Hill brothers—James wrote, 'I played two high-rising balls from Edwin St Hill down in front of me. At the end of the over, without turning his head, the grim-faced Wilton St Hill murmured as he passed, "What you think you will get by playing at those!" Next over I dropped my bat out of the way of a similar ball and was weak enough to steal a glance at him. I was met by a stony stare.'

Wilton St Hill was James's favourite. 'Fires burned in St Hill and you could always see the glow', James wrote. 'As soon as he started to stride to the wicket everyone stopped what he was doing and paid attention.' Tall and slim with 'forearms like whipcord', St Hill 'always had plenty of time. From firm feet he watched the ball until it was within easy reach and only then brought his bat to it with his wrists. He never appeared to be flurried'. But St Hill was not all grace and elegance. 'One afternoon,' James wrote, 'I bowled the first ball of a match which swung from his leg stump past the off. He played forward at it and missed. Full of eagerness and anticipation, I let loose the next as fast as I could, aiming outside the leg stump to swing into him. Out came his left foot, right down the pitch. He seemed to be waiting for hours for the ball to reach, and then he smashed it to the square leg boundary.'

All this took place in the 1920s and St Hill's and James's contemporaries included the legendary Learie Constantine and the 'black Bradman', George Headley. 'No one could appear to play more gaily, more spontaneously, more attractively than Constantine', James wrote, but 'in reality he was a cricketer of concentrated passion, irked during all his big cricket life by the absence of what he found only when he played with Shannon'. Headley made the West Indies' only Test century against Australia in 1930–31 and averaged 60.83 in Tests, third behind Graeme Pollock and Bradman in the all-time averages. When Headley played a shot, James wrote, he hit the ball 'precisely in a certain place. He couldn't think of a stroke without thinking exactly where it was going. Whenever he had scored a century and runs were not urgent, he practised different strokes at the same ball, so as to be sure to command the placing of the ball where there was no fieldsman'.

James also tells us that Headley's 'ideal captain, the man he would have liked to play under', was Douglas Jardine, the architect of the infamous Bodyline, seen by many as the moral low point of the game, because Jardine took it seriously enough to want to win at almost any cost. It was the legacy of this uncompromising attitude that produced the magnificent West Indies cricketers of the 1950s and 1960s, and their intimidating heirs of the 1970s and 1980s.

The incomparable Garfield Sobers was a product of this school. With his creativity and flourish no one looked more cavalier, but Sobers had learned in a hard school. He played his early cricket for the Police Club, in Barbados, and in his biography, *Twenty Years at the Top*, tells the story of playing as a fifteen-year-old boy against one of the stronger clubs, Empire, and being hit in the mouth trying to hook their fast bowler. 'It didn't frighten me,' Sobers said. 'I was ready to start again—and the next bouncer would go out of the ground.' (Sobers also tells of an earlier game when he was asked to play for a country side called Kent, captained by a local builder named Garnett Ashby. Ashby picked him up and took him to the game, on the back of a motorbike. The unofficial patron of the Kent side, a man named Johnny Webster, always encouraged Ashby to bring young players into the club, but expressed surprise that we had brought someone so small. 'You're the one who told me not to judge a book by its cover,' Ashby said. 'Don't take him by his looks.' 'All right,' Webster replied. 'It's only I was looking for someone in long pants.')

Modern Australian cricket was born of encounters with the West Indies in the 1980s, when Steve Waugh began his Test career, and the West Indies attitude of the 1980s can be traced back through the 1960s and beyond. You could argue that modern cricket owes much to the fierce inter-club and inter-island cricket which was played in the West Indies nearly a hundred years ago.

And lest it be thought that the poetry written later at Steve Waugh's urging by the members of his Australian team was something new, here is part of a poem which C.L.R. James wrote in celebration of his hero:

O Wilton St Hill, Trinidadians' pride,
A century and four came from your bat.
And helped to win the victory for your side,
But more than that you did, yes, more than that.

4

A SHOT DUCK

The second tied Test

If cricket was born again in the 1960s through the passion of the players from the West Indies—a re-birth signified by the tied Test played in Brisbane in December 1961—new life was again breathed into the game towards the end of the twentieth century, by a new breed of artists from the sub-continent.

Steve Waugh's sixth Test was the amazing game played in September 1986 in Madras (now Chennai) when, for only the second time in the game's history, a Test match ended with the scores tied.

It was so hot when the Australian team arrived in Madras that Border and Simpson decided to cancel the net practice scheduled for the following day. Border won the toss and chose to bat. In a game marred by disputed decisions and bickering with umpires and between players, Dean Jones's innings of 210, made in almost eight hours, stands out as perhaps the most courageous ever played.

As he approached 200, Jones's physical condition began to deteriorate. Errol Alcott, the Australian team's physiotherapist, said,

It was 38 degrees Celsius, 95 per cent humidity. It was dusty and there was a foul smell coming across the ground from a sewerage stream. I ran out to him because he was starting to cramp up and that's the first sign . . . he couldn't keep the water in, he started to vomit and at lunch he came in absolutely exhausted. We gave him cold baths, cold towels, fanned him, tried to replenish his fluids and he bucked up very well for a while, but by tea he could hardly lift his bat. I think he was 196 at that stage, but I could see he was really a shot duck . . . he urinated all over himself, we had to dress him, change him and he was out there after tea for a short time and got his 210. I had to rush him to hospital and he got three bottles of fluid put back in.

Border was batting with Jones when he started to go downhill. Jones went to him and said he didn't think he could go on, but instead of the sympathy which Jones was expecting, Border said, 'OK, if you can't stick it out I'll get a Queenslander out here'—Greg Ritchie was still to come in.

Boon (122) and Border (106) also made centuries and Australia declared early on the third day at 7 for 574. India replied with 397, Kapil Dev 119 from only 138 balls. At the end of play on the fourth day Australia was 5 for 170, 348 ahead. Border and Simpson discussed the situation and decided to sleep on it. The next morning Border declared. India needed 4 runs an over to win and Kris Srikkanth tore into the Australian bowlers with 39 from 49 balls before he skied Matthews, and Waugh ran from deep mid-off to mid-on to take a well-judged catch. Gavaskar and Amarnath continued briskly and at 2 for 200, with Gavaskar still at the wicket, the declaration looked generous. But when Gavaskar went, caught by Jones at cover off Bright, the tide had begun to turn, and when Kapil Dev top-edged a sweep off Matthews to Bright at square leg, an Australian win looked possible.

The blazing heat and the tension had turned the game into a spiteful affair. Matthews lost his customary cool and traded insults and gestures with Azharuddin and Chandra Pandit; Zoehrer and Chetan Sharma had an ugly exchange; the Australians were openly resentful of some umpiring decisions and Umpire Dotiwalla angrily shook his finger at Allan Border.

Meanwhile Ravi Shastri restored a sense of calm and control to India's batting, but when in the 84th of 87 scheduled overs Ray Bright persuaded Sharma to hit a straightforward catch to McDermott at long-on, and 3 balls later had an appeal for lbw against More approved by umpire Dotiwalla, India need 14 runs from

19 balls, with 2 wickets left. A few balls later, off-spinner Shivlal Yadav charged Matthews and hit him high over mid-on for six.

When Bright began the second last over, 7 runs were needed. Three runs were scored before Yadav tried to sweep, and the ball bounced from his back pad onto the stumps. Maninder Singh survived the last two balls of Bright's over. Matthews started the last over, bowling to Shastri, with India needing 4 runs to win.

Shastri blocked the first ball and edged the second behind square leg, where a slight miss-field by Steve Waugh from a difficult pick-up allowed the batsmen to hurry through for two. He played the third ball to mid wicket and took a single to tie the scores. Border and Matthews spent more than two minutes adjusting the field for Singh, who played a shuffling half-shot to keep the fourth ball at bay.

He repeated the shot, missed the ball and was hit on the pad, the Australians went up and umpire Vikram Raju quickly raised his finger. It was Matthews's fifth wicket in the innings, his tenth for the match. Bob Simpson and the Australian support staff ran onto the field to celebrate, and also to tell them that, because the match had gone way over time, they had to hurry to the airport, where a flight was being held up for them; they had a one-day international to play in Hyderabad two days later.

Allan Border said it was the hardest match he ever played.

In his book, *Cricket Beyond the Bazaar,* Mike Coward wrote that only 29 Australians were there at the end of the game; eighteen cricketers, seven journalists, NSWCA chief executive Bob Radford and three tourists. (Garry Sobers once told me that, although the official attendance at the end of the first tied Test, played in Brisbane in December 1960, was only a few thousand, he had seldom met an Australian who hadn't been there that day.)

Waugh's contribution with the bat was 12 and 2, both not out, with the ball 1 for 44 and 0 for 16. The two remaining matches of the series were tame draws. The one-day series against India was lost 2–3.

5

ATTITUDE

Bob Simpson's contribution

In 1995 when the Australian rugby team, which had won the World Cup in 1991 in such spectacular fashion, failed to defend it, I read that Sean Fitzpatrick, the great All Black hooker and captain, said that he saw the Australians get off a bus when they arrived in Johannesburg in 1995 and, as soon as he saw them, knew they wouldn't win. When asked why, he said, 'Oh, you know, the sunnies, the attitude.'

Sometimes you just know things have changed.

In the past, most of the practice on the morning of a Sydney Test used to be done in the nets behind the Members' Stand. Sometimes a batsman would come out into the main ground for a session of throw-downs against the boundary fence, and usually the fielding side would have a session of ground fielding and catching there before the start of play. When I arrived at the SCG for the Sydney Test in January 1987, climbed to the top of the Noble Stand to try to find a seat, and looked down at the ground, on one side of the oval I saw the English coach hitting high catches to the team gathered 40 or 50 metres away, the same as we used to do at school. On the other side of the ground, the Australians were performing a series of complicated drills involving running, picking up, throwing and backing up. It was noisy and competitive, they seemed to be enjoying it, and so were the crowd nearby.

To see this was to realise that a new element was entering the game. David Boon says Bob Simpson gave structure to their fielding drills, introducing variations, making them competitive—player versus player, one player against Simpson, Simpson versus the team—it made fielding practice interesting and it meant that a lot of fitness work was done during fielding drills.

Boon wrote: 'Simmo's other great strength was his ability to give many players purpose. It would be ridiculous to believe that his methods worked for everybody, but they did for me. He taught me that I should never, ever be satisfied with my performance'.

Although Ian Healy noted that Simpson's practice routines didn't always suit him—Simpson worked on his reflexes, but later Rod Marsh showed Healy it was better to concentrate on finding a rhythm—Healy said:

> Simmo has never received the credit he deserves for his major role in getting the modern Australian team back on track . . . He never gave blokes the easy option, but was always prepared to work with his cricketers to get things right. And like the best players in his teams he was prepared to back his beliefs and judgement, until someone was able to show him there was a better way. There very rarely was.

Boon acknowledges that not everyone got along with Simpson. It is well known that there was no love lost between Bob Simpson and the Chappell brothers, for instance, but according to Boon:

> The fact is that Australia's success was built on a huge quantity of work, and self-belief, and Simpson was the instigator of both . . . He would talk to the players about their attitudes, whether they thought they were becoming satisfied, whether they thought they could improve in this or that area of their game. Of course, he drove everyone mad with it, but that was his job as coach. Simmo was as aware as anyone that playing Test cricket successfully is 90 per cent based on having the correct mental attitude and 10 per cent on natural ability.

Simpson was a great motivator, emphasising the importance of always being able to achieve the maximum, as an individual and as a team: 'Always think you can do better . . . never get complacent'. He said to the Australians: 'We can be the best cricket team in the world', and eventually they were.

Bob Simpson had been coach of NSW since 1984–85 and became coach of Australia before the tour to New Zealand in 1986. His success can be measured by the fact that his methods were eventually adopted by the other State sides, and then internationally.

But success for the Australian team didn't come immediately.

In 1986–87, against a team billed, not for the first time, as the weakest ever to leave England, Australia lost the first Test by 7 wickets. England had appeared weak and divided in the lead-up games, but in Brisbane, Botham scored his first Test century for three years, with 13 fours and four sixes. His 138 from 174 balls was the crucial innings of the match. Waugh used a technique, which was to bring him success through the years, of challenging aggressive batsmen to hook, and Botham eventually holed out to Merv Hughes. De Freitas also succumbed to a short ball and Waugh had Dilley caught by Boon at first slip, giving him 3 for 76 from 21 overs. England totalled 456 and Australia replied with 248 and 282 in the follow-on, leaving England 75 to win, which they did with the loss of two wickets. Waugh made his third duck in Tests, playing a nothing shot at a regulation ball from Dilley for a catch to the 'keeper. In the second innings he made 28 in 54 minutes, with three fours, before coming down the wicket and playing over the top of a well-flighted ball from Emburey.

The second Test was played in Perth, and England put it beyond reach by batting most of the first two days for 592 for 8 wickets declared, with centuries to Broad, Gower and wicket-keeper Jack Richards. Australia's 401 included 125 from Border and 71 off only 111 balls by Steve Waugh, who had gone in as night-watchman at the end of the second day. Brian Freedman, Bankstown president and member of the board of Cricket Australia, told me that Waugh rang his family that night and said, 'This is the most important innings of my life,' or words to that effect. The innings prompted a round of applause from Bill O'Reilly: 'The intriguing power he can deliver to his off side shots from a firmly planted back foot immediately captures one's imagination', O'Reilly wrote in the *Sydney Morning Herald*.

With the Australians 191 behind, Waugh kept them in the match, taking the wickets of Broad, Gatting, Gower, Richards and DeFreitas as England tumbled to 8 for 199 and the game headed for an even draw.

The third Test ended the same way, but Australia looked stronger, batting first and declaring at 5 for 514. Boon made a patient 103 while Waugh continued his good form with 79 not out from 117 balls. The video coverage of the game shows two classic Waugh shots: a cut off the back foot past point from right up on his toes, and a slog-sweep through square leg which made the umpire duck, both off Emburey. A horizontal bat shot from a wide half volley from DeFreitas is smashed to boundary in front of point, and a ball on leg stump from the same bowler is lofted high over mid wicket for another four.

The Australian revival faltered in the Melbourne Boxing Day Test. Border decided to attack the English bowling, but chose the wrong wicket and Botham and Small took 5 wickets each, all but one of them caught, off a series of ill-judged shots. By stumps on the first day they were all out for 141 and England were 1 for 95 in reply. England went on to 349 and on the third day Australia collapsed again, to lose by an innings and 14 runs.

So England kept the Ashes, but Border's team had some consolation in Sydney. Batting first again, they made 343, then held England to 275 as off-spinner Peter Taylor, in his seventh first class game, took 6 for 78. It looked as if Australia would find another way to lose when they stumbled to 7 for 145, but Waugh (73) and Peter Taylor (42) put on 98 for the eighth wicket. Australia's total was 251 and when Peter Sleep, 5 for 72 from 35 overs, bowled John Emburey for 22 to end England's second innings at 264, Australia ended a losing streak that had lasted for fifteen Tests, Australia's longest losing sequence.

Steve Waugh, in his thirteenth Test, had at last played in a winning Test side.

His form in the short game continued in two series played early in 1987. Australia lost all three matches in a four-team challenge series played in Perth early in the New Year, but got to the finals of the World Series Cup after losing two of four to the West Indies and only one of four against England. However, England turned the tables in the final series. In the first final they dismissed Australia for 171 in 44 overs, and passed that score with 6 wickets and 14 overs to spare. In the second final, England made only 187, but Australia never got on top of some tight bowling from Dilley, DeFreitas, Botham and Emburey and could only manage 179 for the loss of 8 wickets.

Waugh, with an 83 not out and 49 not out during the series and consistent performances with the ball, won two man-of-the-match awards and was a strong contender for the man-of-the-preliminary-series award, eventually won by Viv Richards.

6

JUST DO IT

The 1987 World Cup

In the English summer of 1987, Waugh played with Nelson in the Lancashire League and also had four games with Somerset, standing in for Martin Crowe who had commitments for New Zealand in Sri Lanka. Waugh's time with Lancashire was partly spoiled by the weather, but he made some friends there, and in half a dozen innings with Somerset he attracted attention with two powerful centuries against strong fast bowling. Waugh rates a hundred he made against Sylvester Clarke in 1987 as one of his best. Clarke went after him on a green-top at The Oval, but got clobbered, Waugh hitting 15 fours in making 111 from 185 balls. Another hundred at Bristol, facing an attack including Courtney Walsh, attracted attention. He averaged 113.33 for his limited season with Somerset, who were keen to sign him again for the following year.

In October 1987 he was back in India for the World Cup. Having won only seven of nineteen one-day international matches over the past twelve months, and having lost the last five in succession, Australia was not among the fancied sides. England had beaten them the previous summer on their home turf, the West Indies had been in all three finals to date, winning two of them, and India had won the previous final, beating the West Indies at Lord's in 1983.

Pretty much written off in the press, Australia was generally quoted at about 20/1 by the bookies. Channel 9 did not consider there was enough interest to make it worth covering, but Allan

Border said team spirit was on a rise and the team had 'just started to click'.

Australia played India in their first game, in Madras. Boon and Marsh opened with a stand of 110 and Geoff Marsh, with a personal score of 110 from 141 balls, laid the foundation for a solid 270 from 50 overs. Then the Indian top order fired: Gavaskar made 37 from 32 balls, Srikkanth 70 from 83, and Sidhu 73 from 79 balls, including five sixes. India passed 200 with only two wickets down and 14 overs left, before McDermott brought them back to earth by taking the wickets of Sidhu, Vengsarker, Azharuddin and Shastri before they had reached 250. Still, India needed only 15 runs with 4 overs left and 4 wickets in hand. Simon O'Donnell claimed Kapil Dev cheaply soon after, there were two run outs, and 6 runs were needed when Steve Waugh began the final over. Maninder Singh, who had fallen lbw to Greg Matthews to end the tied Test, was facing and worked two runs behind square leg and another two through the gully, bringing India to within one run of another tie, before Waugh knocked back his off stump.

The Australians were comprehensively beaten in a return match with India, played in Delhi, but that was the only match they lost in the qualifying rounds. They had a close call against New Zealand in a match reduced to 30 overs, when Waugh again started the last over, with New Zealand needing only 7 to win with 4 wickets in hand, Martin Crowe on strike. Waugh had Crowe caught by Geoff Marsh in the deep off the first ball, and bowled Ian Smith with the second. Australia won by 3 runs.

After the game Border said, 'The rest of us have had legs of jelly but he seems to just go ahead and do it.'

Despite their performances, Australia were still the underdogs in the semi-final, played against Pakistan in Lahore. Australia batted first and their final over began with Australia 8 for 249, Waugh (14) facing Saleem Jaffer, left arm medium-fast. First ball, good length on off stump; 6 over long-on. Second ball, a foot outside off stump; lofted 4 over mid wicket. Third ball, full toss at knees; hurried 2 past bowler to long-on. Fourth ball, waist-high full toss; 2 through cover. The last ball of the over was a good length ball on leg stump which

Waugh flicked off his toes through mid wicket for 4; 18 off the over, Waugh 32 not out off 28 balls, Australia's total, 267.

Javed Miandad made 70 and Imran Khan 58, but man-of-the-match Craig McDermott, with 5 for 44 from his 10 overs, kept Pakistan under the required rate and they were all out for 249 with an over unused.

The final was played against England in Calcutta before a crowd of 70 000, barracking for Australia. Boon (75 from 125 balls) and Veletta (45 not out from 31) were again the backbone of Australia's innings, but 253 was not necessarily enough; England had reached 2 for 135 at a good pace before Gatting played his now-famous reverse sweep off Border, to be caught by Dyer. McDermott (51 from 10) and Reid (43 from 10) were relatively expensive, but O'Donnell (35 from 10) bowled a tight spell and when Waugh was brought back on the equation was 38 runs to win from 24 balls, with 5 wickets in hand. Alan Lamb, facing Waugh, had scored 44 off 54 balls and, with his eye in, was quite capable of getting half of them in one over.

Waugh, slim and serious—coolly expressionless—starts his stuttering run leaning forward, about a dozen paces, lengthening stride and straightening as he nears the crease, delivering with a quick body action and a pronounced whip. The first ball is short outside leg stump, but keeps low and seems to get on Lamb quickly. It ties him up; he is hit on the leg and scampers for a single. Second ball, shortish, straight, Emburey pulls to mid wicket for 1. Third ball is on a good length, keeps a bit low and cuts nicely off the seam; Lamb tries an ugly short-armed pull but, perhaps again deceived by the pace and low bounce, loses his off stump. End of game . . . except that the incoming batsman is Phil DeFreitas, also a big hitter. He edges for 2, is almost bowled by

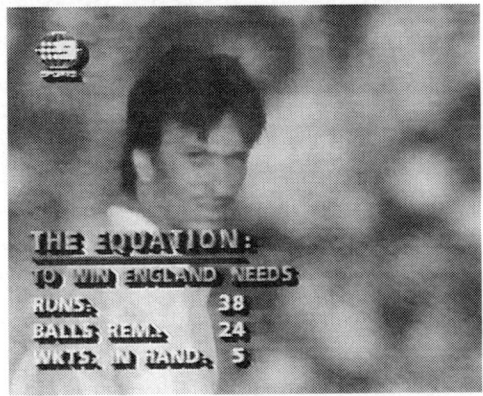

The equation—1987 World Cup. (Board of Control for Cricket in India/TWI)

a slower yorker which just misses off stump, then takes 15 off the next over, bowled by McDermott, including two fours and a six.

The first ball of Steve Waugh's next over, De Freitas backs away and misses; the ball bounces over leg stump and De Freitas and Waugh share a smile. Second ball, there is an appeal for a catch down the leg side; it looks like an inside edge and Dyer indicates a clean catch, but umpire Gupta says not out. De Freitas shakes his head and gestures open-handed—he's innocent, and if he isn't, with the World Cup in the balance, who is going to walk? Ten balls left, 19 runs needed. The next ball is a fullish length and De Freitas tries to lever it into the air but only gets a thick outside edge on it and skies a straightforward catch to Bruce Reid at deep mid-off, fifteen metres in from the boundary rope—if anything is straightforward when the fate of the World Cup depends on it. Nineteen needed off 9 balls now, with Gladstone Small and Neil Foster at the wicket. Game over. Australia wins by 7 runs. Man-of-the-match was David Boon.

In an interview with Greg Baum in the Melbourne *Age*, Allan Border said of Waugh: 'You would never, ever question his nerve. He's one of those guys, you give him the ball in the last over of a one-day game and he backs himself. He's the sort of bloke that you know he's not going to freeze. If he gets hit, it's because the bloke's played a good shot.' Waugh himself said, 'I find that's the best part of one-day cricket. The rest of the game is pretty predictable, but the last 10 overs can go either way. It's a part of the game where it doesn't go to the script every time. It can change, depending on what you do.'

Mike Coward wrote:

At the age of 22 he is laconic, dry, friendly and his country's finest young cricketer . . . Perhaps because he has always lived with the expectation of so many, Waugh prefers to remain in the background. He is more interested in being a cricketer of character, rather than one of the game's characters. He is hard-working, honest, loyal, popular and competitive; a dinkum cricketer.

Bill O'Reilly described Waugh as one of the finest all-rounders in the world. At a press conference when they returned from the 1987 World Cup, Simpson agreed with O'Reilly, but also said, 'It is interesting that at the start of the season Bill suggested that he should give up bowling.'

Looking at tapes of Waugh's bowling, it is obvious that he has an effective slower ball, or perhaps variety of slower balls would be more correct. But much of his effectiveness is enhanced by his ability to cramp batsmen and stop them scoring with a line on middle-and-leg just short of a length, perhaps skidding the ball through. Then he will tempt a batsman to lash out and play a rash shot, looking for a catch from a top-edged bouncer, or an lbw from a slower ball that turns into a yorker.

Mark Waugh's career was also starting to blossom. He had first been selected for NSW in 1985 but hadn't been able to hold his place. A niggling back injury and a dislocated thumb had set him back, although he continued to make runs for Bankstown. But in a 1987–88 pre-season tour to Zimbabwe he was NSW's most successful batsman, and this, with good early-season form for Bankstown and 150 for NSW in a Second XI game against Victoria, saw him selected for the New South Wales Sheffield Shield team. In his third Shield game of the season, against Tasmania in Devonport, he scored his first Shield century. His second was to follow a couple of weeks later against Victoria at the SCG, when Steve (170) and Mark made centuries in the same match. Mark finished the season with 833 first class runs at 64.07 and was now pressing for a place in the Test side.

Late in the season, in a game that looms large in the Bankstown legend, Mark joined Steve at nine minutes to five on the first day of a scheduled two-day game against Balmain, at Balmain Oval. Bankstown were 2 for 45 in reply to Balmain's 161. By stumps they had taken the score to 2 for 184, adding 139 in 69 minutes. Brian Freedman told me that there was no play the following week due to rain, so Bankstown won the match, which got them into the final.

The Waugh twins could only play in the first day of the final—they played on the Saturday but had the final of the McDonald's Cup (the interstate limited overs competition) on the Sunday and were replaced at Bankstown. NSW won the McDonald's Cup (Mark 38, Steve 23 and 2 for 37) and they were able to join the celebrations at Bankstown Oval later in the night, after Bankstown won the final of the Sydney grade competition.

Meanwhile Australia's fortunes on the cricket field had continued to improve. They won a three-Test home series against New Zealand 1–0 and then had a virtual clean sweep of the triangular World Series Cup events with New Zealand and Sri Lanka, losing only one game in eight preliminaries and winning the first and second finals. Steve Waugh performed solidly in the Tests and was man-of-the-preliminary-series in the ODIs. He didn't need to bat in the WSC final series.

A lacklustre drawn Bicentennial Test against England at the SCG and an innings win in a one-off Test against Sri Lanka in Perth rounded out the international season. Steve Waugh took 4 for 33 against the Sri Lankans, including Aravinda da Silva lbw for 6 and Arjuna Ranatunga—plump and unfit-looking even then—caught and bowled off a full toss for 55.

In the 1988 English summer, Waugh was playing League cricket in Birmingham when he got the call from Somerset. Martin Crowe had hurt his back; could Steve take his place? Waugh said, 'I was expecting a couple of days off, I was just at home when I got a call saying Martin [couldn't play] so I was called down to play at Southhampton which was a couple of hours away, drove down there and went in after lunch.'

He arrived at Southhampton to find Somerset 4/64 against Hampshire, went in when the fifth wicket fell and made 115 not out in a total of 308. In 15 matches for Somerset he scored 1314, averaging 73.00, with six centuries—five of them not out—and was voted one of Wisden's five cricketers of the year. One particular innings, 161 from 172 balls against Kent, which took him past 1000 runs for the season, was said by those who saw it to be a most brilliant exhibition of batting. A press report said that those who had seen Waugh bat for Somerset in 1988 regarded the fact that he hadn't yet scored a Test hundred as 'one of the mysteries of the universe'.

Waugh was the same understated individual then that he is now. In an interview at the time he said:

> Maybe there was a bit more pressure on me . . . there's probably a bit more responsibility knowing I'm the overseas player and have to score runs whereas in Australia you've got Border and a couple of other guys who you know are going to get runs and you can rely on them to get runs all the time, so maybe I haven't been . . . quite as single-minded about scoring runs as I have been over here.

Like the man he replaced, Waugh had problems with his back during the season and did very little bowling. Somerset captain Peter Roebuck said:

> I think he's been able with Somerset to release his true talents, which lie with his batting . . . Australia had a great shortage of all-rounders the last few years and therefore Stephen . . . has become a number 6 batsman, late order hitter in one-day cricket. We've used him very much as our dominant, our main batsman in the same way as other teams have got Hick or Allan Border . . . he has batted to their quality.

Steve Waugh, interviewed while playing with Somerset in 1988.

Roebuck says Waugh played his best cricket in England. The backfoot slash with which he scores so many runs is less risky when the ball does not rise so sharply.

He was also a well-respected member of the Somerset team: 'He didn't say much', according to Peter Roebuck, 'but when he spoke, people listened'. Though full of admiration, if Roebuck had a criticism at the time it was that Waugh didn't work hard enough on his technique. Roebuck felt he needed to work out how he was getting out and do something about it.

7

DOWN IN THE DUMPS

Pakistan 1988

In the first Test of the 1988 series against Pakistan, after Pakistan had made 469, with Allan Border out for 4 and Australia 4 for 48, Steve Waugh went in to face the Pakistan spin attack on a wicket that was starting to turn quite sharply. He faced eight balls without scoring before playing back to a ball from Iqbal Qasim which hit him in front but was probably going to miss leg stump. The appeal for lbw was allowed.

This seems to have been the decision which tipped the balance in the Australian camp from a normal level of dissent to an over-the-top response alleging incompetence and bias by the umpires. It had been building for some time, beginning with several close decisions in favour of Pakistan batsmen.

After two days in the field, when perhaps a dozen serious appeals for lbw had been turned down, the Australians were tired and cranky. When Jones and Waugh were given out lbw before Australia had scored 60 runs, Colin Egar, the Australian manager, visited the umpires' room and loudly berated umpires Khizer Hayat and Mahboob Shah. Egar and Bob Simpson then called a press conference at which Egar said, 'The coach and I cannot take any more of it and have taken the decision to let the outside world know we are battling against great odds.'

It didn't take long for the incident to turn ugly, with players talking seriously of abandoning the tour and shunning journalists

33

who did not support their view, the ACB trying to pacify the Board of Cricket Control for Pakistan, and umpire Mahboob Shah, who had been the subject of most of the criticism, lodging a complaint against Egar.

Waugh's lbw decision was the one that brought the most criticism, and when he was given out stumped in the second innings, also off Iqbal Qasim, the allegations were repeated.

In an interview at the time with Ian Chappell, Bob Simpson said, 'I thought Stephen was hardly done by in both innings.' But looking at the video coverage, they don't look like such bad decisions. Iqbal Qasim is a left-armer and the ball that dismissed Waugh was delivered from round the wicket, but Waugh was well back in the crease and it hit him right in front. After many replays it looks a dubious, but not terrible decision. Ian Chappell said, 'I felt the lbw was a decision that could have gone either way, not one that you could start an international incident over.' The video of the stumping is front on, so harder to assess. Waugh comes two paces down the pitch and is comprehensively beaten by a ball that turned sharply. Salim Yousuf takes the ball wide of the off stump and sweeps the bails off as Waugh stabs his bat back inside the crease. Although it is not conclusive, again it does not look like a really bad decision.

Waugh had probably done himself no favours with the umpires when he was bowling during Pakistan's innings. Video coverage shows an appeal against Javed from a short ball that pitched outside off and cut back sharply. It hit Javed, standing on the crease, on the front leg. If given out it would certainly have been a dubious decision, but Waugh appeals loudly, and when he gets no response takes a step towards the umpire with his hands still raised, in an attitude of aggrieved disbelief.

It's also relevant that Waugh had a reputation with umpires in Australia as a batsman who was 'always reluctant to leave the crease'. Amongst themselves, the umpires used to pick their own team of players who never thought they were out, starting with the

openers, through the middle
order and down to the tail, with
a 'keeper and a captain. They
selected a team of bowlers too,
who thought that every appeal
turned down was an injustice.
Steve Waugh was usually captain of the batting team, sometimes captain of both sides.

A few years after the Pakistan
tour, Mike Coward, writing in
the *Sydney Morning Herald*, was
critical of Waugh's attitude,
reflecting the thoughts of many who otherwise admired his cricket:
'Just when will Stephen Waugh lighten up?' Coward asked.

**An exhortation from the SCG crowd,
third Test v West Indies, 1992–93.
(Cricket Australia/Channel 9)**

> He presents an unhappy and unsmiling soul. And this is such a pity,
> for in so many ways he is a very special cricket person . . . unfortu-
> nately he boils over at times and it is not a pretty sight. Because he is
> so proud, so single-minded, so intense, so committed, so ordered,
> so prepared, so poised, he does not believe he is ever out—save,
> perhaps, when he has been bowled—or that any of his appeals when
> he is bowling should be refused. This trait has irritated his contem-
> poraries and critics and, to his cost one fancies, alienated umpires.
> It is not too late for Waugh to rid himself of the chip he so need-
> lessly carries on his broad and able shoulders.

Peter Roebuck, some years later, put the same thought more
succinctly and rather more gently when he described Steve Waugh
as often 'looking like the bloke whose lawnmower has broken
down'.

Which is not to say that there weren't some bad decisions against
the Australians in Pakistan in 1988. Australia lost 46 wickets during
the series, 12 of them lbw; Pakistan lost 47 wickets, of which 7 were
lbw. There were other disputed decisions, including a number of
bat/pads. There was then a sense of inevitability about results in
Pakistan: Allan Border said after the tour, 'I could have written

down the scenario before I got here, exactly what was going to happen.' After the first Test was lost on an under-prepared pitch, Border said, 'The next two tests will be played on bland pitches and will be drawn. It's the same old story in Pakistan.'

And that's how it happened. In reply to Pakistan's 469, Australia made 165 in the first innings of the first Test and collapsed again in the second innings for 116, only Ian Healy, batting at number 8, making more than 20. The second Test was drawn in Pakistan's favour; needing 374 to win in the fourth innings, Australia was 3 for 67. Waugh made 1 and 19 and had match bowling figures of 1 for 80.

However, they lifted their game significantly in the third and final Test. Australia batted first, making 340, Pakistan replied with 233, then Border declared at 3 for 161, leaving Pakistan to score 268 on a difficult wicket. Pakistan were lucky to avoid defeat, struggling to 8 for 153.

Waugh's contribution of 59 in the first innings of the third Test was his best innings of the tour. But with scores of 0, 13, 1, 19, 59, two wickets for the series and, most uncharacteristically, several dropped catches, it had been an unhappy time for Waugh, and he let it get to him.

Writing in the Melbourne *Herald* after the second Test, Rod Nicholson said:

> Desperately out of form all-rounder Steve Waugh will endure another Test in this land he loathes—simply by default. After a horrendous tour of dubious decisions, demoralising scores and psychological anguish, he will almost certainly still be in the third Test line-up against Pakistan at Lahore on Friday. But this must be his last chance. Waugh does not deserve to be in the team. He is mentally down in the dumps and his batting, bowling and fielding are completely lacking in confidence. Waugh knows it—and so do his team-mates and opposition.

The Australian press made things more difficult, making out that the cricketers were poor losers and, led by Mike Munro, knocking on doors trying to get team members to criticise each other. When he got home after the tour, Waugh was upset and angry when he saw the file that his then girlfriend Lynnette Doughty had kept of the coverage of the tour. But he himself said, 'I got depressed and let myself down in every way. I like to think it wouldn't happen again.'

An icy exchange in an interview of Bob Simpson by Ian Chappell is a reminder of the atmosphere on tour:

> **Chappell:** Bobby, now that the players have cooled down a bit, do you think they're sorry they talked of quitting the tour?
>
> **Simpson:** I don't think in any way, Ian. I believe, and it seems to have been proved over here even, with stories in the paper saying what really is going on in this country, that the stand we've taken has been long overdue. I think we've had a situation developing in Pakistan where teams have gone home, complained bitterly, but none of those complaints have gone to the ICC via the various bodies. Colin Egar and I, in taking the decision we did, realise of course the ramifications, but believe that in the interests of not only this team but of world cricket, something should be said and said very clearly.
>
> **Chappell:** Do you think quitting a tour is the right way to make that statement?
>
> **Simpson:** I don't think we were ever going to quit, Ian, and I'm surprised that you of all people would even suggest an Australian team would do that. As far as I was concerned there was never any chance that the tour would not go on.

The exchange between Simpson and Chappell shows how the tour emphasised a problem that had existed for some time and had to be sorted out. Less than a year earlier, in a Pakistan–England Test at Faisalabad, England captain Mike Gatting and umpire Shakoor Rana exchanged sharp words and Rana refused to start play on the third day unless Gatting apologised. Reluctantly, he did, but not before a day's play had been lost.

Echoing Simpson's comments, Egar released a public statement:

Other visiting teams have drawn attention to pitches and umpiring decisions which are clearly unsatisfactory and contrary to the spirit of the game. The situation is unacceptable and damaging to the reputation of international cricket, yet nothing seems to be done. We appeal to the Pakistan Board and the International Cricket Conference to take a long and honest look at the situation confronting visiting teams, for the sake of their own reputations as well as that of the players whose careers are put at risk.

After the tour, Allan Border summed it up with his usual informed directness: 'If Pakistan is to continue to want to play at an international level, then a lot of things will have to change there'. And of course they have.

September and October are the hottest months of the year in Pakistan, with temperatures regularly in the mid-30s and higher. The heat, and the fact that it is hard to prepare good wickets so soon after the monsoon, mean that it is not the best time to have a Test series there. However, the Australian Cricket Board's contractual arrangements with PBL Marketing required that Australia had to play a home series during the Australian summer, so the Australians had to go to Pakistan in the off-season.

Imran Khan, 'the Lion of Lahore', Pakistan's most influential cricketer, felt so strongly about the issue that he refused to play in the 1988 series against Australia, which was unfortunate, because Imran, who had played a season with NSW in 1984–85, helping them to win the Sheffield Shield, had great respect from the Australians, and his presence and influence might have prevented some of the problems on what was one of the unhappiest tours undertaken by the Australian cricket team.

As it was, Imran was critical of the Australians. In a foreword to Mike Coward's book, *Cricket Beyond the Bazaar*, he wrote:

For me, the disappointing aspect of the Australian attitude to Pakistan has been their inability to accept the country as it is—a third world country with its own culture . . . I feel they have an attitude problem. Instead of looking for wine, women and Western culture they should consider their visit an opportunity to explore the history and culture of a country quite different from their own.

8

COUNTING BOUNCERS

Marshall, Ambrose, Walsh and Patterson

In the three-Test 1988 series in Pakistan, Steve Waugh made 92 runs at 18.40 and took 2 wickets for 108. After 20 Tests he had made 768 runs at an average of 27.43 and taken 30 wickets at 36.70. Allan Border was quoted as saying: 'It would be nice to have him playing well because he's got so much talent, but at the moment he's under a bit of pressure'.

Waugh still had some doubts about whether he was good enough for Test cricket; Bob Simpson's encouragement was important to him at this stage of his career, assuring him that he had the ability and that what he had to do was learn how to make the most of it. In hindsight, the tough time Waugh had in Pakistan is the sort of experience that, if you survive it, stands you in good stead throughout a career. It's like choking at golf—all the great golfers have done it, and the next time the pressure is on, you've been there before and it's that much easier.

The Pakistan experience hardened Steve Waugh. He had decided that he wanted to make the most of his opportunity in cricket and that to do this he would have to give it absolutely 100 per cent. At the start of the 1988–89 series, Waugh said, 'I've been very lucky that the selectors have helped me a lot because there were times when they could have said I wasn't going well enough and dropped me. But they stuck by me and I'm grateful for that. Right now I'm still feeling confident. I'm hitting the ball pretty well and I hope a hundred is just around the corner.'

He was soon back in the runs. In the opening Sheffield Shield game of the season, against Queensland in Brisbane, with Australian selector John Benaud watching, Craig McDermott bowled Mark Taylor for 2 and had Steve Smith caught in the gully for 0. Maguire dismissed Dyson for 5 and Tazelaar had Mark Waugh caught by Healy for 0. Then, with NSW 4 for 29, Steve Waugh and Greg Matthews put on 195, Waugh batting 272 minutes for his 118, with 14 fours.

There was more pain to follow for the Australian XI. The West Indies toured in the summer of 1988–89, with one of the great teams of modern cricket. If their batting was strong—Greenidge, Haynes, Richardson, Hooper, Richards, Logie, Dujon—their bowling was awesome—Marshall, Ambrose, Walsh, Patterson.

In Brisbane, Australia batted first and made only 167. The West Indies passed them with only three wickets down, but were restricted to 394, McDermott and May taking 3 wickets each and Waugh 2 for 61 from 18 overs. Waugh's wickets were Desmond Haynes and Carl Hooper and there was a good deal of comment on his treatment of Viv Richards. Bill O'Reilly wrote:

> The most significant incident of the Brisbane Test, in which the Australians played like a pack of half-baked apprentices, was the salutation young Steve Waugh served up, in the form of three successive bouncers, to visiting captain Viv Richards . . . I took it immediately as an uncompromising message to the opposing skipper that Waugh was sick to death of the bouncer policy that the West Indies have for so long adopted as their standard method of attack. Didn't you? And I nodded my head and murmured to myself, 'Good on you Steve, I agree with you entirely.'

Waugh's defiance continued with the bat. Dropped at 18, a straightforward chance to Greenidge at second slip off Marshall, he went on to top score in the second innings, making 90 in 250 minutes, from 167 balls. He showed the usual strength on the off side and played some adventurous cuts over the slips and gully. He also took several hits on the body and, although he played and missed a number of times, seemed to be about to record his first Test hundred when he tried to slash a widish ball from Marshall through point, only to be caught by Haynes.

West Indies won by 9 wickets, and Australia was on the receiving end again in Perth, where West Indies won by 169. The West Indies continued their ferocious attack, bowling at the batsman most of the time—Geoff Lawson's jaw was broken by a short ball from Ambrose—but Australia showed a lot of fight in their first innings, Graeme Wood making 111 in four hours and Waugh (91) again getting close to a century. Man-of-the-match honours went to Merv Hughes, who took 5 for 130 from 36 overs in the first innings and 8 for 87 from 37 overs in the second, but the difference between the teams in Perth was an innings of 146 from 150 balls by Viv Richards, who threw the bat at everything within reach.

In Melbourne, on a wicket described as 'sub-standard', West Indies made only 280, Australia replied with 242, then Richie Richardson, with 122 scored in six and a half hours, guided the West Indies to 9 for 361, leaving Australia with 400 to win. Steve Waugh, after taking 3 wickets for 77 in the West Indies' first innings, took 5 for 92 in the second, and managed, with Merv Hughes, to get up the nose of Patrick Patterson, bouncing him and sledging him until, at one stage, with Waugh talking to him from square leg all the way through Merv Hughes's run to the wicket, Patterson pulled away and glared at the Australians. After the day's play he appeared in the Australian dressing room, telling them that he would 'sort it out' on the field the next day.

This was perhaps one of those occasions when sledging was counter-productive: Patterson took 5 for 39 from 15 overs and the Australians, needing 400, succumbed for 114. Looking at the video coverage, the Australians appear shocked at the ferocity of the attack. Typically, Waugh was dismissed by a ball from Ambrose delivered from wide of the crease, short and straight at the body, which he fended to third slip. Any batsman who stayed at the crease for any length of time was injured. Border and Peter Taylor had bruises on their arms, bodies and fingers, Waugh and Ian Healy had crushed fingers and Waugh also had a cut on his jaw.

In *Hands and Heals*, Ian Healy wrote: 'We'd all had a gutful of getting beaten and getting beaten up . . . we'd spent much of the Test counting the bouncers and wondering why the umpires didn't find them intimidatory'.

The series was lost and the slow Sydney wicket was more to the Australians' liking. It was Mark Taylor's first Test and Border's 101st. The Australian captain took 7 for 46 from 26 overs of his unpretentious left arm orthodox spin bowling, and West Indies were all out for 224. Australia replied with 401 (Boon 149, Border 75, Waugh 55 not out) and, after West Indies made 256 in their second innings (Border 4 for 50), Australia reached the 80 runs needed for victory with the loss of 3 wickets.

On the placid Adelaide wicket, Dean Jones made his second Test double century in Australia's total of 515, but by the time the West Indies had replied with 369 (Mike Whitney 7 for 89 from 30 overs) it was fairly obvious it was going to be a draw.

In the Test series against the West Indies, with 331 runs at 41.38, Waugh was third in the averages, behind Dean Jones and David Boon. His overall bowling figures were not impressive, but in the third Test he took 3 for 77 and 5 for 92. Dick Tucker in Sydney's *Daily Telegraph* wrote: 'The Steve Waugh knockers have suddenly disappeared. The talented Test all-rounder has silenced them with a brand of batting courage and aggression that has been outstanding in a generally depressing summer for Australian batsmen'.

Waugh said, 'I have become a lot tougher since Pakistan. I read the reports while I was over there and they weren't totally correct, but I expected that: players are built up and then chopped down by the media—it happens all the time. The Pakistani experience has hardened me. At the start of the season I was itching to prove my detractors wrong . . . I was just so determined. I approached every game positively and gave 100 per cent.'

Pakistan joined the West Indies and Australia for the triangular series. Away from home, Pakistan were outclassed but, against the odds, the Australians gave as good as they got against the West Indies.

The first game of the series was against Pakistan in Adelaide and was Mark Waugh's first one-day international. The twins did not have a lot to do; Steve took 1 for 27 as Pakistan were all out 177 from 45.4 overs, then Australia made the runs with the loss of only one wicket. The next game was in Sydney and, chasing 220, Steve made 40 and Mark, 18. According to press reports, Mark ran out both his brother Steve and Allan Border, although this is not mentioned in Mark's biography—perhaps, as is often the case with run outs, the fault was not all his. With Australia on 219, needing 1 to tie, 2 to win, Craig McDermott hit a full toss from Ambrose—the last ball of the innings—straight to Viv Richards at mid wicket.

Steve suffered a groin strain during this game, and while travelling to Cronulla for treatment from team physiotherapist Errol Alcott, was involved in a car accident which shook him up and gave him a stiff neck, although no serious injuries. There was some doubt about his fitness, due mainly to the groin strain, but Alcott's treatment, which included wearing the bottom part of a wetsuit for support and warmth, kept him in the series.

Successive losses to the West Indies and Pakistan followed, then four straight wins got Australia into the final series. The first of these wins was in Melbourne where Steve's contribution of 34, 0 for 36 from 10 overs and a catch at a critical stage, won him the man-of-the-match award. West Indies had been 5 for 189, chasing 226, with Viv Richards and Roger Harper hitting out, when Harper hit McDermott very high, straight back over his head. Waugh ran back about 25 metres from mid-off, watching the ball over his shoulder, with the sightscreen looming up in front of him and Merv Hughes (fielding as a substitute) bearing down on his left. He took the ball high, in both hands, then managed to swerve to his left to avoid the sightscreen, if not the waiting arms of Merv Hughes. It was described as one of the most difficult catches ever taken. A Dunlop advertisement for cricket boots appeared soon after, asking 'How did Stephen Waugh cover 40 metres to take the catch of the season?'

Australia won the first final. On the difficult Melbourne wicket, West Indies fell 2 runs short of Australia's target of 204. In Sydney, the West Indies top order all got runs and Australia fell 92 runs short

How did Stephen Waugh cover 40 metres to take the catch of the season?

" "

DUNLOP

of a target of 278. The third final, in front of a crowd of 73 575, was ruined by rain; although Australia's innings was reduced to 38 overs, an unbeaten 93 from 82 balls by Dean Jones put Australia in a strong position. In 17 minutes at the crease, Steve Waugh made 27, including a six off the back foot over extra cover from the last ball of the innings, bowled by Curtly Ambrose. But after further rain, the West Indies only had to score 108 from 18 overs. They were 2 wickets for 4, then Desmond Haynes (40 from 36 balls) and Viv Richards (60 from 40 balls) took over and they made the runs with four overs and 8 wickets left.

Steve's one game for Bankstown in the 1988–89 season is recorded in the Club's history, *Bankstown Cricket Club 50 Not Out*, by Mick Stephenson:

> Under difficult batting conditions he scored 93 in 217 minutes with 3 sixes and 7 fours to guide Bankstown to 187, after they had been precariously poised on 4 for 46. The Bulldog supremo then blasted through the Dragons batting lineup. With his lively mediums he captured an amazing 5 for 13 from just 9 overs and the

The catch of the season: Harper c Waugh b McDermott 15. Australia v West Indies, MCG, January 1989. *(Cricket Australia/Channel 9)*

Dragons were unceremoniously bundled out for a paltry 67. At one stage St George had slumped to 4 for 11 and Tugga had the lot.

Then came the English summer of 1989, when all his dreams came true.

9

HOW TO PLAY CRICKET

England 1989

When he arrived in England in 1989, Waugh had been in the Australian Test team for four seasons and had played 26 Tests without scoring a century. He was averaging 30.53 with the bat and 39.33 with the ball. He had earned a reputation as a cool head in a crisis with a series of crucial performances as a bowler, which had played a major part in winning the World Cup in 1987, and he had reached the nineties twice, averaging 41 against the West Indies, a team that included Marshall, Ambrose, Walsh and Patterson, perhaps the most feared pace attack in the game's history.

But the lack of a Test hundred was a trigger for the press and a monkey on his back. In public he said the press was more interested in it than he was, and pointed out that many an innings of less than a hundred was worth more to a team in a difficult match than a hundred when the going was easy. In private, he said it was like having King Kong on his back.

Waugh had good experience in England, having played for Essex and Somerset and been voted one of Wisden's five Cricketers of the Year for his performances for Somerset in 1988. However, his form coming into the 1989 Ashes series was not encouraging, with only a couple of half centuries in the county games and scores of 35, 43 and 35 again in the Texaco Trophy one-day series.

Honours had been even in the one-dayers, with a win each and a tied game, and England, following their dominance in the two previous Ashes series, were firm favourites in the press. But as often happens, the media had missed the sea change that was taking place. Australia, at least in its batting, had the foundations of the team that would take it to the top of world cricket by the mid-1990s. In contrast, the English selectors couldn't settle on a side; they chose no less than 29 players in the six-Test series. Australia chose twelve.

In the first Test of the series, played at Headingley, Waugh joined Dean Jones on the second morning at the fall of the fourth wicket. It was overcast and most of the players wore their sweaters throughout the day. Taylor was out for 136, Australia was 4 for 283. Tom Graveney, the elegant English batsman of the 1950s, would

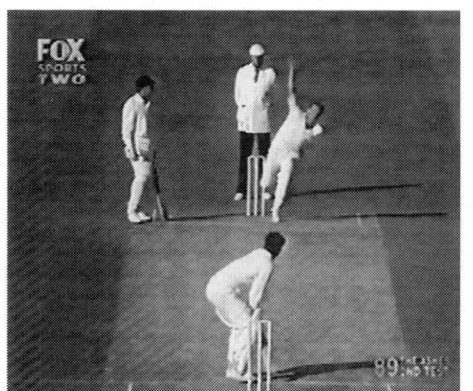

How to play cricket. Waugh drives during his first Test century, Headingley 1989. *(England Cricket Board)*

later write: 'They should have made a video of the stand between Waugh and Jones and given it to every coach in the land'.

Early in Waugh's innings, a four off DeFreitas is little more than a forward defensive shot. There is no follow-through, but it is so well timed that it races to the rope wide of mid-off. Richie Benaud comments, 'I'll swear that was nothing more than a defensive push.' A flick off his toes to the leg boundary and a square cut, both off Pringle, are so decisively struck that there is no need to think about running. All these shots with the absolute minimum of effort, the maximum of timing. Waugh smashes Pringle past point to reach 50 (71 balls, 84 minutes), raises his bat and acknowledges Jones's congratulations, all the while chewing what seems to be a very large wad of gum.

A perfect cover drive—this is how to play cricket—a cut over point soon after: 'It stood up and Steve Waugh waited and waited and cracked it square'. Always intense when he is on the cricket field, Waugh looks to be calm and totally in control, 'coolly expressionless', as one commentator described it. In all

Steve Waugh after scoring his first Test century at Headingley. *(England Cricket Board)*

his innings that I have watched I have never seen Waugh look better: the economy of movement, the simplicity of his stroke-play—there is no flourish, the back-lift is short, the follow-through curtailed—it's all about when you transfer your weight.

A rare edge through slips off Phil Newport takes him to 99 and he reaches his century (124 balls, 160 minutes, 16 fours) with a square cut for a single, doffs the baggy green cap he has worn throughout the innings, waves his bat, allows a modest, rather shy smile, and the Australian dressing room and the crowd rise to him.

Bob Simpson remembers the first time he saw Steve Waugh in action, soon after Simpson had taken over as coach of NSW, when

Waugh was about eighteen. 'It was obvious from the start he was somebody special. I can't remember seeing a batsman who hit the ball so hard or so sweetly.' Later, after Simpson became coach of the Australian team in 1986, he said of Waugh: 'He is a very rare, even unique, talent. He has to be in that area of excellence we saw with young Doug Walters and Greg Chappell. He is the hardest hitter of a ball in the side, yet he plays so straight. He hits the ball with both hands whereas most power players stand a long way away from the ball to get that power into their swing'.

I spoke to Bob Simpson early in 2004. 'It's like chopping,' Simpson said. 'If you only used one hand chopping wood, you'd break your wrists. I say to people when I'm coaching, imagine that bat you are going to pick up is an axe; no one will ever pick up an axe with their hands apart—you use both hands together— but with a cricket bat, a lot of people use the top hand as a guide and the action and the strength is in the bottom hand. I'm basically a bottom hand player, Bradman was a bottom hand player, but Steve is one of the rare ones who seem to be able to use both hands.'

Ian Chappell says, 'England suits Steve because he doesn't pull or hook, and the bounce is less over there—that is particularly important when you are driving off the back foot, which Steve Waugh does a helluva lot. If you're driving a ball off the back foot from waist high, it's a lot easier than trying to drive one from chest high, and that's why you generally find that Australian batsmen tend to cut, rather than drive, off the back foot. You'll get exceptions like Norm O'Neill, who was a magnificent back foot driver, but in general Australian batsmen prefer to cut because the ball is more likely to be at chest height. Steve doesn't cut so much; in England he tends to force off the back foot, in Australia he often plays a sort of half-and-half shot—it's half a cut and half a forcing shot—and I think you'll find that that's because the ball bounces a bit higher in Australia. So English conditions are ideal for his technique because they allow him to score a lot of runs off the back foot.'

In his autobiography, *Hands and Heals*, Ian Healy wrote:

I was out in the middle with Stephen when he reached what was his maiden Test hundred, after three and a half years of trying. The relief and joy were palpable. But unlike many cricketers who might have been satisfied with three figures and lost concentration for a second, Stephen put his head down, determined to get as many as he could. That was his way of savouring the moment. When he reached 137, he looked up to the players' balcony and waved at Tubby Taylor, who had made 136. 'Gotcha!' he signalled.

Border, who had set the tone for Australia's batting throughout the series with an aggressive 66, declared at 7 for 601, Steve Waugh not out 177. In the conditions, and against that attack, it was not a particularly tough hundred—over the years, of course, there would be plenty of tough ones to come—but Waugh himself has said, 'I was a different man after that innings'.

England replied with 430 (Alderman 5 for 107) and Border declared a second time at 3 wickets for 230. Needing 402, England made 191. David Boon said England bowled far too short; Simpson told the Australians to bowl a full length, and Alderman was the key to their success. Boon says Alderman didn't swing the ball a huge amount, but you always thought he was going to, then he would bring it back in off the seam and hit you on the pads. With 5 for

England v Australia, first Test, Headingley, Leeds, 8–13 June, 1989

Result: Australia won by 210 runs

AUSTRALIA

GR Marsh lbw DeFreitas	16	c Russell b Foster	6
MA Taylor lbw Foster	136	c Broad b Pringle	60
DC Boon c Russell b Foster	9	lbw De Freitas	43
*AR Border c Foster b DeFreitas	66	not out	60
DM Jones c Russell b Newport	79	not out	40
SR Waugh not out	177		
+IA Healy c & b Newport	16		
MG Hughes c Russell b Foster	71		
GF Lawson not out	10		
Extras	21		21
Total	7 for 601		3 for 230

FoW 44 57 174 273 411 441 588   14 97 129

Bowling	O	M	R	W	O	M	R	W
DeFreitas	45.3	8	140	2	18	2	76	1
Foster	46	14	109	3	19	4	65	1
Newport	39	5	153	2	5	2	22	0
Pringle	33	5	123	0	12.5	1	60	1
Gooch	9	1	31	0				
Barnett	6	0	32	0				

ENGLAND

GA Gooch lbw b Alderman	13	lbw Hughes	68
BC Broad b Hughes	37	lbw Alderman	7
KJ Barnett lbw b Alderman	80	c Taylor b Alderman	34
AJ Lamb c Boon b Alderman	125	c Boon B Alderman	4
*DI Gower c Healy b Lawson	26	c Healy b Lawson	34
RA Smith lbw b Alderman	66	c Border b Lawson	0
DR Pringle lbw b Campbell	6	c Border b Alderman	0
PJ Newport c Boon b Lawson	36	c Marsh b Alderman	8
+RC Russell c Marsh b Lawson	15	c Healy b Hughes	2
PAJ DeFreitas lbw b Alderman	1	b Hughes	21
NA Foster not out	2	not out	1
Extras	23		12
Total	430		191

FoW 35 81 195 243 323 338 392 421 424 430   17 67 77 134 134 153 153 166 170 191

Bowling	O	M	R	W	O	M	R	W
Alderman	37	7	107	5	20	7	44	5
Lawson	34.5	6	105	3	11	2	58	2
Campbell	14	0	82	1	10	0	42	0
Hughes	28	7	92	1	9.2	2	36	3
Waugh	6	2	27	0	5	3	4	0
Border	2	1	5	0				

44 in the second innings, Alderman was man-of-the-match. Five of his 10 wickets for the match were lbw.

Waugh received the first of many man-of-the-match awards in the second Test, played, as always, at Lord's. Here England won the toss and clawed their way to 286, Merv Hughes (4 for 71) doing most of the damage, well supported by Alderman (3 for 60).

England's bowlers were hammered again and Waugh went in late on the second day with Australia 4 for 221. He stayed for most of a bright, sunny third day, finishing not out 152 in a total of 528, which included a 130-run partnership with Geoff Lawson (74) for the 9th wicket. Waugh's batting was of the same quality as in the first Test. Two shots in particular stand out: a mere flick at a ball on leg stump from Dilley which left midwicket standing, and a square cut at full height off the same bowler—'And every so often he produces a shot like that, which is sheer beauty,' said Richie Benaud.

England (359, Gower 106) made Australia bat a second time, but only for half a day. They passed the England score with four wickets down, Waugh not out 21, having made 350 runs in the series without losing his wicket.

Ian Healy wrote:

In two Tests, Steve Waugh had gone from being potentially a good Test cricketer to being definitely an outstanding one. I can still picture him at one point on this tour, padded up in the dressing room and commenting, 'You know, Heals, I feel great again today'. He wasn't being cocky, just displaying that supreme confidence that comes when you are really on top of your game. I reckon he eagerly looked forward to every innings on that tour.

The English journalist Murray Hedgcock put Waugh in the category of 'those exotic, exciting, gifted-to-the-point-of-genius players who make the ground sit up and buzz when they stride to the crease'. Hedgcock said Waugh brought to mind the famous remark of 'the Governor-General', Charles Macartney, who came down to breakfast on a perfect sunny day, rubbed his hands together and remarked, 'By cripes, I pity any poor cove that has to bowl to me today.'

But Steve Waugh's best was behind him, at least for this tour. In the drawn third Test he made 43 before a good length off-cutter from Angus Fraser took his off stump, leaving him with a total for the series to date of 393.

In the fourth Test, after England had made 260, Waugh went to the wicket with Australia 4 for 274 and top-scored with 92 with some of the same exquisite timing he had shown in the first two Tests. (Richie: 'Goodness me! He's just given that a little flick of the wrists and it's fairly raced away through cover'.) His dismissal was unusual: he tried to pull a bouncer from Fraser, but misjudged its pace, took his eye off the ball and top-edged it gently to Tim Curtis

Why Steve Waugh doesn't hook: Waugh, on 92, caught by Tim Curtis trying to pull a bouncer from Angus Fraser. Fourth Test, Old Trafford, 1989. *(England Cricket Board)*

at mid wicket. As he left the field, the video shows he is obviously displeased with himself, shaking his head and saying, 'Fuck, fuck'— as you would.

Australia won the fourth Test by 9 wickets, regaining the Ashes. Batting first in the fifth Test, Australia was 4 down for 453 when Steve Waugh went to the wicket. Geoff Marsh had made 138 and Mark Taylor 219. Wearing a helmet, Waugh faced seven balls without scoring before flicking a fired-up Devon Malcolm low to Gower at mid wicket. Australia went on to 602 for 6 and won by an innings and 180.

During a match against Essex, played between the fifth and sixth Tests, Mark Waugh, who was having a season with Essex, scored 100 not out for the county and Steve scored 100 not out for Australia.

The sixth Test was drawn in Australia's favour, Dean Jones scoring 122 and Alderman taking 5 for 66 and 2 for 30. With 41 wickets at 17.37, Alderman was man-of-the-series. Mark Taylor, on his first tour, made 839 runs at 83.90 and Dean Jones made 566 at 70.75. Steve Waugh disappointed in the sixth Test, with 14 and 7 not out, but topped the Test averages with 506 at 126.50, scored at 3.76 per over, slightly faster than the rate of 3.70 at which Don Bradman scored his 974 runs in his legendary 1930 performance.

More than one journalist was calling Waugh 'the new Bradman', a tag which Waugh politely denied. (The previous 'new Bradman' had been Ian Craig, who had a terrible slump in England in 1956 and when asked by the Queen if this was his first tour, said, 'Yes, and it looks like my last, the way I'm batting.')

After more than a decade in the doldrums, Australia, led by Allan Border, was at last on the way up. The batting was strong. They lacked a great bowler, but the bowling was consistent and intelligent and Bob Simpson had the team well-organised in the field. Border was by now an experienced and respected leader, and in Merv Hughes the touring party had a genuine funny man, always an asset on tour. It was a very happy tour, as winning tours usually are.

(News Limited)

The only source of dissatisfaction was the continuing ban on wives. A player could visit his wife or girlfriend at her hotel, but only when they were not playing, or during county games—wives and girlfriends were not allowed in the team's hotel until the last two weeks of the tour. Steve Waugh's fiancée, Lynette Doughty, went to England for part of the tour, as did David Boon's wife Pip, with their daughter Georgina. In his autobiography, *Under the Southern Cross*, Boon wrote:

> We had a couple of days off, so Pip, Georgina and I were looking around London with Steve and his then fiancée, Lynette. In keeping with the tour rule, I was obliged to make the girls stand on the sidewalk, while I went up to my room to fetch something. If sharing your life with a wife or girlfriend doesn't affect your performance when playing cricket in Australia, I don't see how that lifestyle will hurt your performance on tour.

According to Ian Healy:

> The Fourex sponsorship never impinged on the cricket . . . most of the photo opportunities and appearances were squeezed into a

hectic period at the beginning of the tour. After that we just had to attend a Fourex function on the night before the rest day of each Test. The touring party would split up, three or four of us together, and journey to different locations, usually clubs or pubs, in the neighbourhood. Rather than being a grind, I found these functions gave me an escape from the 'What are we doing tonight?' routine of the tour.

Meanwhile praise was being heaped on Steve Waugh in the Australian press. In the *Sydney Morning Herald*, Phillip Derriman wrote: 'Suddenly he is Australian cricket's hottest property, whether he likes it or not. He is said to be in big demand for product endorsements, and he is certainly in big demand from the media'. Waugh had signed a contract with the English bat-maker Gunn & Moore for the 1989 England tour, reported to be 'a lucrative three-year deal, including a $1000 bonus for each Test hundred'. Derriman continued: 'He seems to be liked by everyone he deals with. Some see him as a throwback to an Australian cricketing type of the past—undemonstrative, hard-boiled, decent, respectable and successful'.

Ian Chappell wrote:

> I couldn't help thinking that the Australian selectors deserved a pat on the back for their foresight and their faith . . . Watching Waugh has been one of the great pleasures of this tour in a summer where the sun has shone and the Australian captain has come of age as a leader. A man should be satisfied with such enjoyment, but to see it all come together against England has made it a summer to savour.

When the team came home, the people of Sydney lined the city's streets for a tickertape parade as they were driven from the Regent Hotel in George Street to a reception in Darling Harbour.

10

'SORT OF TENSE'

Dropped from the Test team

After the 1993 tour of England, when Shane Warne was man-of-the-series, Steve Waugh gave an insight into the pressures imposed by success such as he had had in England in 1989: 'People will be expecting Shane to win games every time he walks through the gate,' he said, and, 'After even the smallest run of outs there will be someone saying, "He's lost it". It's a tough situation.'

Waugh's back had given him trouble towards the end of the England tour in 1989. He was diagnosed with stress fractures and when Australia went to India in October 1989 for the Nehru Cup, a one-day tournament with India, Pakistan, England, the West Indies and Sri Lanka, Waugh went as a batsman only.

Australia failed to qualify for the final and came home to play a Test against New Zealand in Perth. Boon made 200 in 451 minutes and, with New Zealand following on, Mark Greatbatch took 462 minutes to make a hundred as the game crawled to a draw.

In December 1989, a draw in Brisbane in the first of a two-Test series against Sri Lanka was a pointer to a new power in world cricket. Australia made 367 (Moody 106, Waugh 60) and were surprised by the depth and strength of the Sir Lankan batting. Aravinda de Silva's 167 earned him man-of-the-match. Other names, such as Ranatunga, Gurusinha, Ratnayeke, Wickremasinghe and

Ramanayake, were to become well known in the world of cricket over the next decade or so.

In Hobart, the second and last Test of the series, Australia made only 224 in the first innings (Ratnayeke 6 for 66) and Sri Lanka replied with 216. However, centuries to Mark Taylor (108), Dean Jones (118) and Steve Waugh (not out 134, a rare second innings century for Waugh) allowed Border to declare at 5 for 513. Sri Lanka made 348 and were far from disgraced, but it was not enough. Waugh bowled 6 overs in the first innings but did not bowl in the second.

In the triangular series, which included Pakistan, Waugh bowled a few overs in the first few games, but none after that, and he batted without great distinction, being named twelfth man when Mark came back into the eleven for the second final, which Australia won comfortably, having lost only two games throughout the series.

The disappointments continued for Steve in a three-Test series at home against Pakistan in January and February 1990. In Melbourne he made 20 and 3 and got the vital wicket of Javed, lbw for 65 in the second innings. Australia won the Test by 92 runs, but Steve pulled up sore and Errol Allcott ordered more scans, which showed that the stress fractures in his lower back had not fully healed. Alcott explained that while Steve has an easy, relaxed run to the wicket, he has a very quick, vigorous body rotation on the delivery stride, which causes the problems with his back.

In the drawn second Test, played in Adelaide, Waugh made 17 in the first innings, lbw to Wasim Akram's trademark in-swinging yorker, and only 4 in the second. He did not bat or bowl in the Sydney Test, which was reduced to two days' play by rain.

It was a hotch-potch of a season. One Test in New Zealand followed, in which he made 25 in each innings and which was lost by 9 wickets after Australia collapsed for 110 in the first innings, Richard Hadlee taking 5 for 39 from 16 overs. A five-match triangular series with India in New Zealand followed, won by Australia, in which Waugh didn't bowl and had a top score of 36. Then in April–May 1990 there were four games in the Austral-Asia Cup in Sharjah, where Australia lost in the final to Pakistan. Ian Healy wrote: 'Pakistan were much too good for us in the final, winning by

90 runs, and it was amazing afterwards to see huge sums of money changing hands, as supporters rewarded players from the successful team for their match-winning performances'.

This was followed by two exhibition games against Pakistan in the United States, replacing India, who had pulled out. They were not official ODIs, but the players had five days in New York and five days in Los Angeles, stayed in top hotels, won one and lost one, and even if the money ended up being a little less than was expected, they had a fine time to end the season.

Steve Waugh had been playing cricket without a break for five years. During the winter of 1990, he had a six-month layoff. He and Lynette spent much of the winter working on and painting the split-level brick house they were having built, looking out over a valley at Alfords Point, on the Georges River in Sydney's southern suburbs. He also spent a lot of time on an exercise bar and doing other routines to strengthen his back. X-rays had revealed a slight abnormality in the bone structure in his lower back, described as 'a gap on the left side of his fifth lumbar vertebra which widens when he rotates in his bowling action, putting excess strain on the right side, where the stress fracture has occurred'. Exercise and diet was the solution.

At the start of the 1990–91 season Waugh said, 'I have taken off some weight and put on some muscle to strengthen my back and stomach. I'm not 100 per cent right yet but I am building up.' He said he was ready to bowl again, although Errol Alcott warned, 'It's quite all right at the moment but whether his back can stand the rigours of five Tests and the limited overs internationals remains to be seen.'

He had a busy few months ahead of him.

OCTOBER 1990

14	FAI Cup v Queensland	Brisbane
16	FAI Cup v Tasmania	Sydney
20	FAI Cup semi-final v Victoria	Sydney
27	FA Cup final v WA	Perth

NOVEMBER 1990

2–5	Sheffield Shield v Tasmania	Sydney
16–19	Sheffield Shield v Victoria	Melbourne
23–25	First Test	Brisbane
29	ODI v New Zealand	Sydney

DECEMBER 1990

2	ODI v New Zealand	Adelaide
9	ODI v England	Perth
11	ODI v New Zealand	Melbourne
16	ODI v England	Brisbane
18	ODI v New Zealand	Hobart
20–23	Sheffield Shield v WA	Perth
26–30	Second Test	Melbourne

JANUARY 1991

1	ODI v England	Sydney
4–8	Third Test	Sydney
10	ODI v England	Melbourne
13	ODI First Final	Sydney
15	ODI Second Final	Melbourne
19–22	Sheffield Shield v SA	Sydney
31–3 FEB	Sheffield Shield v WA	Sydney

Waugh made useful runs in Shield and FAI Cup games in the lead up to the Tests, but started the series badly. He made only 1 in his only innings in the first Test of the season, against England in Brisbane, where Australia won by 10 wickets. A series of one-day internationals followed and for once he could not find his form in the short version of the game. In six games in the triangular series against England and New Zealand he had a highest score of 16. Three of his innings were not out, but he had his chances in other games and was not able to make the most of them. His bowling, too, was less effective than usual.

His double century in the Sheffield Shield game against Western Australia in Perth would have assured his place in the Test team,

SHEFFIELD SHIELD

AUSTRALIAN CRICKET BOARD

MATCH WESTERN AUSTRALIA v NEW SOUTH WALES

AT W.A.C.A. PERTH on 20, 21, 22, 23 DEC 1990

1st INNINGS OF NEW SOUTH WALES

DATE 20, 21 DEC. '90

UMPIRES PRUE T.A. - EVANS R.J.
CAPTAINS MARSH G.R. - LAWSON G.F.
WICKET-KEEPERS ZOEHRER T.J. - EMERY P.A.
12th MEN CAPES P.A. - BEVAN M.
TOSS WON BY WESTERN AUSTRALIA
TEAM BATTING FIRST NEW SOUTH WALES
SCORERS BULL C.A. - NICHOLLS A.J.

LUNCH SCORES O'NEILL 4
3-111 WAUGH M.E. 0
OVERS 29

TEA SCORES 4-242 WAUGH M.E. 55
OVERS 59

WAUGH S.R. 62

STUMPS SCORES 4-375 WAUGH M.E. 128
OVERS 93 WAUGH S.R. 112

	BATSMEN	HOW OUT	BOWLER	RUNS	BALLS	4's	6's
1	SMALL S.M.	C WOOD	REID	26	31	5	
2	TAYLOR M.A.	BOWLED	REID	57	78	10	
3	BAYLISS T.H.	C ZOEHRER	REID	20	52	2	
4	O'NEILL M.D.	C ZOEHRER	McLEAN	9	41	1	
5	WAUGH M.E.	NOT OUT		229	343	35	1
6	WAUGH S.R.	NOT OUT		216	339	24	
7	MATTHEWS G.R.						
8	EMERY P.A.						
9	LAWSON G.F.						
10	WHITNEY M.R.						
11	HOLDSWORTH W.J.						

TOTAL 4/601

DEC.

INNINGS TIME 564 MINS

RESULT WON
POINTS:— HOME TEAM VISITING TEAM AWARD:—

WAUGH M.E. - WAUGH S.R. 250 RUNS PSHIP IN 234 MINS 450 RUNS IN 400 MINS
TAYLOR: BAYLISS 50 RUNS PSHIP IN 43 MINS.
WAUGH M.E. - WAUGH S.R. 50 RUNS PSHIP IN 52 MINS.

SWITCH WAUGHS
Mark for Steve cou be sound ... positic

BROTHERS AT WAUGH
Mark in for Steve

OH BROTHER – STEVE FOR AXE

THERE'S WAUGH IN THE FAMILY
Mark set to repla...
Steve i...

WAUGH'S LAST CHANCE

Steve gets ... promotion to regain touch

WAUGH FACING SACK

were it not for the fact that most of his runs were made in partnership with the one player who was challenging for that place, his brother Mark.

Coming together with NSW 4 for 137, the twins put on a record fifth wicket partnership of 464 in 407 minutes. The WA attack, with Bruce Reid, Terry Alderman, Chris Matthews, Tom Moody and Ken MacLeay, was regarded as one of the strongest in the Shield competition. MacLeay at one period bowled consistently half a metre outside off stump, prompting Mark to charge him and smash a six fifteen rows back over the offside field. Mark finished with 229 and Steve with 216, both not out, in NSW's total of 4 for 601 declared.

The Boxing Day Test brought no joy; on 19, Steve played inside a good ball from Angus Fraser which straightened slightly from leg and took the off stump. He was bowled sparingly and didn't bat in the second innings, as Australia cruised to an 8-wicket victory.

At the start of the 1990–91 season there had been conjecture in the press about the brothers' claim on a place in the Test team. Ian Chappell was quoted as saying Steve needed a big score to hold his place, Keith Miller said both should be in, and Rod Marsh asked, 'Why change a winning team?'

As the season progressed, the headlines suggested Steve's time was up: 'Is time running out for Steve Waugh', 'Waugh's last chance', 'Waugh facing sack', 'Tough times on the Waugh front', 'There's Waugh in the family', and 'O brother—Steve for Axe'.

An interview with AAP correspondent Howard Northey began with Steve asking a question: 'This isn't going to be another sack Steve Waugh story, is it?' When asked if he might improve his Test performance by trying to hit his way out of trouble he replied, 'I got into the Test team by hitting the ball along the ground and I'm not like, say, Dean Jones, who can go out and immediately start hitting the ball over the top . . . changing the way I play isn't going to help me.' Steve Waugh was not one to make excuses, but he talked about the problem he had batting number 6 in one-day cricket, because he got so used to having to go in and score quickly, as opposed to playing himself in for Tests.

Nevertheless, in the Sydney Test, starting on 4 January, he went on the attack. Devon Malcolm bowled short and whenever there was any width Waugh smashed him though the off-side field. He raced to 48 from 61 balls, but then he fended at a well-directed bouncer from Malcolm, took his eye off the ball and lobbed an easy catch to Stewart at short leg. In the second innings he came in after Border and Jones had gone in successive balls, facing a hat trick from Tufnell. The commentator said he was dropped at silly point first ball, although video coverage seems to show that it hit the front pad, not the bat. On 14 he tried to steer Eddie Hemmings through the gully, but only managed to edge it to Jack Russell behind the stumps.

This Test was drawn and the calls for Waugh's replacement in the Test team were renewed, but there were three World Series matches and a Sheffield Shield game against South Australia to come before the Test team would be announced. On January 10, against England in Melbourne, Steve top-scored for Australia with 65 from 82 balls, while Mark was run out for 36. In the first final, played in Sydney on 13 January, Mark was bowled by Morrison for a duck, but took 3 wickets for 29 from 10 overs. Steve was not out 16. Two days later, back in Melbourne for the second final, neither of them took a wicket. Mark was not out 3 and Steve did not get a bat, as Australia recorded another comfortable win.

A well-made 60 in the Shield match at the SCG, watched by Test selectors John Benaud and Bob Simpson, might have been enough to keep Steve in the Test team, but again he was upstaged by his brother. Writing in the *Telegraph*, Mark Gately said:

> Mark's second century this season was his twelfth Shield ton, his 13th for NSW and his 25th in first class cricket. He struck two sixes, both off former Test tweaker Tim May, and eleven fours in an innings that was a banquet of everything that excites the palate of a cricket lover. Power, timing, aggression, solidity, speed, daring, inventiveness, dominance and artistry were all there.

Another report said: 'Mark's superb knock of 112 . . . made it simply impossible for the selectors to continue to ignore his talents'.

A few days later Bob Simpson phoned Steve to tell him that he was out of the Test team, replaced by Mark. Mark had moved away from home too by that time, but Steve knew he was at their mother Beverley's place and went straight there. Younger brothers Dean and Danny were there too. Steve walked in and said, 'Congratulations you're in the team.'

Mark asked, 'Who got dropped?'

'Me.'

'Oh, bad luck.'

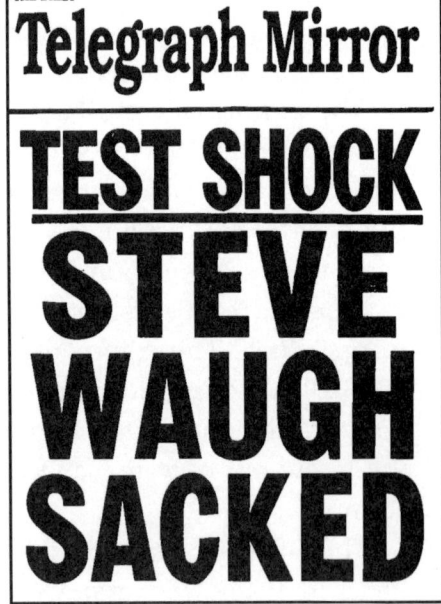

THE DAILY

Telegraph Mirror

TEST SHOCK
STEVE WAUGH SACKED

(News Limited)

'Don't worry about it. I'm just another player.'

Mark has been quoted as saying, 'It was sort of tense.'

Bev Waugh told the papers Steve took it well; he said the worst thing was that he wouldn't have an excuse to get out of helping Lynette paint their new house.

Lynette kept a list of people who rang.

In the *Sydney Morning Herald*, Daniel Williams described Steve Waugh at this time as 'hating fuss, loathing baloney . . . far from being the confident, dogmatic, even terse cricketer he appears, Steve is a pleasant, shy fellow . . .'.

Later, Steve said, 'It doesn't really sink in until the plane is ready to leave and you're not on it.'

In Adelaide, Mark became the fifteenth Australian to make a century in his first Test match.

11

PICNIC POINT ROAD, PANANIA

Growing up

After his success in England in 1989, Steve Waugh was asked by the *Sydney Morning Herald*'s Peter Bills: 'To whom do you attribute your batting success?' Waugh replied, 'I cannot honestly think of anyone. I never really had a coach when I was young, I just played the game at home with my brothers. I was playing club cricket by the time I was seven and I suppose I always felt if I was keen enough to put in the hard work, things would come my way.'

Later, the Waugh brothers used to go to Barry Knight, who had nets and coaching classes in the city, but Mark said it was more for practice and going to McDonalds afterwards than for the coaching. Knight told them they were naturals and to 'stick to the way we were playing . . . we never worried too much about technique . . . it was mainly all natural, just the way we worked it out for ourselves'. Steve said, 'I can't remember actually watching anyone or copying them . . . we used to go out there and it would just come naturally . . . you would hit the ball and away it would go. You never thought too much about it.'

Beverley Bourne was nineteen and Rodger Waugh was twenty when they were married. Bev was a teacher with the NSW Department of Education and Rodger worked with the National Bank in Sydney's CBD. Their twin sons, Stephen and Mark, were born

Picnic Point Road, Panania, September 2003.

in Canterbury Hospital on Wednesday 2 June 1965. Under her bond with the Department, Bev had to go back to work when they were six weeks old. Their parents-in-law helped out—they were living with Rodger's parents at the time.

The next year the family moved to 56 Picnic Point Road, Panania. The area hasn't changed much: Picnic Point Road is a wide, fairly busy, tree-lined street of small- to medium-sized houses. The Panania Primary School is just down the street and the Georges River is at the end of the road, a few minutes drive away.

Bev and Rodger were both very good tennis players. Rodger had beaten Tony Roche in a NSW under-14 grass-court final and, with John Cottrill, won a national under-19 doubles final. Bev had won a South Australian under-14 singles title and, with Ray Ruffels, the NSW under-19 mixed doubles. Later in life, she took up squash and twice in the 1990s won the Australian Women's Masters Championship.

Bev's brother Dion was a stalwart of the Bankstown Cricket Club, which might account for the twins' early interest in the sport, although they say that he 'encouraged' rather than coached them. Like many great sportsmen, they mainly figured out how to do things for themselves.

They were quiet kids who entertained themselves, liked Lego and trains but were happy playing with cardboard boxes or whatever was at hand. Steve was the more active and adventurous. Even when he was young Mark liked to look clean and groomed. Rodger was a strict father and they were well-behaved, did what they were told. They were rather shy. Mark, in particular, hated getting into trouble.

As they grew up, the boys watched a lot of sport on television. They would watch for hours, then, when it was finished, would go out into the yard and play whatever they'd been watching—cricket, golf, soccer, tennis. When they got into teams they had some coaching, but Mark says they really learned how to play cricket from watching TV. When they could, they went to the Tests at the SCG and watched all day. If they couldn't go to the game or watch it on TV, they listened to the radio, or played in the yard. Bev describes herself as 'an enthusiastic backyard cricketer but not very good at soccer'.

Bev and Rodger used to play in tennis tournaments in the country. The boys loved the weekends away: the trips in the car; then, while their parents played tennis, playing sport with the other kids all day.

At the age of seven Steve and Mark were chosen in Bankstown's under-10 side. Playing in teams a few years above their age meant they did a lot of fielding; it didn't do them any harm— they were good at it from their backyard games—and as Mark Gately says in *Waugh Declared*, it meant 'They knew how the also-rans felt'.

Both were good bowlers from an early age, Mark perhaps the better, bowling medium pace. Even then, Steve wanted to bowl

(Bev Waugh)

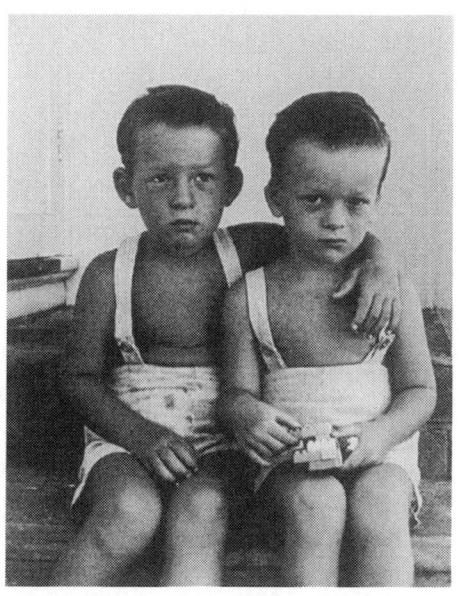

bouncers all the time. For a time, when they were about twelve, Mark bowled leg spin and later said he regretted having given it up. From about that time they started to dominate their age group and were picked in representative sides. It was then that Steve said he started to realise that they could get to the top level if they wanted to.

Steve enjoyed going away with the rep sides: 'It used to be great fun staying awake at night and playing tricks on each other. It was an adventure'. They had a lot of success, and not just at cricket. Panania Primary won the State cricket carnival in 1976 and 1977, the State soccer carnival in 1976, and were runners-up in the tennis carnival in 1977. Mark was captain and Steve vice-captain of the NSW Primary Schools cricket team which won the national cricket carnival. Mark also captained the tennis team, which won the national championships, and Steve was captain of the soccer team.

Their brother Dean was born when the twins were three, and Danny when they were ten, and with four boys in the family and both parents working, their home life was extremely busy, sometimes tending to the chaotic. There wasn't much time for housework and the boys were too involved in sport to be of much help on the domestic front. But they were generally quiet and disciplined, and they didn't fight with each other much—if they did, Rodger came down on them very hard.

Rodger hung a cricket ball in pantyhose in the garage for them to practise cricket with. Steve said it taught him to play straight. Bev drove them everywhere in the family's white Ford Falcon station wagon. She was concerned that their success should not go to their heads and told them not to take themselves too seriously. Just because they won things, she said, it didn't mean they were any better than other people; they might be good at some things, other people are good at other things.

As a teacher, her observation was that kids involved in sport use up their energy and are less likely to get involved in drugs, but she did worry about them wearing out their bodies with all the activity. The twins had a lot of aches and pains in their joints and backs during their adolescence.

In a radio interview with Debbie Spillane, Steve said, 'The schools I went to were always big on sport, it seemed to be almost more important than education. That was all we lived for in those days, sport. We never knew anything else. School was only a way to play more sport. I don't think we took school too seriously. I could never see the point of going home and studying for two hours when you could be out playing sport . . . I'd much rather be having fun than sitting down with my nose in a book or trying to make my running writing neat. There were better things to do than that.'

Nevertheless, the boys' school reports are complimentary: 'Mark is a great student. Everything is done to perfection with great attention to detail'; he is also described as 'polite and well-mannered'. Steve is more 'sensitive', 'too energetic at times' but with 'a keen sense of humour'.

In their later years at school, Mark remained a fairly conscientious student, but Steve often wagged, especially maths. He and his mates used to go to the beach or to a friend's house. He still scored more than 300 in the HSC, equivalent to about 60 per cent.

When in Year 12 their careers adviser asked them what they wanted to do, both said, 'Play cricket in England.'

I spoke to Peter Horwitz, who, with the then Director of NSWCA coaching Peter Spence, was part of the birth of modern coaching at State junior level in the 1970s. Horwitz coached the State under-age teams, starting with the under-13s and going through to under-16s, at the time the Waugh twins were starting their representative careers. 'I started off with the under-13s,' he said, 'and the plan was that the one coach would take that whole group through to the under-16 national championships. I started off with Sydney Metropolitan with Steve and Mark Waugh and Brad McNamara and Gavin Robertson, and I'd take teams from Sydney Metropolitan to Newcastle and to Wollongong—we got a couple of thrashings from Newcastle and Wollongong, so we realised we had to widen the scope to include all the country areas—and it ended up I'd be taking these sides away for ten or twelve days and we'd playing cricket every day.

'I reckon at that age group you need to have pretty athletic boys and I had a bias towards athleticism—I mean, assuming cricket ability to be about equal, then I tended to pick the most athletic sides.

'One year we picked Mark, but we didn't pick Steve. We'd had some trials down at Drummoyne Oval and I had players there from Wollongong, Newcastle, Dubbo, all over, and you really had to pick them on what you saw that day, and Steve just batted like an old sheila that day and I thought, you know, if I pick him on reputation, there'll be a howl all round, because he'd got out more than any other player, and some players were just fault-free. So I didn't pick Steve that year. I've subsequently heard the story that Steve reckons he didn't get picked because he "scored too fast", but that's bullshit—anyway, the next year Steve came along and he batted great and he was back in the squad and I took them right through then to the under-16s.'

Horwitz says the Waugh twins changed the landscape of Australian cricket. 'They were the first of the outstanding athletes to choose cricket as their main sport, and from the time Steve and Mark started playing Test cricket, there was a huge surge forward in the athleticism of our Test side. This had two wonderful side effects. The first was that other great athletes chose cricket as their number one career pursuit and, second, that every cricket team in Australia—down to the Under-10s in Woop Woop—realised that athleticism in the field was vital and that poor fielding was unacceptable.

'In my day, you'd be lucky to have five good fieldsmen in a Sydney first-grade side. Today it's a given that all eleven players are skilled and athletic, both in the field and between wickets.

'I can say this about Steve and Mark: they are two of the most naturally gifted athletes I've ever had the pleasure of coaching. Mark in particular, Mark could do anything. From the moment he came to a net, from the moment he played in his first trial games, you'd say to yourself, here's a bloke you'd be pretty confident would go all the way, provided he had the right attitude, because he just seemed to have everything. He was amazing.'

I suggested to Peter Horwitz that perhaps Steve's ultra-competitive attitude might be a reaction to the praise that was always heaped on Mark for being so naturally graceful and doing everything so easily—maybe that gave Steve the determination to succeed, even though he wasn't as naturally gifted as Mark.

Horwitz said, 'You might have something there, but on the other hand, I can still remember when we played against Victoria in Launceston in the final of the national championships, I remember the Victorian captain going forward and playing a cover drive and I thought, "Well that's four"—then he made the mistake of just walking forward to admire the shot and Steve came across so quickly, with one hand picked up and threw out middle stump, and I thought, "You have to be something special to be able to do something like that", you know, not many people could ever do that, at any age—he was 15.'

Were they aggressive on the field then?

'I never noticed it, no. I don't recall sledging being a big factor then. They were terrific boys and their parents Rodger and Bev were always extremely supportive, particularly Bev. The most important thing I remember about them was their athleticism—that stood out. The other thing I remember was that from an early age, say 13 or 14, they instinctively always wore helmets, wherever they were batting, in the nets, in trial matches, didn't matter if it was a flat track or whatever, they wore their helmet. And I actually think, when I look back on it, that—it's a pretty important factor, because I can still remember Mark in the nets one day he went for a hook, missed, got hit on the helmet and he just nonchalantly turned round and threw the ball back, whereas if you or I went for a hook when we were kids and got hit on the head with our caps on, we'd remember it.

'Steve never really played the hook even then, but, you know, if a rubbishy bowler dropped short he'd pull and so forth, but I don't remember him playing what you or I would call a genuine hook to a bouncer.

'I remember him down at the championships in Launceston. In the first match we played against WA, and I remember talking to the openers before they went out and I said to them, "Look this is no harder than a Green Shield game and you've all done well in Green Shield and you just go out and treat it like it's another Green Shield game." I was just trying to motivate them and get their confidence up, but when they went out to bat Steve came up to me and said, "I heard what you said to those blokes. This is tougher than Green Shield, you know," and I said, "I know that Steve, but I didn't want them to think it's tougher than Green Shield. I wanted them to feel that they're capable of handling it." But he knew.

'Even then he had this habit of playing very late, but I honestly think he's like a good wine: he's just got better and better with age. He did struggle when he first got into the Test team, and maybe they put him there a bit soon—it was hard times for the Australian team then—but when he got on that first tour in England, and he blossomed, there was no looking back. And how he ended up handling some of those West Indies bowlers—that was pretty ferocious stuff. I mean, it got to the stage where he was a real warrior, you know. Nothing seemed to worry him.'

When Bob Simpson first saw the young Steve Waugh, he was impressed at how hard he hit the ball and knew Waugh was something special. At that time, Waugh was a real thrasher, to the extent that it sometimes got him into trouble—he was once pulled out of the nets at a coaching clinic by an angry Barry Richards for smashing balls all over the place.

Then, from the age of about sixteen, he started to come up against good bowlers in grade and realised that he had to temper his aggression. Brad McNamara, who played for Western Suburbs and was the same age as the Waugh twins, was one of the bowlers he found he had to treat with some respect.

Steve had played in Bankstown's Green Shield (under-16) side when he was thirteen, and in 1980–81, when he was 15, he topped both batting (355 at 51) and bowling (12 at 16.58), and his mature captaincy received a mention in the club's records. He also started that season in fifth grade and was soon promoted after an innings of 118 against Sydney University. In five innings in fourths he made

292 runs at an average of 146, and in two innings in thirds he made 138 not out and 43.

The next couple of seasons were spent mostly in Bankstown's second grade, as well as playing Poidevin-Grey (under-21) and in the NSW under-19 side.

The National Championships for the under-age teams were a chance to meet and make friends with other top players from around Australia—Brad McNamara in particular became a lifelong friend of Steve's. They did some early drinking together and apparently ended up in some funny places.

By 1983–84 Steve was a regular member of Bankstown's first grade side, was the Combined High Schools Sportsperson of the Year, and was picked in the Australian under-19 side and made 187 against Sri Lanka. Five hundred runs and 27 wickets in first grade before Christmas 1984–85 earned him a place in the NSW Sheffield Shield side.

Steve had left school by this time and was going out with Lynette Doughty, who he had met at a school dance. When they met, Lynette had no interest in cricket. In Mark Gately's book, *Waugh Declared*, she recalls that the first time Steve went to dinner at her house—this was some time after they met—someone asked Steve what he was going to do for a living. 'Play cricket for Australia,' he replied. Lynette said, 'The whole table just went quiet.'

Steve had enrolled at Milperra Teachers' College, but lasted only a few weeks. He had been away for the first two weeks of term playing for the Australian under-19 side against Sri Lanka, and when he came back he found himself one of three boys in a roomful of girls studying to be teachers; it wasn't his scene. He made some money umpiring for indoor cricket, did some casual work for Kingsgrove Sports Centre and Bankstown Council, and spent three months on the dole. But he knew by this time that he was going to make his living from cricket.

The twins could probably have had a career in tennis or soccer, too. Steve was the more promising at soccer and had a real opportunity to make a career from it. The boys played at Bankstown, then at Auburn, where they were coached by Len Quested, a former professional player from England. According to Quested, Steve was a flamboyant player, with an ability to make something happen. He said that at that age he was a better player than Robbie Slater, who later became a Socceroo. (The Bankstown coach, Ron Mannell, also noted that Steve 'always had that surprised look when he was fouled'.)

Australian soccer legend Johnny Warren, who had got the Commonwealth Bank to sponsor junior soccer and used to go to games and coach as part of his promotional activities, saw Steve play in July 1983 and wrote in the *Sydney Morning Herald*:

> I have not seen a better goal this year than one scored by East Hills High School's Stephen Waugh in the Commonwealth Bank Cup at Mt Druitt Town Soccer Centre last Wednesday evening. It was a goal of which the legendary Franz Beckenbaur would have been proud. Waugh began a 50 metre slalom run well inside his own half and beat seven opponents before smashing a 20 metre drive past the Springwood goalie.

East Hills defeated Springwood 3–0 and advanced to the quarter finals.

At the time, Steve was playing soccer for Croatia's reserve team, but when the training schedule began to clash with cricket, soccer was the loser—once it got serious, there was just too much training with soccer. Mark was the better tennis player, but the waiting around at tournaments got to him, so he decided to concentrate on cricket. Bev had steered them away from tennis because it was such an individual sport, less sociable and character-building than team sports. Steve and Mark liked being in a team environment, and cricket was the game where training was more fun; cricket was the high profile game you played for your country.

Interestingly, if you wanted to pick two sports to play that would help you to become a good cricketer, it would be hard to choose better than tennis, with its emphasis on placement and hand–

eye coordination, and soccer, where the essentials are balance and footwork.

In his Sheffield Shield debut, against Queensland at the 'Gabba in December 1984, Steve was picked as much for his bowling as his batting. He batted at number 9, and was bowled by Jeff Thomson for 31 in the NSW total of 357. Waugh bowled 23 overs for only 34 runs, without taking a wicket, as NSW limited Queensland to 315 and took first innings points.

(Bev Waugh)

According to Bankstown folklore, Steve hit Jeff Thomson, who had played his early cricket for Bankstown, for 4 during this innings and got seriously abused for his trouble. When Waugh got down the bowler's end, he said to Thomson, 'My uncle asked me to say hello to you,' and Thomson replied, 'Who the bloody hell is your uncle?' When he found it was Dion Bourne—the famous 'Lunch', who had done so much for Thomson in his Bankstown days—he eased up on the verbal abuse, if not the bouncers.

Waugh failed in his second Shield game, against Tasmania, and was dropped. He was back in against Queensland at the SCG, but made 0 and didn't bowl; then he made 94 against Victoria at the SCG, adding 178 with Greg Matthews, contributing to an outright win that put NSW at the top of the Shield table for the final against Queensland.

Played in March 1985 at the SCG, the final was a Sheffield Shield classic. Allan Border won the toss and Queensland batted first, making 374; Trevor Hohns, later to become Chairman of Selectors, top-scored with 103. NSW were 7 for 226 when Steve Waugh came in to bat. He attacked the bowling from the start, scoring 71 of 92 runs made while he was at the wicket, and being last man out with the total at 318. The young Steve Waugh was impressed by Queensland and Australian captain Allan Border, who ran across to shake his hand and say, 'Well done' as he left the field. Imran Khan then took 5 for 34 as Queensland collapsed for only 163, leaving NSW 220 to win. Jeff Thomson and Carl Rackemann ran through the top order, and Waugh joined Peter Clifford at 6 for 140 and added 21 in a 33-run partnership. Both were out with 45 runs still needed, but the bowlers stood firm, and NSW reached the target with the last pair, Bob Holland and Dave Gilbert, at the crease.

In Ken Piesse's book, *The Taylor Years*, Mark Taylor says Waugh likes to talk about one of his early Sheffield Shield trips, when he roomed with Imran Khan. They used to get a lot of phone calls, Waugh said, all for Imran, who was out most of the time. Steve used to answer the phone: 'Hello,' he would say. 'When would you like to come up?'

Later, Taylor tells a story against himself. Australia was 1 for about 300 in a Test in Hobart against New Zealand, but Taylor had been rather stodgy and the crowd became quite abusive. When he came back into the dressing room, and was complaining at length about the crowd's ignorance and slow handclapping, Steve Waugh said, 'Actually it was us, mate. We started it.'

After the 1984–85 Sheffield Shield final, Bill O'Reilly wrote in the *Sydney Morning Herald*:

> One would have to be blind not to recognise the amazing ball sense of Waugh who, strangely enough, is being handled as if he were still ploughing painfully through some graduation course. How would the Australian selectors in 1930 have gone down in history if they had not picked their bunch of youngsters. In the Leeds Test of that year Don Bradman, as a rosy faced boy, scored 309 runs in one eventful day. This lad Waugh must be sent to England this year

and I implore our three selectors to give the young man the chance he thoroughly deserves.

Waugh wasn't picked, but in view of what happened in England four years later, it's obvious that O'Reilly knew that he would succeed in English conditions.

Instead, in the 1985 off-season, Waugh signed to play League cricket in England, but when Dave Gilbert, who was playing with Essex, was called up to play for Australia, Waugh took his place at Essex, playing for the second XI. He played some spectacular innings: 100 off 29 balls against Chelmsford, 184 against Brondes-bury, and 200 in a 50 overs under-25 match against a Sussex side that included the Australian all-rounder Tony Dodemaide.

He also had an unexpected windfall. Dave Gilbert, whom Waugh replaced at Essex, had been called up into the Australian team because of the rebel tours organised by the South African Cricket Union. The rebel team included players such as Kim Hughes, John Dyson, Steve Smith, Trevor Hohns, Steve Rixon, Terry Aldermann and Carl Rackemann and, fearing that the rebels might sign up promising young players, the Packer organisation offered several of them, including Steve Waugh, three-year contracts not to play in South Africa. Waugh said, 'I hadn't even thought of going to South Africa . . . It was big dollars. I did nothing over the three years, just collected the cheques. It enabled me to buy my first block of land. I was really lucky.'

However, he was on his own at Essex, staying with another player and his wife who were paid to have him but didn't

Steve Waugh in 1986.

make him very welcome. He had to organise his own washing and ironing for the first time in his life, ate out most of the time, and was missing Lynette.

He was glad to be home, and celebrated in October 1985 with his first Sheffield Shield century—107 not out against Tasmania, in Hobart. Mark made his Shield debut in this game, opening with Mark Taylor and making 13 and 28. Both failed in the next Shield match and Mark was dropped, but in December, against South Australia, Steve made a spectacular 119 and the selectors included him in the squad for the Melbourne Boxing Day Test against India. It was thought he would be twelfth man, but when Greg Ritchie was injured, Waugh came into the eleven.

12

THE KITCHEN SINK

Failure and technique

The five years since that 1985 Melbourne Boxing Day Test had ended in disappointment. Steve Waugh had been dropped for the fourth Test of the 1990–91 series against England, and for almost two years he was on the outer, playing only two of Australia's fifteen Tests during that time.

But, as Greg Baum wrote in *The Age*, 'He remained physically close to the team, an estimable one-day player and solid citizen tourist. But he appealed to and confided in no-one; not coach Bob Simpson, nor captain Allan Border'. Border said, 'He's the sort of bloke you don't really need to spend too much time chatting to. He knows. He's got his own stuff mapped out. You don't need to prop him up too much.'

Waugh himself was philosophical:

You've got to expect a bad trot at some stage in your career, because you're playing against high-quality opposition. It's a matter of getting yourself right mentally, getting fit again, and really wanting to score runs at that level. You're playing with a lot of guys with a lot of experience and they're occasionally going to help you out, but there's no one person I go to directly and say, 'How can you help me out?' It's got to come from within most of the time.

In the 1990–91 Sheffield Shield season he played five matches for 516 runs at an average of 86, second only to his brother Mark,

Bowling for NSW in the late 1980s.

who averaged 97.40. This earned Steve selection for the tour of the West Indies, and although he was not selected for the first two Tests, he impressed the selectors on tour with his attitude, commitment and hard work at training. He said the break may have done him some good: 'I thought about what I was missing out on . . . I figured that cricket was my life, my job, and I really missed it, and that shook me up a bit, so I have a new commitment and desire'.

As in the past, it was the one-day game that kept him in contention. And Australia had an unexpected success in the one-day series in the West Indies, due in part to Waugh's ability to impose his will on events at critical moments. In the first match, played in Kingston, Jamaica, with the West Indies 1 for 48, chasing 244, and with Richardson and Greenidge starting to dominate, Gordon Greenidge gave Waugh the charge, but the bowler saw him coming and dropped it short, on off stump cutting to leg; it went straight through Greenidge and flattened his stumps.

Twenty runs later, Steve Waugh got a sliding off-cutter through Carl Hooper for an lbw decision. Then when the West Indies, through Richardson and Logie, had re-grouped to 4 for 190, with plenty of overs left, the Waugh brothers combined to turn the game again. Mark, bowling medium pace, had Logie hole out to Steve, deep at square leg, and Australia went on to win by 35 runs. They then won the second game, lost the third, and won the fourth and the fifth. Man-of-the-series was Geoff Marsh, with scores of 26, 23, 81, 113 and 106. Without being a match-winner, Steve Waugh played a part with runs or wickets in every game.

The first Test was drawn. Australia lost the second Test, a 297-run stand for the second wicket between Desmond Haynes (111) and Richie Richardson (182) being the deciding factor. Mark Waugh, with Boon and Marsh, had been the best of the Australian batsmen, and in the third Test, played in Port-of-Spain, Trinidad, Steve was selected alongside his brother, the first time that twins had played together in a Test. In a drawn match, shortened by rain, they batted together for an hour and a half, putting on 58 before Steve edged Walsh to Dujon and was out for 26. Mark went on to make 64 and took 1 for 9. Steve took 0 for 10 from 5 overs.

I had the good fortune to go to the fourth Test of the 1991 series in the West Indies. Walking along the road towards Kensington Oval, not far from the centre of downtown Bridgetown, Barbados, a schoolboy leaned out of a bus and asked, 'Hey, you Aussies?' We said we were. 'Only thing you gonna win is the toss, man.'

Despite a warning on the back of our tickets that 'Musical instruments, drums, cymbals, radios and loudspeakers are NOT permitted for use in stands', the stand next to ours had trumpeters, cymbals and a bass drummer supported by a rhythm section on a variety of home-made instruments. We were in the Hall-Griffith stand, quite sedate in comparison, although not without the characteristic Caribbean humour. A couple sitting in front of us seemed to be running a business on their mobile phone and we commented on the number of calls they were taking. The next time their phone rang, they turned around and handed it to us, saying, 'It's for you.' On the rest day, with Australia facing defeat, we hired a Mini-moke and toured the island. At a roadside stall, we bought soft drinks from an old woman who asked, 'You takin' your licks peaceful?'

Both Waughs were retained for the Barbados Test, which the West Indies won by 343 runs after making only 149 in the first innings. Mark made 20 and 3, Steve 2 and 4 not out. Mark took 4 for 80 in the West Indies second innings of 9 for 536, which included Gordon Greenidge's epic 226 made in 11 hours and 17 minutes. Steve was dropped for the fifth Test, in Antigua, where an Australian win was set up by an unbeaten 139 from Mark Waugh in the first innings.

Steve Waugh's statistics in first class cricket to the end of the 1990–91 season were:

Sheffield Shield	39 matches	2438 runs at	42.77
Tests	42	2065	38.24
ODIs	111	2295	32.79

Stephen and Lynette Waugh.

Steve had been going out with Lynette Doughty for eight years, and on 16 August 1991 they were married. Brad McNamara was best man. He was playing with Oldham in the Lancashire League in England at the time, and he flew home for the wedding but had to get back to England within four days to meet his cricket commitments.

The next month Waugh was in Zimbabwe with an Australia B side led by Mark Taylor and managed by John Benaud, who was also an Australian selector. Benaud, in his delightful account of the tour in his book, *Matters of Choice*, said there were several motives behind the selection of Australia's B team: to see how Mark Taylor went as captain, to look at leg spinners Shane Warne and Peter McIntyre, and 'the fervent hope that Steve Waugh could drag himself out of a form slump'.

Waugh made three centuries on the tour, but it didn't get him back into the Test side. Warne, however, was picked for the Sydney Test and his book *Shane Warne—My Own Story* has a revealing cameo. After he was told of his selection for the Australian team, he was asked to go down to the Board office to talk to the press. He had a very bad hangover from celebrations the night before and was driven there by his father: 'I remember telling Graham Halbish that I was nervous and a bit queasy and that if he could hold off the media for a while I'd appreciate it. I headed straight for the safety of the toilet but didn't quite make it in time'.

(For me, Shane Warne is in the J.P. McEnroe class; he is so good to watch that I'll watch him no matter how badly he behaves. There is a perfect reference to Warne in Sarah Macdonald's book *Holy Cow—An Indian Adventure*. She describes a meeting with two young boys; they exchange 'the usual dialogue of the traveller' which involves 'admitting we are Australian and agreeing that Shane Warne is a great cricketer but a naughty man'.)

Won by Australia 4–0, the 1991–92 series against India was also notable for the emergence of Sachin Tendulkar. The 18-year-old Tendulkar, with centuries in Sydney and Perth, was the more impressive at this stage; Warne took 1 for 150 in Sydney and 0 for 78 in Adelaide and, along with Mark Waugh and Geoff Marsh, was dropped for the fifth Test.

Steve Waugh made 448 runs in Sheffield Shield games at 49.78 in 1991–92, and he played in the winning Australian side in the triangular one-day series against India and a lacklustre West Indies. His top score for the series was 34, but as in the past, to the detriment of his form in the longer game, batting at number 7 he seldom had the chance to play a proper innings. Stan McCabe's biographer, Jack McHarg, attributed Waugh's slump to batting down the order in one-day games, where he usually had to go in and have a whack. Writing in *Australian Cricket*, McHarg said he felt that Steve had a limited future in Test cricket at this stage.

In the *Sydney Morning Herald*, Peter Roebuck wrote:

Of late he has been inclined to throw hands, bat and kitchen sink at everything remotely tempting. He has particularly slashed at rising deliveries outside off stump without first moving his feet across and without closely watching the ball . . . Sceptics will say his problems are mental but I believe they are more a matter of technique. Because he never moves across he finds it difficult to step inside deliveries. Because his weight is not properly balanced between his feet he can be immobile.

On the positive side, after an FAI Cup match against Queensland, Waugh said, 'It's probably the first time in two years I've bowled without any sort of pain in my back . . . I think I put an extra yard on my bowling today and that's what I've been looking for.' In the one-day series, he generally bowled his 10 overs and had several 2 and 3 wicket hauls.

Australia didn't carry its form into the 1992 World Cup, played in Australia and New Zealand and won by Pakistan after a spectacular display of fast swing bowling by their captain, Wasim Akram. Again, Steve Waugh performed creditably, but not well enough to earn him a place in the touring party to Sri Lanka at the start of the 1992–93 season.

In an interview with Waugh reported in the *Telegraph*, Mark Gately said, 'You've got a reputation as a very intense guy but you don't strike me as someone who finds it difficult to relax and enjoy his cricket. Are you?'

Waugh replied, 'No, I still find it a lot of fun. It's just the way I come across. More than anything it's the way I concentrate, it's not the way I am. I find if I'm out there mucking about and laughing when I'm batting, I'll get out. That's the reason I'm like that. Especially with my bowling, I've got to be aggressive. I know if I try and relax and have a bit of a joke when I'm bowling I bowl a heap of garbage. If I try to knock someone's head off I bowl a lot better.'

Without the Test commitments, Waugh had a little more spare time. Gately asked him how he spent his time off the field: 'The last two years it's been with the house. Every spare minute we've been putting work into our house. It's been a pretty big project and it's coming to an end. Beside that I just relax by going to the movies or around to friend's places for tea. Pretty simple really'.

The 1987 World Cup-winning Australian team at the Red Fort in Delhi.

Interview at the end of the
1995 West Indies tour.
(West Indies Cricket Board/TWI)

With Greg Dyer, Greg Matthews and David Gilbert in India in 1986.

With Bob Simpson at the Man-of-Match awards, fourth Test, Kingston, Jamaica, 1989. *(West Indies Cricket Board/TWI)*

Steve Waugh being interviewed by Shane Warne before the Semi-final against the West Indies, 1996 World Cup. *(Board of Control for Cricket in India/TWI)*

With Brian Freedman at the Bankstown v Sutherland Sydney First Grade Grand Final, 1996-97. *(Channel 10)*

'No need to think about running': Waugh cuts for 4 during his first Test century. First Test, Headingley, 1989. *(England Cricket Board)*

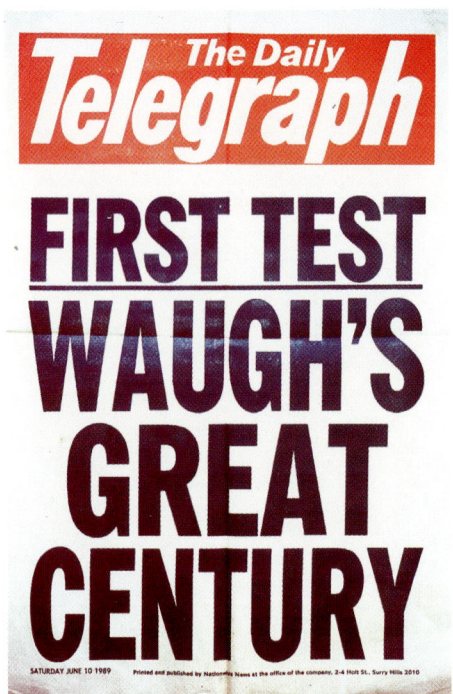

(News Limited)

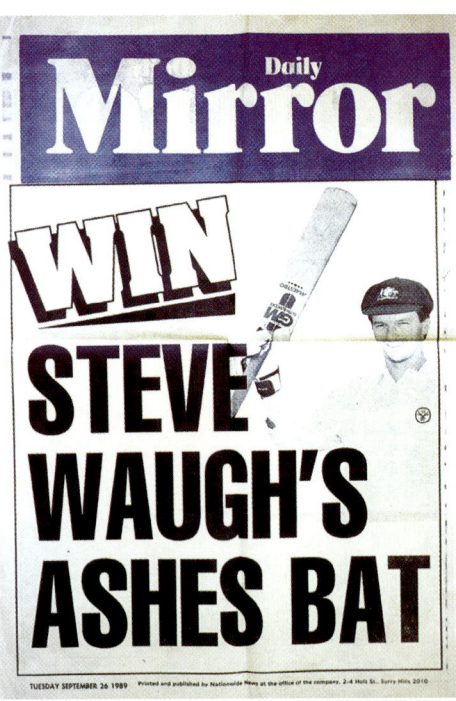

(News Limited)

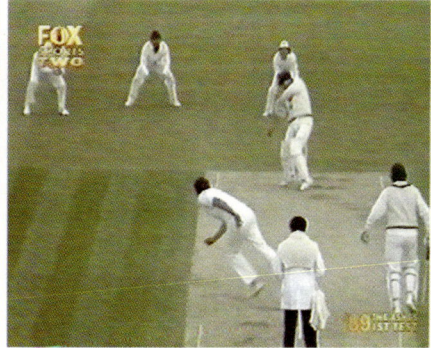

The disputed Lara catch, first Test, Bridgetown, Barbados, 1995. Michael Holding said, 'It hits the ground, actually,and then he scoops it up'. *(West Indies Cricket Board/TWI)*

'Don't cuss me, man': the confrontation with Curtly Ambrose, third Test, Port-of-Spain, April 1995. *(West Indies Cricket Board/TWI)*

Crowd sign, 1989–90

Opposite page top: The Waugh family in the late 1980s: Steve, Rodger, Danny, Mark, Beverley and Dean. *(Bev Waugh)*

Opposite page bottom: 'Runs in the family': *Time* Australia cartoon, May 1995. *(*Time *magazine/ Mark Sofilas)*

With Lynette, October 1989. *(*Woman's Day*)*

Starwaughs: Steve with his Symonds Tusker bat and brothers Danny, Dean and Mark at Bankstown Oval.

13

UP THE ORDER

Batting number 3

Although Waugh missed the tour to Sri Lanka at the start of the 1992–93 season—he and Lynette had a delayed honeymoon in the United States—he started the season in good form. He made 81 and 83 in State trial matches, then, batting number 3, made a man-of-the-match 85 not out and took two wickets in a Mercantile Mutual Cup (one-day) game against South Australia. This was followed by 48 against Victoria, and 131 from 140 balls and 3 wickets against Queensland, for another man-of-the-match award.

Bob Simpson said, 'The off-season at home has helped Steve . . . he was getting a bit overwrought, there's no doubt about that . . . As you know I've been very close to Steve and he appears more relaxed and determined to enjoy himself . . . the tenseness is gone and his footwork is looking good.'

Waugh had done a lot of work with Simpson on technique over the years. Simpson told me: 'There was always a concern about him with the shorter ball; for a while he wanted to be all macho and hook—he got a bit carried away I think. Once he came back, he thought everything was going to be right, and it wasn't right, the blokes worked him out again, and they started to bowl the line that he didn't like, which was in here—into the ribs—and they could tie him up there and he didn't play a shot, so he really had to come up with something to get over that. What I explained to Steve at the time was; it doesn't matter how you look, your job is to survive the ball you've just received, and the reason he was having the trouble was because he was so side on. It's OK to be side on if the ball is on the off stump or wider, but if it's in at the body, you've got to be open, to be able to ride it.

'So I said, "First, you've got to understand it doesn't matter how bad you look avoiding the bouncer, it's better to avoid it than try to play it down if you're not capable of playing it down." So he accepted that and that was a big breakthrough, you know, the macho thing was gone. Then I just taught him how to ride the ball, get inside it and play it down, but more importantly to get off strike.

'And that's when he really appreciated the full significance of singles. Stephen had always been a four hitter, so we worked very hard on the ball coming in to the body: move across to the off, all the weight on the right foot and you can roll through it, push it away to leg, get off strike so the bloke can't get at you again. That was the most important thing, it gave Steve a weapon to get away from the fast bowlers so he wasn't being subjected to over after over of it. I don't care who it is, if you get enough short bouncers, you start to worry about them—anyone who says they like fast bowling is an absolute liar.

'So that was the big difference, and the concentration—we punched that fairly heavily, you know, the need to be able to survive the good ball—and letting the ball go, he got better at that, too.'

In the first innings of a Shield game against Victoria, Merv Hughes welcomed Waugh with a bouncer which he turned away from and fended to Paul Nobes close in on the leg side—but then he made 95 and 100 not out in an Australian XI match against the West Indies at Bellerive Oval, Hobart. Other members of the Australian XI side were Matthew Hayden, Damien Martyn and Darren Lehmann.

He was back in the Test team, and with Geoff Marsh and Dean Jones gone and David Boon opening with Mark Taylor, there was much discussion about who should go in to face the West Indies quicks when the first wicket fell. Ian Chappell said Waugh was not the man for the number 3 spot, because of his technique against the short ball, but Waugh saw it as an opportunity: 'I didn't so much volunteer, I was asked about [batting at] three and it was a challenge and a good opportunity to stay in the side, so I thought, "Yeah, why not?"'

'A lovely slower ball': Carl Hooper beaten and bowled by Steve Waugh for 47. First Test, Brisbane, 1992–93. *(Cricket Australia/Channel 9)*

Writing in the *Sun-Herald*, John Benaud pointed out that in the last Test Waugh had played, in the West Indies, he was effectively a bowling all-rounder, batting at number 7, and asked: 'Was his jump in the order by the hand of his captain, Border, alone, or did Waugh stick up his hand for the job? It doesn't really matter, the bottom line was the message it announced: Steve Waugh, you're a batsman!'

And so to Brisbane. Border won the toss and chose to bat and after about 20 minutes Taylor edged Ian Bishop to the 'keeper and Waugh was in, facing Ambrose and Bishop with Courtney Walsh and Patrick Patterson looking forward to their turn. Waugh stayed for half an hour and made 10 in the first innings, then made 20 in an hour and a half in the second.

The West Indies made sure they bowled their full quota of bouncers at him and it worked in the first innings, although he was unlucky. He shaped to glance a short ball from Ambrose, then took his hands away; the video shows he missed it by six inches—the deflection was from his hip.

When West Indies batted, his 14 overs for 46 included the wicket of Hooper, bowled with a lovely slower ball; full length, Hooper thought it was going down leg and shaped to turn it, but it straightened and he played inside it.

In the second innings, Ambrose was no-balled for excessive short-pitched bowling to Waugh, who after 90 minutes edged a

Hooper caught and bowled by Waugh for 3, second Test, MCG 1992–93.
(Cricket Australia/Channel 9)

rare good length ball from Ambrose to the 'keeper.

It was a game Australia should have won. Needing 231 in the second innings, the West Indies were 8 for 133, saved by a fighting 66 by West Indies captain Richie Richardson, made in 235 minutes.

Again there were calls for Waugh to be dropped. Ian Chappell in particular, and not for the first time, insisted that if he was to be in the team, his vulnerability to the short ball, and inability or refusal to hook, dictated that number 3 was not the place to bat him. Dennis Lillee said Waugh was a great one-day player but 'wasn't up to it at first drop in Brisbane' and should be replaced by Justin Langer (like Lillee, a Western Australian).

But he stayed. Bruce Reid and Greg Matthews made way for Shane Warne and Mike Whitney. It was Warne's fifth Test and, even at this early stage, he had gained some notoriety. Warne had been a somewhat reluctant and rebellious student at the Academy of Cricket. On a trip to Darwin he had bared his bum out a hotel window and been sent back to Adelaide in disgrace, and was then kicked out of the Academy. He had had two Tests against the Indians and two in Sri Lanka without much success. Then, in the second innings of the second Test, with West Indies 1 for 143, chasing 355, he bowled Richie Richardson with a flipper and West Indies collapsed to be all out 219, Warne a match-winning 7 for 52. In *Shane Warne—My Own Story*, Warne wrote: 'All that practice with Jack Potter at the Academy, trying to get the flipper right, had paid off in one delivery . . . looking back now I can say definitely that that ball was the turning point in my career'.

In Australia's first innings, Mark Waugh (112) and Allan Border (110) had put them in a strong position with a total of 395. Steve Waugh made 38 and 1. He batted well in the first innings before again edging Ambrose, this time to Lara at first slip. In the second innings he smashed a wide ball from Bishop high to Phil Simmons at gully.

In Sydney, he was lucky to be let off early, a missed stumping chance off Hooper, but went on to 100, his first Test century in more than three years. He brought up the hundred with a back foot straight drive off Ambrose for 3, and put on 94 in partnership with Mark (57) before Mark ran himself out with a misjudged single. Steve's 100 took nearly four and a half hours and included only five fours. Border declared at 9 for 503 and, as Lara deftly stroked his way through the gaps in the field to 277—the third highest score in Tests against Australia—a draw became inevitable.

Then came the cliff-hanger in Adelaide. Now one up with two to play, a win would secure the series for Australia. In seven series against the West Indies, going back to 1978, Australia had lost six series and tied one. The last series win against West Indies had been under Ian Chappell in 1975.

Richardson won the toss. Haynes and Simmons saw off the new ball and were starting to look dangerous at 0 for 84 when Steve Waugh deceived Simmons with a slower ball which he top-edged to cover where Merv Hughes took a well-judged catch. Hughes then took 5 for 64 from 21 overs as the West Indies were confined to 252. On an uncharacteristically responsive Adelaide wicket, Curtly Ambrose took over where Hughes had left off, taking 6 for 74 and limiting Australia to 213. Hughes was again the star with 43; Steve Waugh, batting at five in this Test, was second top score with 42. David Boon, who at one stage retired hurt after being hit on the elbow by Ambrose, carried his bat for 39.

Australia trailed by only 39, but then off-spinner Tim May, on his home turf, came on and took 5 for 9 from only 6.5 overs, and the West Indies were all out 146—as David Boon said, 'The Frank Worrell trophy was only 186 runs away.' Ambrose had Boon lbw for 0, Australia 1 for 5, then 2 for 16. Mark Waugh and Langer put on 38, but when Mark went, it was 3 for 54 and 10 runs later Steve miss-hit an attempted cut off Ambrose to Arthurton in front of point.

Four for 64. Border, Healy and Hughes went cheaply, and at 7 for 74 it looked to be all over. Warne and Langer took it to 8 for 102. May then joined Langer and the score had reached 144 when Langer edged Bishop to be out for a very fine 54 in a little over four hours at the wicket. Forty-two runs for the last wicket looked unlikely at first, but after 88 agonising minutes, numbers 10 and 11 had taken the score to 184. One to tie, two to win. It was the 26th of January, Australia Day, surely . . . but no, Walsh bowled short, McDermott tried to get out of the road, it flicked a glove, and Junior Murray did the rest.

The Perth Test was a massacre. The West Indies with their four quicks had the advantage, and it must have been with some misgiving that Allan Border chose to bat when he won the toss. Ambrose, probably at the peak of his career on a wicket described as having too much moisture and seaming all over the place, took 7 for 25 from 18 overs. By stumps on Day 1 the West Indies were 1 for 135, already 16 runs ahead of Australia's first innings total. It was all over half way through the third day. Steve Waugh made 13 and a duck—once again dollying a catch off a short ball—and he was back under pressure.

AAP correspondent Patrick Keane wrote:

> The rising delivery that cut short another Steve Waugh innings against the West Indies at the WACA Ground yesterday may well have prematurely ended the Test career of the 27-year-old New South Welshman. Waugh perished to another short ball in the fifth Test when he could not defend himself against fast bowler Ian Bishop, lobbing a gentle catch to substitute Gus Logie in the gully . . . Waugh has not had the technique to cope with the difficult No 3 position.

He averaged 25.33 in the series against the West Indies. Mark averaged 37.77, bettered only by David Boon's 61.25.

Robert Craddock wrote in the *Telegraph*:

> Steve Waugh has read a million times this season that he is vulnerable against the short ball . . . Waugh said 'Half the time you don't want to pick up the paper because you know it's going to be some

sort of headline saying you are likely to be dropped. I know guys say they don't read the papers, but we all feel the pressure'.

Waugh himself acknowledged how hard it was to score against the West Indies, especially in Perth, and noted that he had not scored a boundary off Ambrose during the entire Test series. An appropriate last word on the series was provided later by Richie Benaud: 'One thing that should always be remembered is that Steve Waugh put his hand up to go in at number 3 against the West Indies in Australia last summer, not the kind of thing which leaps to everyone's lips when volunteers might be sought'.

The West Indies again proved to be Australia's nemesis in the one-day series, winning both finals. Although Steve Waugh generally had a satisfactory series, he suffered every bowler's worst nightmare in a preliminary game against Pakistan, played in Hobart. Bowling the last over, with Pakistan trailing by 16, he took a wicket with the first ball, then went for 4.1.4.1. A six was needed off the last ball to tie. Asif Mujtaba had just reached 50, so he had his eye in, and when Waugh's attempt at a full length turned into a full toss, Mujtaba smacked it over the mid wicket fence to level the scores.

In a three-Test tour of New Zealand, where Shane Warne continued to enhance his reputation with 17 wickets at 15.06, Waugh performed solidly with runs in each Test—62, 75 and 41. On the softer New Zealand wickets, some of his batting had the compact, classic look of his innings in England in 1989, but his concentration seemed to let him down, with false shots when he was well set. With Hadlee gone, New Zealand were rather less formidable, but they managed to share the series 1-each with a 5-wicket win in the third Test.

On the second day of the first Test, played at Lancaster Park in Christchurch, Allan Border became the leading run-scorer in Test history when he reached 50 with a pull to the boundary off Dipak Patel. He finished with 88 and a tally of 10,161 runs, 39 more than Sunil Gavaskar.

14

STUCK IN THERE

Maturity and consistency

From his selection for the first Test against the West Indies in Australia in 1992–93 to his retirement from Test cricket in January 2004, Steve Waugh was never again dropped from the Australian Test team. In this period, too, unlike the1980s, the Australians won a lot more Tests than they lost. England was crushed at home in 1993, losing the one-day series 0–3 and winning only the last Test, when they were already 0–4 down in a six-Test series.

For this series, Steve Waugh went back to number 6, where he had made all those runs against England in 1989. Border said, 'I've always felt that he's better down the list having a dash at the old ball . . . he's good batting with the tail because he still does hit fours, even though the field is out . . . He's a different sort of player over here, he looks so much in command.' Australia's batting was always too strong. In the first four Tests (after which the Ashes were retained) Steve Waugh came in at 4/225, 4/234, 4/591, 3/197, 4/81 and 4/321. He did very little bowling—only 32 overs in the series—but batted consistently, with scores of 3, 78 not out, 13 not out, 13, 47 not out, 157 not out 59, 20 and 26. He topped the averages with 416 runs at 83.20. No doubt he would have made more runs if he had been batting up the order. Boon made 555 runs at 69.38 and Mark Waugh 550 at 61.11.

Australia's bowling was dominant too. Warne set the tone in the first Test when, after Australia had made only 289, he was brought on with England making good progress at 1 for 80. His first ball was the famous, perfectly pitched 'ball from hell' that dipped and drew Mike Gatting forward, landed outside leg stump, then bit and spun past the outside edge of Gatting's bat to take off stump. Gatting looked bewildered and Warne never looked back, with 34 wickets at 25.79. In his book, *Shane Warne—My Own Story*, Warne wrote: 'After stumps that day the England players came into our dressing room for a drink and Gatt just looked up at me and said, "Bloody hell, Warnie, what happened?"'

Warne didn't do it all on his own. Merv Hughes took 31 wickets at 27.26, Tim May took 21 at 28.19 and Paul Reiffel had the best average: 19 wickets at 20.84.

Although it was a successful tour for Steve Waugh, his only innings of note was 157 not out in the fourth Test, and even this was overshadowed by Border's 200, also not out, in Australia's first innings total of 4 for 653. Australia won by an innings and 148, and England's performance cost Graham Gooch the captaincy, replaced by Mike Atherton.

Perhaps a more important innings for Steve Waugh was his 47 not out in the third Test on a bright sunny day at Trent Bridge, where Australia needed 371 to win and had collapsed to 4 for 81 when he came in. Mark had been bowled by Andrew Caddick for 1, and soon after, Australia was 5 for 93, and then 6 for 115. Although Waugh's timing was not always at its best, he and Brendon Julian (56 not out) saw out the last two hours to save the game.

After being dropped on 0, Waugh made 59 in the first innings of the fifth Test, including a partnership of 153 with Mark, who was at his graceful best in scoring 137. It was an interesting contrast in styles: Mark is more flexible and gets his power from subtle transfers of weight, rocking backwards from bent knees, whereas Steve sets himself in position and gets his power from his hands and arms.

Egged on by the crowd, England fast bowler Martin Bicknell tested Waugh with some well-directed short stuff in the fifth Test. He made him play one or two false strokes and gave him some unsolicited advice—'Nice of Martin Bicknell to enquire if Steve Waugh was OK,' said Richie.

Writing in *Inside Edge*, Richie also said:

> There is always a lot of talk about technique as regards playing against both pace and spin and one thing of which we can be reasonably certain is that the starting point for technique is footwork. The reason I mention footwork in relation to Steve Waugh is that his footwork against the pace bowlers always seems on the flamboyant side. It has always seemed to me that he has been too correct and much too side on to be a really successful player of short-pitched bowling. That is merely an observation from experience because I have seen few batsmen who have been very side on in defence able to provide a proper counter to the ball coming in at their ribs.

Also in *Inside Edge*, Kerry O'Keeffe took a different view:

> My videotape collection of [Steve Waugh's] dismissals over the past twelve months is littered with instances of squaring up and drawing his hands towards the rising ball. Against Ambrose in particular, his right leg—carrying virtually all his bodyweight—would screw his shoulders front on and present him with difficulties in dealing with the steepling delivery.

Everyone is different, of course; watching Garry Sobers on video is interesting: he doesn't move his feet much but you notice that he keeps his head very still—everything revolves around his head and he gets his power from the great flourish from his arms.

Ian Healy described a sledge that worked: during the fifth Test, with England 8 down in the second innings late on the fourth day and Thorpe on 60, defending well and farming the strike, Waugh said to Healy, loud enough for Thorpe to hear, 'You watch, he'll play for the not out.' Soon after, Thorpe went down the wicket trying for a big hit from Warne and was stumped by Healy. Healy wrote that England didn't like Australia's on-field bravado, but did nothing to confront it or to find out how the Aussies went about their work. 'I have always felt that if a team was beating you the one place you must go is their dressing room, to try to discover what they're doing right', Healy wrote. 'Had they come into our dressing room we would gladly have shared a beer with them, but we never saw them.'

David Boon (now a Test selector) details the contest between Hayden and Slater for the second opening spot at the start of the tour. It was won by Slater. 'While Slats' Test career has gone from strength to strength', Boon wrote, 'the highly gifted Queensland opener has played just one Test match . . . quite possibly he may never play for his country again'. Which goes to show that the average Test player (or selector) may not know a lot more than the rest of us.

It was on this tour that Steve Waugh started writing his diaries. Before laptops were common, his target was two pages a day on foolscap paper. His first book, *Steve Waugh's Ashes Diary*, with a foreword by Shane Warne, was in the bookshops in time for Christmas 1993. The text is mainly a straightforward account of the team's day-to-day activities. When they are playing cricket, the match is the focus, but not to the exclusion of everything else: Waugh writes up where they went, how they got there, what they ate, who did something silly. The photographs—many of them taken by Steve Waugh himself—are well-chosen and numerous.

'The downside of life as a touring cricketer is the time spent away from your family, especially for those guys with young children', Waugh wrote. 'On this tour, wives and families are not allowed to stay in the team's hotel until the last two weeks of the campaign. They can, of course, live in England if they choose, although that isn't much of an option, as they only end up trekking round after the team without spending much time with their companions, at a great financial cost.' Lynette arrived in England on Day 57 of the tour, along with Helen Healy and the Healys' two-year-old daughter, and stayed until the end of the tour—Day 122, August 24—with a week away from the tour on a trip to Italy. Waugh wrote: 'The trip allows them some time away from the cricket. It can be very tiring and sometimes boring for them to continually follow the team around and watch cricket day in and day out'.

During this series in England the squad formed two groups, Nerds and Julios (after Julio Iglesias) for intra-squad competition at fielding practice, touch football, tenpin bowling and similar competitions. Julios were cool and stylish, captained by Errol Alcott and including Mark Waugh, Shane Warne, Brendon Julian and Craig McDermott. Qualifications included use of hair gel, having posed as a model for a newspaper article and walking as if 'carrying a watermelon under each arm'. Nerds were captained by Tim May and included Simpson, Border, Boon, Taylor and Steve Waugh; they were characterised by being 'ugly, poor dressers, good drinkers, and non-use of gel in their hair'. Other aspects of the tour were the revival of the Daktari suit for dumb behaviour, introduced on the Australia B tour to Zimbabwe in 1991, and Plucka Duck, as featured on the TV show 'Hey Hey It's Saturday'—a replica had to be carried everywhere by the last player to make 0.

After England won the last Test, Waugh wrote:

> With the series over, all the players from both sides got together for a drink and a chat. But not for long. Half the English team were on the motorway home before they had finished their beer, which was something we couldn't believe, especially as they had just won a Test match. They weren't even going out together to celebrate. This to me explains why we were a much tighter-knit group. We enjoy our victories together and moments like these bond everyone together in a link which is so important when times get tough.

Early in the 1993–94 season in a grade match between Bankstown and Fairfield, Bankstown made only 84 in the first innings and Fairfield made 183. In the second innings the Waugh twins put on 160 from 132 balls and were able to leave Fairfield 129 to win from 35 overs—not a big ask. Mick Stephenson's history of the Bankstown Cricket Club records:

With Mark and Steve intimidating the Fairfield batsmen by standing just metres away on either side of the pitch, and a fired up Scott Thompson, capitulation was inevitable. It took just 96 minutes and 24 overs with Scott Thompson taking 8/29 . . . brilliant, aggressive and uncompromising captaincy from the man who was destined to lead Australia.

Waugh had not recaptured the brilliance of his 1989 form in England in 1993, but he had become a much more measured player, less volatile, more reliable. How had it happened? Perhaps it was anger at criticism from the press. Perhaps it was almost a business decision, recognition that if he could stay at the top he would make a lot of money. Perhaps it was just experience. Probably it took elements of all of the above.

Over the next two years, Waugh made a significant contribution to every series he played in, usually with the bat but sometimes also with the ball. New Zealand was overwhelmed by Australia's batting in a three-Test series in Australia late in 1993. The Perth Test was drawn after Australia declared at 1 for 323 in the second innings. The Hobart and Brisbane Tests were won, Border declaring at 6 for 544 and 6 for 607. Steve Waugh made 216 runs for once out, with a highest score of 147 not out, while Boon, Taylor and Mark Waugh also made more than 200 runs in the series and Michael Slater made 305 at an average of 76.25.

Australia also dominated the three-way one-day series with New Zealand and South Africa. In Australia's fourth game of the series, Waugh tore a hamstring while batting and had to retire hurt. It was a bad tear, but he had ten hours of treatment per day and within two weeks got it to a stage where he could play again. Geoff Lawson wrote in the *Sydney Morning Herald*: 'A Christmas at home rather than in a Melbourne hotel is a pleasant change of pace for the elder Waugh brother, although he has spent more of the festive season in the company of the NSW physiotherapist than his family'.

With his fitness in doubt he decided to prove he was OK by making himself available for the Sheffield Shield side, and the NSW selectors took the opportunity to make him captain. Against South Australia, after trailing by 70 runs in the first innings, Waugh, to the surprise of his team-mates, declared NSW's second innings closed when they were only 265 ahead on the placid Adelaide pitch. He then asked off-spinner Gavin Robertson to open the bowling—another surprise—and after NSW had won by 109 (Robertson 5 for 43), Waugh organised for the team to stay over in Adelaide that night instead of flying home, so they could have a proper team celebration.

Michael Bevan, with 103 and 89, had played a major part in NSW's win, but Waugh had made 73 and 46, and he led NSW into the next Shield game against Tasmania in Hobart, where he made 190, although Tasmania took first innings points. During this game bushfires were threatening his home at Alfords Point in Sydney's southern suburbs. Family and friends, including team-mates from Bankstown Cricket Club, helped Lynette prepare as the fire approached. Eventually she had to evacuate the house. Waugh kept in touch as best he could and left the ground in Hobart to return home, but before his flight was due he heard that the danger had passed. Waugh said they had been lucky to save the house: 'The fire went right over the house and around it, burnt all the yard, front and back, and took the fences out'.

The match also had its share of drama, with Waugh criticising Tasmanian captain Rod Tucker's tactics of giving NSW easy runs in their second innings in the hope that NSW would give them a reasonable target. Tucker's ploy worked; NSW declared and Tasmania won outright. Waugh called it a 'Teddy Bear's picnic' and Tucker angrily told him to mind his own business.

The first of three Tests against South Africa started on Boxing Day 1993. Rain spoiled this Test, which was drawn; then in Sydney, on a black day for Allan Border, needing 117 to win in the fourth innings, Australia made only 111. Craig McDermott's 29 was top score, Fanie de Villiers took 6 for 43, Alan Donald 3 for 34.

Damien Martyn had replaced Waugh for the first two Tests against South Africa, but Waugh was back in the side for Adelaide.

He made 164 in Australia's first innings, and took 4 for 26 (Hudson, Rhodes, Cullinan and McMillan). Australia won by 191; Steve Waugh was man-of-the-match and, despite having played only one Test, man-of-the-series. His only blemish for the match was a shake of the head and an angry stare at umpire Terry Prue when he was given out caught behind trying to glance, for which he earned a reprimand. Waugh apparently didn't think it had carried to the 'keeper, but the video coverage and the commentators seem to support the umpire. Waugh wasn't the only dissenter; South African Peter Kirsten was referred to the match referee for questioning lbw decisions and was fined 75 per cent of his match fee.

Waugh's confidence was now up and he was getting to the stage in first class cricket that he had occupied in grade as a youngster: of being able to impose his will on a game in a way that very few cricketers are able to do. He had had a cortisone injection in his back early in the summer and was bowling more freely than he had for three or four years. His bowling in the Adelaide Test particularly, which at one stage reduced South Africa from 2 for 173 to 6 for 203, was a triumph of thinking cricket, as he sought the danger spots in a cracking wicket, varied his pace and outwitted his opponents.

The return series, in South Africa, which was preparing for the elections which brought Nelson Mandela to power, was the first by the official Australian team since 1969–70. It was to be Allan Border's farewell series and it produced some quality cricket.

South Africa won the first Test comfortably, Hansie Cronje's 122 in the second innings the deciding factor in a game where runs were hard to come by. A contributing factor may have been the provocative nature of the crowd. There is an element in South African crowds, especially in Johannesburg, that expresses genuine ill-will to outsiders; the Australians weren't used to it, and it got to them.

On the third day, after Hudson had made a gritty, three-hour hundred, Warne, who had been heckled and upset by the crowd, bowled Hudson round his legs. Warne wrote: 'I lost it completely and started yelling, "Fuck off! Go on Hudson, fuck off out of here!"'

Warne started to follow Hudson off the field, still yelling abuse, and Ian Healy had to restrain him. Later in the game Merv Hughes had an altercation with a spectator in the 'players' tunnel' which protects them from the crowd as they go on and off the field. Hughes yelled abuse and slammed his bat into an advertising sign. Both Hughes and Warne were fined nominal amounts by the match referee—Warne says $1000, Steve Waugh says $250, Ian Healy and David Boon say $400—but when the incidents were replayed on televison back in Australia they were widely condemned and the Board imposed an additional $4000 fine. The players were upset at the additional fine; it seemed to be a knee-jerk reaction to the press campaign at home. Their tour contract said that such matters should be dealt with by the tour management, and when ACB chairman Alan Crompton and CEO Graham Halbish arrived later in the tour they received a cool reception.

At Newlands, South Africa made 361 and Australia totalled 435—Boon 96, Steve Waugh 86. South Africa then crumbled to 164 all out, Steve Waugh a match-winning 5 for 28 from 22 overs. The wicket was keeping low, which suited Waugh's skidders. Boon said this was the best he ever saw Steve bowl. Waugh said, 'The cortisone injection I had earlier in the summer seems to have done the trick. It has meant a lot less pain and I'm freer with my action.'

Border's last Test was a drab affair. Australia took more than a day to make 269 and after South Africa ground their way to 422 a result could only come if Australia collapsed. An unbeaten 113 from man-of-the-match Mark Waugh in a little under five hours made sure this did not happen. Steve's contribution was 64 and 3 for 40, which earned him man-of-the-series. Allan Border said,

Hansie Cronje caught and bowled by Waugh, the first of his 5 wickets for 28 in South Africa's second innings. Second Test, Cape Town, 1994. *(United Cricket Board of South Africa)*

'There's a greater maturity about his play. He has really settled on his technique now and he's playing superbly.'

The one-day series was played either side of the Tests; South Africa led 4–2 with two to play. At Newlands for the seventh game, Australia made 242—Taylor 63, Mark Waugh 71—then the bowlers starved the South African top order. McGrath and May both bowled their 10 overs for 38 runs, Warne bowled 10 overs for 31 runs and 3 wickets, and Reiffel bowled 7 overs for 18 runs. South Africa lost only 5 wickets but made only 206 runs. Needing to win the eighth game to tie the series, Australia made only 203 (Boon 45, Steve Waugh 42) and South Africa needed only 6 to win from the last over. Damien Fleming managed to restrict them to 4 runs only and tie the series. Man-of-the-series was again Steve Waugh, who had made a contribution with bat, ball, or both in every game.

Following the success of his *Ashes Diary* from the 1993 England tour, Waugh wrote another diary of the tour to South Africa:

> I guess my aim with these tour diaries is to give everyone a feel of what it's like being on tour with the Australian cricket team. A sort of sneak look at touring life with hopefully a few insights into what happens on the field and how we prepare and relax off it. It doesn't always come easily—believe me, I stare at blank paper for a while.

The diaries do give a feeling of what it's like to be on tour, how busy it is, how mundane in some respects—eating, sleeping, catching the bus—but surreal in others—attending a camp for 200 young cricketers at Soweto, picking up the newspapers to learn that you are in doubt for a Test match because of a spider bite, going out in front of a hostile crowd to face Alan Donald. It would have been interesting to have some background to the Warne and Hughes incidents. Waugh deals with the results—the fines—in his book but unlike Warne, does not deal with what Warne and Hughes actually did, or why.

As the 1994–95 season approached, John Benaud wrote in the *Sun-Herald*: 'In an extraordinary move, the Cricket Board had decided to interview four candidates for the captaincy . . . On Tuesday, in the Board's rooms in Melbourne, Mark Taylor, Steve Waugh, David Boon and Ian Healy will front up to face questions from the directors'. A statement from the Board's chief executive Graham Halbish said that the interviews were 'to discuss the captaincy and things in general'. Benaud favoured Taylor and said, 'The directors should spend about five minutes on the captaincy question. Meaning they'll have plenty of time to quiz the four senior players on "things in general"'. As more than one commentator said, it was strange to find the Board of such a large and public institution having to interview its senior players to find out what they thought.

Ian Chappell wrote that he would have chosen Mark Waugh: 'He has got a good cricket brain—you can see when he is bowling that he's always trying to work out how to get people out . . . He would lead from the front. If he told people in the team to go out and attack, he would do it himself. Steve is not that sort of player. Nor is Taylor'.

However, no one was surprised when Taylor got the job. He had been made captain of his grade club, Northern Districts, when he was 22, and had proved himself there and with the Australia B side in Zimbabwe in 1991. He had captained NSW with success and he had captained Australia (with Steve Waugh as vice-captain) in three Australasia Cup games in Sharjah after the South African tour. There was some surprise at the appointment of Healy as vice-captain—many thought that Steve Waugh had the better credentials—but Healy was widely respected and it's possible his open, extroverted approach was preferred to Waugh's perceived dourness and introversion.

Their next commitment was the Singer World Series in Sri Lanka, also involving India and Pakistan. Australia reached the semi-finals, but the tour is best remembered for the level of security required and the fact that it was here that Mark Waugh and Shane Warne had their first meeting with 'John' the bookmaker. In James Knight's *Mark Waugh: The Biography*, Waugh tells how John introduced himself at the team's hotel and gave him $US4000 and Warne $US5000 in return for 'general information about pitch and weather conditions and the Australian team's mood, tactics and selections' for the rest of the 1994–95 season. Waugh says he accepted the offer because it seemed to be no more than he and other players did quite often when interviewed on the radio. More sinister approaches were to follow soon after.

In Pakistan in 1994–95, with the same team management as in 1988—Bob Simpson as coach and Col Egar as manager—the series began in Karachi with one of the great Test matches. Australia made 337 (Bevan 82, Steve Waugh 73) and led by 81, Warne and Joe Angel taking 3 wickets each. Despite Taylor's second duck in his first Test as captain, Australia looked comfortable at 2 for 171, leading by 252, near the end of the third day. Ian Healy wrote:

> I started to pack up my gear, but Warney saw me and quipped 'Geez Heals, you wouldn't want a couple of wickets to fall'. I just laughed. Seven balls later, I was out there, after Pakistan's awesome duo, Waqar Younis and Wasim Akram, blasted out Junior, then Bevo, then Tugga . . . It was typical Pakistan cricket. They could go along at their own pace and then boom, boom, boom, they changed gear.

Despite a staunch, undefeated 114 from the redoubtable David Boon, the last 8 wickets fell for 61 and Pakistan needed 314 to win. At 7 for 184, then 8 for 236 and 9 for 258—56 needed and 1 wicket left—Australia seemed a certainty, but Inzamam-ul-Haq and leg-spinner Mushtaq Ahmed decided to hit out and quickly closed the gap. Healy says that Warne bowled superbly and should have won the game for Australia when, with 3 runs needed, he and Taylor decided to leave an opening at mid wicket for Inzamam, in the hope that he would try to play through there against the spin. It worked: Inzamam went out of his crease to force Warne to leg, but the ball bit sharply and beat the bat. It beat Healy too, went through his legs for 4 byes and the Test was lost. Healy says it was the worst miss of his life. He still finds it hard to look at photographs of the end of the game.

History repeated itself. As Border had said after Pakistan had won the first Test in 1988: 'The next two Tests will be played on bland pitches and will be drawn'. At Rawalpindi, after Pakistan had trailed by 261 in the first innings, man-of-the-match Salim Malik saved the game with 237. Whatever else might be said about him, Malik was a stylish and inventive batsman, especially against spin, and the duels between him and Shane Warne are compulsive viewing.

For Australia, Michael Slater made 110 and Steve Waugh a brave 98 in the face of an onslaught of bouncers from Waqar and Wasim on the second day. Both fast bowlers had spent long periods off the field on the first day and reacted angrily when a new ruling from the ICC prevented them from bowling for a similar period on the second. Waugh was hit on the body several times, had to pull away more than once to ask the umpires to stop the close in fieldsmen from talking, and, when the barrage was at its peak, couldn't resist the temptation to ask after Wasim's bad back, which had kept him off the field on the first day. Gavin Robertson said, 'Akram bowled at an incredible pace, targeting the batsman's chest and head. He ducked and weaved and was hit excruciating blows on the arms and under the ribs.' Waugh said he had never faced a faster spell of bowling. 'It was quick, short and nasty,' he said, 'but this is Test cricket and you don't expect any favours out there.'

Steve Waugh missed the third Test with a shoulder injury. It too was drawn, and Salim Malik was again man-of-the-match, but the Pakistan captain's alleged activities off the field had been even more remarkable. On the night before the final day of the first Test, he phoned Tim May and Shane Warne and asked them to meet him. May said he was too tired, but Warne went and later said that he had been offered $US200,000 to bowl outside off stump on the last day of the Test, to ensure a draw. Warne rejected the offer. It was discussed amongst the players but not made public.

Three weeks later, at a reception on the eve of a one-day match in Rawalpindi—on that tour the one-day games were played between Tests—Malik approached Mark Waugh and offered the same amount for Waugh to 'get four or five players and throw the game tomorrow'. Waugh rejected the offer and made 121 the next day, although Pakistan won the game by 9 wickets. The issue was discussed more generally among the touring party after the second offer, but did not become public until Phil Wilkins broke the story in the *Sydney Morning Herald* five months later. For the record, Australia won the one-day series against Pakistan and South Africa.

Steve Waugh did not publish a diary of this tour, although he and his friend Gavin Robertson put out a weekly newsletter titled the 'No Whinge No Wine Tour', which included interviews and profiles, and generally poked fun at everybody on tour. Tim May and Damien Fleming also kept the touring party amused by recording video interviews with the local Pakistanis about the relative prospects of Hawthorn and North Melbourne in the AFL Grand Final.

In his autobiography, *Opening Up*, Mike Atherton, English opening bat and captain, wrote:

> I saw Waugh for the first time on our 1990–91 tour and, like many others, I thought he flinched and looked unsure against short, quick bowling. Indeed, so unsure did he look that he was dropped at Adelaide in favour of his twin brother, Mark. Six months before our next tour there, I unwisely mentioned this flaw in a newspaper inter-view. He hadn't forgotten the comment and when I was batting against Shane Warne in the first Test of the [1994–95] series, Waugh asked Mark Taylor if he could field at silly point for me. 'I've waited a long time for this,' he snarled, as he took up residence under my nose, and he continued to growl and snarl throughout my stay. That was unusual for Waugh. His sledging, or 'mental deteri-oration', as he called it, was usually indirect. He would often pass comment to a team-mate, designed of course for the opposition player and within his earshot. 'Hey Warnie,' he might say as he passed Nasser mid-pitch, 'Hussain plays with a really open face, doesn't he?' He avoided full on confrontation, and by picking his comments and his targets carefully he was much more effective.
>
> That was as much communication as we had in the thirteen years we played against each other, until after my last match at The Oval, when we chatted and shared a beer.

The 1994–95 Ashes series in Australia was going pretty much as predicted after Australia won comfortably in Brisbane and Melbourne. There was a glitch in Sydney when, after leading by 193 on the first innings, England declared at 2 for 255, leaving a day and a half to bat and 449 to make, but the wicket was a feather bed and openers Slater (103) and Taylor (113) gave Australia the start it needed to save the game. England won the fourth Test, dismissing Australia for only 156 in the fourth innings in Adelaide, to put some interest back into the series, but they were crushed in Perth for a 3–1 series loss. Michael Slater made 623 runs at 62.30. The bowling of man-of-the-series Craig McDermott (32 at 21.09) and Shane Warne (27 at 20.33) was a major factor.

Steve Waugh made 345 at 49.29. Commentating during the first Test, Greg Chappell said, 'His footwork has improved terrifically over the last season or so.' Later, after Waugh had been left 99 not out in the fifth Test, Geoff Boycott said, 'He had a difficult time this morning, but he's a gritty player and it's been a gritty sort of innings. He's really stuck in there, fought his way through the difficult times, the hard parts of his innings when he was playing and missing this morning at the quick bowlers and the new ball.' Still carrying the shoulder injury suffered in a one-day match in Pakistan, Waugh did not bowl during the Tests.

The one-day series was played between England, Australia and Australia A. England did not make the finals, in which Australia defeated Australia A 2–0.

It had been ten years since Steve Waugh's Test debut. The skinny, nervous youth with the long hair was now a seasoned, established Test player, and generally regarded as the world's best one-day cricketer.

The really big reputations are won by players who save or win the Test matches that matter. Waugh had taken a long time to get into this category, but he was close. In his thirteenth Test—against England at the SCG in January 1987—his first Test in a winning side, his second innings 73, coming in at 4 for 110 was important—but the series had already been won and Waugh's contribution was overshadowed by Dean Jones's 184 in the first innings. He played two great innings in England in 1989, 177 at Leeds and 152 at Lord's. But he came in with the score at more than 200 in both cases, and the balance of the sides was such that Australia would probably have won without those innings.

It must have been galling for him when, five years after his debut, India was back in Australia but he was not in the Test side. Another two years on, he found himself batting number 3 against the West Indies in Australia; his 100 in Sydney was a good innings, but in a drawn game where Brian Lara made 277.

He had come closest to true greatness in the third Test against South Africa, played in Adelaide in 1993–94. The series was in the balance and South Africa was a strong side. He went in at 4 for 183, so Australia had a reasonable start, but his 164 was chanceless. It gave Australia a winning platform and was followed by bowling figures of 4 for 26, all class batsmen—Hudson, Rhodes, Cullinan and McMillan. It won him man-of-the-match and, even though he had only played this one Test, man-of-the-series.

His 98 against the fired-up Wakar and Wasim at Rawalpini in 1994 was brave and resourceful, the sort of innings very few batsmen could have played. He had also played a significant part—as a bowler—in winning the 1987 World Cup, and as an all-rounder in winning many a one-day international. And the Steve Waugh package was more than the sum of the parts. He could bat, he could bowl, he was brilliant and reliable in the field, he had a good cricket brain and was a feisty competitor; Steve Waugh was the man to turn to in a crisis, good for team morale on and off the field. To outsiders he might have seemed dour and moody, but he was a lively companion on tour, and a tonic for team spirits, taking the mickey without malice. As Allan Border said, 'He's a very positive bloke. He never believes we're going to lose. He always believes something is going to happen.'

15

THANKS BUT NO THANKS

The search for Steve Waugh

In the early 1980s, when I became editor of a (now defunct) cricket magazine called *World Cricket Digest*, it was suggested that I should get Bill O'Reilly to write a piece on leg spin. I looked in the phone book and there he was, W.J. O'Reilly, Hatfield Street, Blakehurst. I rang him and he agreed to write the piece, then he asked in his big booming voice, 'And how much did you propose to pay me for this privilege?'

'What would you say to . . . ?' I mentioned a sum—I can't remember how much.

'I'd say that was modest,' O'Reilly said, 'but I'll do it. It's a subject I know something about.'

One of the joys of my life was getting to know Bill O'Reilly. He went on to narrate a documentary for me and I spent 'many hours in his glorious company', as cricket writer David Frith once put it in a letter to me.

Bradman was not so easy to meet. I wrote, asking him to be involved in a documentary, but he politely declined. Later, I met him when he wanted to make video versions for the Bradman Museum of talks which he used to do on coaching and cricket history. From this he got involved in helping me identify and catalogue a mass of archival cricket film which I had gathered, and this led to his involvement in two programs I made for the ABC.

Like O'Reilly, Bradman was good company, and both had

charming wives. I thought Bradman and O'Reilly were alike in many ways; both were stimulating in conversation, full of ideas but keen to hear the opinions of others, humorous, interested and interesting. It still puzzles me why they didn't get on—I think it puzzled Bradman too, he didn't seem to have any particular animosity towards O'Reilly, and O'Reilly never really explained what Bradman had done that made O'Reilly so cranky with him.

Twenty years ago it was much easier to get in touch with Test cricketers. Over the years, I interviewed Garry Sobers, Neil Harvey, Ray Lindwall, Rod Marsh, Alec Bedser, the Chappell brothers. With the ex-Test players, someone would have their number, or the State cricket association would give it to you, and you would just ring them up. Miller was the only one I couldn't interview. He was happy to talk on the phone but he was reluctant to be quoted and he wouldn't do interviews for television; he said he couldn't be bothered.

In 1989 I did a book of interviews with cricketers and others involved with the game. I spoke to David Boon, Trevor Hohns, Merv Hughes, Dean Jones, Tim May, Mark Taylor and Tim Zoehrer, all Test players at the time. I had wanted to talk to Steve Waugh, but his then manager, Austin Robertson, who looked after several high profile players including Dennis Lillee and Allan Border, said I wasn't offering enough money. From memory, apart from Waugh, Merv Hughes was the only one I spoke to who had a manager. Generally, I paid the players and ex-players for interviews. There were exceptions—the Chappells would never take any money.

In 1997, I had the ABC interested in the idea of a documentary series featuring Waugh and Peter Roebuck, which was to be called 'The Best XI' and was to review all the Test players through the ages and come up with the best team of all time. I spoke to Waugh on the phone a couple of times but again dealt mainly with his agent, now Colleen Adamson at Advantage International. The project fell through partly because Waugh was Australian vice-captain and about to become captain of the one-day team—it was hard to find the time. As always with film and television projects, finding the funding was also a problem.

Waugh is now managed by TEAM-Duet and I know Harley Medcalf, a principal of the firm, reasonably well—we were team-mates on a cricket tour of India some years ago. In September 2003, after I had been commissioned to write this book, I phoned Harley, to try to arrange an interview with Steve. Harley said he did not think Steve would be pleased to hear that someone was writing a biography, but he would talk to him. A week or so later I was told that Steve had said he would not talk to me or co-operate in the publication of the book.

Soon after that I spoke to Harley again, saying that when the book was near to completion there would be a number of things I would need to check, and asking if he would think about revisiting the issue with Steve then. Harley asked me to confirm the request, which I did by email:

4 November 2003
To Harley Medcalf DUET-Group
Hullo Harley

Whether or not Steve agrees to talk to me will have some bearing on how I do the book and as I am just about finished researching and about to start writing, it would be helpful if I could clarify the situation now.

I would be asking for two things. First, for answers to a list of specific questions where I am not sure of facts—this could be done in writing if Steve wished. Second, for an interview of up to an hour, if possible with Lynette present for at least some of the time.

I think you are aware that this is a serious, factual book about someone I think is an important figure. Also that I have made some sort of contribution to cricket through collecting and preserving archival film and making documentaries including 'The Bradman Era', 'The Story of Cricket in Australia', 'The Cricket Archives' etc.

I'm not in a great hurry to talk—I'd like to get a fair bit of the book written first—but I'd appreciate your advice re whether Steve will talk to me as soon as it's convenient.

All the best
Jack Egan

Unfortunately, I never received a reply. I also hoped to be able to interview Glenn McGrath:

15 October 2003
To Warren Craig Titan Management
Hullo Warren

As discussed earlier [on the phone] I have been commissioned by Allen & Unwin to write a biography of Steve Waugh—a fairly serious book, an objective look at a major figure in sport, which says something about him and something about cricket, in Australia and internationally . . . I'd like to talk to Glenn mainly about Steve as captain, reasonably technical stuff such as how they work out strategies for different batsmen—Lara, Atherton, Jayasuriya, Tendulkar etc. Also about Steve as a batsman—how Glenn bowls to him on the rare occasions they have played against each other.

I suppose this is a difficult one, but I'd also like to talk about the sledging issue; Glenn has been involved in a couple of incidents while Steve has been captain and I'd like to get Glenn's side of the story, to see the issue from his perspective. We could talk over the phone, but I'd prefer to go and see him if possible.

This is not an authorised biography, but I have been in touch with Harley Medcalf and asked if I can put some questions to Steve (to check specific facts etc.) and also talk to Steve down the track, when I have finished my research.

Cheers
Jack Egan

November 4 2003
Jack

I have been advised by Stephen Waugh's management that they are not in support of this project and accordingly Glenn will not make himself available to be interviewed for this book.

Kind regards
Warren Craig

I had similar responses from New Zealand captain Stephen Fleming and former England captain Nasser Hussain. The New Zealand and England media managers asked if the book was endorsed and when I told them it wasn't, politely declined: 'Stephen [Fleming] has said thank you for the opportunity but no thanks'. I was unable to contact another former England captain, Mike Atherton. The England media manager was most helpful, and gave me a contact who said she would forward an email, but I didn't hear back from Atherton. Colleen Adamson, Steve's former manager at Advantage International, also declined to be interviewed.

Cricket Australia were helpful at first, giving me contact details for overseas players and Boards, but when I asked for contact details and clearances to interview the current coach John Buchanan and physiotherapist Errol Alcott, the media manager simply did not reply, despite a follow up email, a message left on his mobile and a message left at Cricket Australia's switch.

The South African Board's media officer happily put me in touch with South African captain Graeme Smith, although he did suggest that I wait until Smith returned from the tour of Pakistan. Other players or ex-players who agreed to be interviewed were Ian Chappell, Bob Simpson and Tim May, in his capacity as executive officer of the players' organisation, the Australian Cricketers' Association.

It's an irony that the players of previous generations, who didn't make much from the game, were usually happy to talk and not too worried about getting paid for it, while today's players, who make a lot of money, are difficult to contact and often reluctant to talk.

The demand on their time is a factor. There is so much more cricket being played, commercial opportunities and media outlets have mushroomed, and with them the demand for interviews, appearances and endorsements.

Management is another factor: they need their managers to organise their time, as well as to oversee their contracts and maximise commercial opportunities. But if the player isn't getting paid, the manager isn't getting a percentage.

When I asked Bev Waugh if she would agree to an interview about the twins when they were growing up, she said: 'I'd have to speak to the boys . . . they lead such a busy life that the decisions are left to people they pay well and . . . [Steve] says, "Look, these decisions have got to be made by my management and I've got to go along with them." . . . You mightn't like what they're doing,' Bev says, 'but you haven't got the time to do it yourself and that's what you're paying them to do, so sometimes you've got to go by their judgement, whether you think it's right or not.'

16

IN YOUR DREAMS

West Indies 1995

The West Indies side of the late 1980s and early 1990s—Haynes, Greenidge, Richardson, Richards, Hooper, Logie, Dujon, Marshall, Ambrose, Walsh and Patterson—was one of the great teams of all time. By 1995, Haynes, Greenidge, Richards, Logie, Dujon, Marshall and Patterson had gone. Lara was probably the only replacement who represented an improvement, and he had not yet reached the stage where his mental approach matched his physical and technical genius. But in Richardson, Lara, Adams and Hooper, the West Indies had four very good batsmen, and Ambrose and Walsh were still great bowlers.

At the start of the 1995 tour, Mark Waugh said, 'I think the teams in the past had been scared, but we weren't going to give up. It's always tough going to the West Indies, but we thought we had a side that was equipped to do well. We thought the Windies had lost a bit of their aura of invincibility, so we thought we were a chance.'

If the West Indies were in decline, the results of the one-day series did not show it. They won 4–1 despite being without Richie Richardson for all but the first game. Richardson was back for the Tests and, in what looked like the last straw for the Australians, Craig McDermott, the main strike bowler, tore ligaments in his ankle before the first Test and was out for the series. Damien Fleming was also on the plane home with an injured shoulder.

Before the Test series started, Bob Simpson handed out a

question and answer sheet asking why players felt they had not done as well as they might in the one-day games and what they would need to do to lift their performance. According to Mark Waugh: 'Many of the players considered this a critical moment of the tour because they were really encouraged to think deeply about the position they were in. The discussions that followed during an intense meeting motivated the players as individuals and as team-mates. The timing was perfect'.

Bob Simpson told me: 'They were given the form and they had to bring it back to me. I wanted to set out the guidelines for the rest of the tour, and I used the question and answer technique to get responses from the team about how they would react in certain situations, to get their ideas and feelings out in the open, so I would know where they were coming from. We used this information in discussion at team meetings'.

Mark Taylor spoke at length at the pre-Test dinner, recalling how in the West Indies in 1973, when Dennis Lillee had broken down and Bob Massie had lost form, Max Walker and Jeff Hammond had stepped up and helped Ian Chappell's side to an unexpected series win. They also discussed tactics for the West Indies batsmen, which could be boiled down to 'Bowl tight to the top order and bounce the tail'.

When it came to bowling tight, Paul Reiffel and Glenn McGrath stepped up and were the ideal pair, and the left-armer Brendon Julian, slanting the ball away from the right-handers, was a good foil for them. And then there was Shane Warne.

The first Test was played in Bridgetown, Barbados. Richardson won the toss, West Indies batted, and within 25 minutes Stuart Williams had slashed at Julian and been caught by Taylor at first slip, Sherwin Campbell had edged Reiffel to Healy, Richie Richardson had also tried to smash Julian through cover but had edged to Healy, and West Indies were 3 for 6.

It seemed the West Indies' game plan was to intimidate the weakened Australian attack. Lara and Hooper continued to play their shots, Hooper greeting Shane Warne by hitting his first three balls to the boundary. They took the total to 130 before Julian struck again, Hooper on 60 edging to Taylor; twenty minutes later McGrath claimed Adams, caught by Warne in slips. Lara remained the danger, but soon after Adams's dismissal, he cut Julian hard to Steve Waugh at gully. Waugh fumbled and fell, scooping at the ball as it landed, then rolling over and claiming the catch.

Lara went, then hesitated when the crowd protested, but eventually accepted Waugh's confirmation that he had caught it. An umpire with access to the slow motion replay would not have given it out; it certainly looks as if the ball hit the ground—you can see it bounce as Waugh tries to scoop it up. But as he fell, Waugh had to take his eyes off the ball, so he may not have known it bounced. Possibly, all he knew was that he grabbed for it and came up with it clutched against his chest. Viv Richards, who should have known better, said, 'The player must have known it had hit the ground—some Aussies have been doing it for years . . . it's a poor thing when you have to resort to that.' As is often the case with decisions like this, most of the Australians thought it was out; most of the West Indies thought it wasn't.

A couple of weeks later Waugh had the opportunity to watch a replay of the catch. He wrote in his tour diary:

> As I watched the slow motion replays from all angles, I couldn't believe my eyes. To me, the replay confirmed my impression of the catch, for the ball bounced off my right hand at exactly the same time I hit the ground and then rebounded up and landed on my left wrist, making it a fair catch. I was astounded, dumb-founded, you name it, to think that all these so-called cricket experts could claim it appeared to be a non-catch. There was no way they could determine that conclusively from the slow motion footage. Needless to say, I was immensely pissed off.

The replay I have seen has commentary from former West Indies fast bowler Michael Holding, who says, 'There is the ball, up near to his chest. It hits the ground, actually, and then he scoops it up'.

Lara was out for 65, West Indies were 6 for 156, and they were all out 39 runs later for 195, with a couple of hours left for play on the first day. At stumps Australia were 2 for 91, Taylor not out 42, and the next day they took the total to 346, Healy's 74 not out with seven fours and a couple of sixes being the main contribution, supported by Steve Waugh 65, Taylor 55 and Mark Waugh 40. McGrath (5 for 68) and Warne (3 for 64) disposed of the West Indies a second time for 189 and Australia made the 39 needed without losing a wicket.

The second Test, at St John's, Antigua, the scene of Brian Lara's world record 375 against England a year earlier, was spoiled by rain. Neither side gained an advantage and the West Indies, apart from a vicious spell of short bowling on the second day, seemed a little flat. Ambrose in particular, perhaps not fully recovered from a shoulder injury, was below his best. Walsh was by now their most feared bowler.

'A clever piece of cricket': Lara caught Boon bowled Waugh for 88. Second Test, Antigua, 1995. *(West Indies Cricket Board/TWI)*

David Boon recounts a clever piece of cricket that was responsible for Lara's dismissal in the first innings. Waugh put Boon at short mid-on and said he would bowl outside off stump to a packed off-side field, hoping that Lara would eventually try to force him away on the leg side but, on the slow wicket, not time it properly. After a couple of overs it duly happened and Boon held a very good catch high to his left.

At Port-of-Spain, on a grassy, under-prepared pitch, which, as Mark Waugh said 'spat violently at both teams', it was more like a game of chance than a Test match. The Australians thought 150 would be a good score. They made 126 and 105, losing 5 wickets for only 2 runs at one stage in the second innings. West Indies made only 136 in their first innings and needed 96 to win. The Australians still rated themselves a chance, but Williams and Richardson threw the bat at everything and got away with it. It was all over half way through the third day.

The match is remembered for the encounter between Curtly Ambrose, who was back at close to his best, and Steve Waugh on the first day. Waugh, who had been heckled and abused, both on and off the field, because of the dispute over the Lara catch in the first Test, was pretty fired up himself, and he and Boon had defied the West Indies quicks for some time, with Waugh taking several hits on the body, but flashing and usually connecting whenever

there was any width. After Waugh had cut him over slips for four, Ambrose bowled a bouncer which went high over Waugh's head, and followed it down the wicket to give him the stare. As it seemed to be going on for longer than usual, Waugh eventually said, 'What the fuck are you looking at?' to which the tall Antiguan replied, 'Don't cuss me, man.' What Waugh said next has not been recorded, but it was obviously short and to the point. Then, as Ambrose continued to look menacing at close range, Richie Richardson came from slip, grabbed him by the left arm and pulled him away. Richardson, who had to pull quite hard to get Ambrose to move, looks angry and obviously spoke sharply to his senior bowler.

In an interview later in the day, Waugh said, 'I'm out there with the bat, he's out there with the ball, we're trying to do our best, you know. Sometimes tempers flare over, but I thought it was played in the right spirit.'

Sabina Park, in Kingston, Jamaica, with its polished pitch, is the scene of many a humiliation for visiting teams. When they arrived, the Australians were greeted with cheering and applause from the large Australian contingent in the crowd, although Steve Waugh wrote: 'The warm-ups were conducted amid an atmosphere that lent itself to a heavyweight title bout, which I guess wasn't too far from the truth'. Mark Taylor (who always called 'tails') got it wrong for the fourth time in four Tests, and Richie Richardson, reckoning that the team that batted last would lose, chose to bat.

Richardson then played a very fine innings for an even 100, supported by Lara with 65, but no one else. West Indies totalled 265. In an interview, Steve Waugh said:

> To get them out for 265 was a good result, but we've got to cash in tomorrow. If we can get a lead of 150 or 200 I think it'll start to play a few tricks the last couple of days . . . it's certainly time the batsmen put their hands up. The bowlers have been doing a great job over here, probably better than anyone expected, and our fielding has been first class . . . all the batters have been in good touch, we've just been getting starts and not going on with it. But tomorrow I'm sure you'll see a couple of guys put their hand up and say, "I'm going to go out there and make a big hundred". That's what we need tomorrow—we need a lot of determination and someone to go out there and get a big score for us.

The next morning Australia lost Taylor at 17 and Boon at 50; then, when Slater was caught by Lara off Walsh with the score at 73, Steve Waugh joined his brother Mark and stepped out of the way of the obligatory first ball bouncer from Kenny Benjamin. With life in the wicket early, the West Indies quicks pounded it in short for over after over, but it was often too short and often wide. The twins kept their concentration, punishing anything off line. Steve was dropped on 42—an edge off Kenny Benjamin that flew straight to Courtney Brown and should have been taken—but they put on 101 between lunch and tea and gradually wore down the attack. Richardson had to bring on Hooper, Adams and Arthurton.

Mark got his eighth Test hundred, clipping Hooper to mid wicket for a single, and when Steve took 2 through mid wicket to reach his century—also his eighth in Tests—the twins had a classic encounter in mid-pitch: there is the briefest of handshakes, Mark says something, Steve says a couple of words in reply, then Mark hunches his right shoulder to loosen his sleeve and turns and walks back to the bowler's end.

On 126, with the total now 304, Mark turned Hooper into the hands of Jimmy Adams at short leg. Ian Healy said it was 'the finest partnership I have ever seen in cricket, a stirring stand of 231 built on great skill and impeccable concentration. Everything we talked about in the batting meeting before the Test was played out perfectly in this partnership'. Interviewed together at the end of the day, Steve and Mark agreed that the innings they played were among their best, but Steve deflects any attempt to make too much of the event: 'It is, I suppose, something you dream of, but, you know, we managed not to run each other out today'. Mark smiles and looks around the place, a bit embarrassed (reminding me of film of Keith Miller). Steve is wearing his baggy green cap; Mark, his collar turned up as ever, wears an off-white tour cap with a green visor.

Steve was 110 at the end of the second day and had taken his score to 195 on the third day, when he was joined by number 11, Glenn McGrath, who had two balls to face from Kenny Benjamin. He survived a bouncer and a yorker. Waugh had the strike against Hooper and took a single, McGrath took another single and, with one ball to go, Richardson brought the field in. Waugh went to charge the last ball of the over, Hooper saw him coming and speared it down the leg side, but Waugh managed to turn it through square leg and reached 200 with an all-run four. He was mobbed by Australians from the crowd, including Greg Ritchie— 'Fat Cat, what are you doing here? You should know better,' Richie Richardson said to him.

'Something you dream of': Steve and Mark Waugh after their 231-run partnership. Fourth Test, Kingston, 1995. (West Indies Cricket Board/TWI)

West Indies v Australia, fourth Test, Sabina Park, Kingston, Jamaica, 29 April–3 May 1995

Result: Australia won by an innings and 53 runs

WEST INDIES

SC Williams c Blewett b Reiffel	0	b Reiffel	20
*RB Richardson lbw b Reiffel	100	c & b Reiffel	14
BC Lara c Healy b Warne	65	lbw b Reiffel	0
JC Adams c Slater b Julian	20	c SR Waugh b McGrath	18
CL Hooper c ME Waugh b Julian	23	(6) run out	13
KLT Arthurton c Healy b McGrath	16	(7) lbw b Warne	14
+CO Browne c Boon b Warne	1	(8) not out	31
WKM Benjamin lbw b SR Waugh	7	(5) lbw b Reiffel	51
CEL Ambrose not out	6	st Healy b Warne	5
CA Walsh c Boon b SR Waugh	2	c Blewett b Warne	14
KCG Benjamin c Healy b Reiffel	5	c Taylor b Warne	6
Extras	20		27
Total	265		213

FoW 0 103 131 188 220 243 250 251 254 265   37 37 46 98 134 140 166 172 204 213

Bowling	O	M	R	W	O	M	R	W
Reiffel	13.4	2	48	3	18	5	47	4
Julian	12	3	31	2	10	2	37	0
McGrath	20	4	79	1	13	2	28	1
Warne	25	6	72	2	23.4	8	70	4
SR Waugh	11	5	14	2	4	0	9	0
ME Waugh	4	1	11	0	1	0	1	0

AUSTRALIA

*MA Taylor c Adams b Walsh	8
MJ Slater c Lara b Walsh	27
DC Boon c Browne b Ambrose	17
ME Waugh c Adams b Hooper	126
SR Waugh c Lara b KCG Benjamin	200
GS Blewett c WKM Benjamin b Arthurton	69
+IA Healy c Lara b WKM Benjamin	6
BP Julian c Adams b Walsh	8
PR Reiffel b KCG Benjamin	23
SK Warne c Lara b KCG Benjamin	0
GD McGrath not out	3
Extras	44
Total	531

FoW 17 50 73 304 417 433 449 522 522 531

Bowling	O	M	R	W
Ambrose	21	4	76	1
Walsh	33	6	103	3
KCG Benjamin	23.5	0	106	3
WKM Benjamin	24	3	80	1
Hooper	43	9	94	1
Adams	11	0	38	0
Arthurton	5	1	17	1

After batting for almost ten hours, Waugh said he was in a trance-like state and felt as if he could have batted for another 10 hours, but a few balls later Kenny Benjamin speared in a throat ball and he fended it to Lara at slip.

Australia's total was 531, a lead of 266. West Indies were 3 for 63 by stumps on the third day, with Richardson and Lara both out. Reiffel and Warne took 4 wickets each and Australia won by an innings and 53 runs.

Greg Ritchie among the Australians congratulating Steve Waugh on reaching 200. Fourth Test, Kingston, 1995. *(West Indies Cricket Board/TWI)*

In the Bankstown Cricket Club's history, Steve Waugh is quoted as saying, 'It was the innings you dream of, playing your best when everything is hanging on it'.

Before the tour, Waugh had to decline a sponsorship deal. In his book *Run Out*, Graham Halbish, former CEO of the Australian Cricket Board, wrote:

> He had a fantastic offer from Pepsi for the 1995 tour of the West Indies. The Australians were not happy with the sponsorship money they were getting for the tour from Coca-Cola. Pepsi was offering Steve a private deal for the same amount of money as the whole team put together. It was a six figure sum and we had a couple of thorny meetings with so much at stake. I had a series of talks with Steve and his manager at the time, Austin Robertson . . . but this was one case where I simply had to say no because Coca-Cola was a major ACB sponsor.

It must have been frustrating for Pepsi. Waugh was player-of-the-series and topped the Australian aggregates and averages with 429 runs at 107.25. He also rose to the top of the Coopers & Lybrand world ranking of batsmen. Mark was second in tour aggregates and averages with 240 at 40.00. After the tour they had a few days to wind down in Bermuda with wives and girlfriends. While they were there tour manager Jack Edwards told Mark Taylor to 'take the party to a decent restaurant and have a good night'. It was a matter of pride with Australian touring teams that whenever the Board offered to pay for dinner, they should always make the most of the opportunity. They drank Moet all night and the bill came to $US6777.

When they got home they were given another tickertape parade in Sydney, where an estimated 150 000 people lined George Street as they made their way from the Town Hall to a presentation in Martin Place.

17

'LUNCH'

Dion Bourne and Bankstown

I played cricket for 30 years in Sydney's City and Suburban competition for a club called I Zingari. IZs had a centenary in 1988 and published a history, and Bruce Collins, who started the Bradman Museum in Bowral and knew Don Bradman, asked The Don to write a foreword for the book. His foreword was humorous, informed and informative, and toward the end of it Bradman wrote: 'My cricketing life was dominated by my being on display in the shop window as it were, whereas I have always gone out of my way to emphasise that the health, welfare and future of cricket lies not there, but in the hands of the thousands of club and social cricketers who gave birth to the game and nourish its existence'.

It's clubs like Bankstown which maintain the health, welfare and future of Australian cricket, and it's people like Stephen and Mark Waugh's uncle, Dion Bourne, also known as 'Lunch', who run those clubs and provide the structure for young players all over the world to learn and prosper.

The Waughs make the point that they were encouraged rather than coached by Dion Bourne, and Bourne probably had more influence with another couple of high profile players than he did with Stephen and Mark Waugh. Bourne captained the young pace men Jeff Thomson and Len Pascoe in their early days in first grade, not always an easy job, as they sometimes seemed to be more interested in surfing—and other things—than cricket. Thomson used to roar up for training in his Mini Cooper S, travelling very fast but often very late. For repeated lateness Thomson was once dropped to the thirds, but soon earned his place back in the top grade by taking all 10 wickets against St George. Despite an age difference of a decade or so, Bourne and the young quicks became firm friends and, when lack of interest or lack of discipline might have seen them slip away from cricket, Dion Bourne was instrumental in keeping them in the game.

I met Len Pascoe on one occasion. This might seem strange now, but until the Number 2 Oval and the old Sydney Sports Ground were redeveloped into the Sydney Football Stadium in the 1980s, there was a 'members' net beside the State squad's net on the Number 2 Oval, and SCG members could practise there alongside the State players. I was bowling in the members' net one day when the batsman hit one straight back to me and it cannoned off my foot into the State squad's net next door. Lennie was just starting his run and I thought there was time to duck across and retrieve the ball, but I misjudged it and he had to abort. 'Get out of the road, you silly old prick,' he roared. Startled, I looked up. Lennie gave me a nice smile. He'd been kidding.

There are many such stories about Len Pascoe. I interviewed umpire Dick French some years ago and he told me that in a one-day international in Melbourne in 1980, Pascoe was bowling to Geoff Boycott, who tried to glance but missed and it brushed his pad on the way to the keeper. Marsh went up and Pascoe jumped the stumps and set off to embrace him. French said, 'I thought, "This is going to be fun," then I said, "It's not out". Lennie stopped in his tracks. He looked at me. He glared at Boycott. Then he called out to Marshy, "Hey Bacchus, before you chuck the ball back, take that splinter out of it, will you?".'

Mick Stephenson's *Bankstown Cricket Club—50 Not Out*, a history of the club, is rich with such stories. On one occasion, Sid Boddy, one of the founding members when the club was formed in 1951, umpiring in the lower grades with Bankstown fielding, 'forgot himself momentarily and appealed vociferously for a catch behind'. A medium pace bowler named Glen Keane, well-endowed with freckles, was known as 'Leopard'. He was normally a model of accuracy, but on an off day he was all over the place, and a wit called out from the field: 'For heaven's sake Leopard, can't you keep 'em on the spot?'

Ken Thorpe was one of the club's leading run-getters in the 1960s. As his son grew up, there was some discussion in the club about whether he would follow in his father's footsteps. Eventually Ken had to tell them that the boy didn't seem to have great ball skills—although he was quite good at swimming. Another who has had success in the world outside cricket is Frank Cicutto, who played several seasons for Bankstown in the early 1970s and opened the batting in first grade before being transferred to work in Melbourne. In the days before people wore helmets, Cicutto was hit on the head when fielding close to the bat, suffered a fractured skull and spent months in hospital. He was secretary of the club for two years before he went to Melbourne, and later became CEO of the National Australia Bank.

Len Pascoe, Dion Bourne and Jeff Thomson. *(Bankstown Cricket Club)*

A group of boys including the Waugh twins at Bankstown Oval in the 1970s.
(Bankstown Cricket Club)

Grahame Thomas was Bankstown's first Test representative; an opening batsman and a stroke-player who liked to hit the ball hard, Thomas played eight Tests in the 1960s. Maurie Lilienthel, who, like Sid Boddy, was a founding member, was a delegate from the club to the New South Wales Cricket Association and became chairman of the Association's Country Committee, which involved travel all over the State looking for and encouraging young cricketers. In 2001, Lilienthal was awarded the Order of Australia medal for his services to the game.

During the 1930s and 1940s Bankstown played in the Sydney Shires competition. Jack Fitzpatrick, who lived in Bankstown but played for Cumberland and was good enough to play several games for NSW in the late 1930s, together with local businessman Harry Toohey and others, worked hard to get the club into the grade competition. Don Bradman played a promotional game for the club in the 1930s and was impressed with the strength of cricket in the area. Later, NSWCA president Sid Smith promised Fitzpatrick that if the club could win two Shires competitions they would be admitted to Sydney grade. This they duly did and the grade club was formed in 1951 with Jack Fitzpatrick as secretary and Harry Toohey as president. In 1958–59 Bankstown won both the first grade premiership and the club championship, a feat repeated twice since. The club has won all the grades and the Poidevin-Grey (under-21) and Green Shield (under-16) competitions on numerous occasions.

Physically, Bankstown Oval has always been an attractive ground. A photo from the 1920s shows a picket fence and a classic, Federation style grandstand in what had previously been known as Fripp's paddock. White ants wrecked the stand, and after the first reconstruction took place in 1961 the oval earned a reputation as one of Sydney's better grounds. The second reconstruction, which included the Stephen and Mark Waugh pavilion and the 600-seat Kevin McCormick grandstand, was opened in 2000 and has given the ground facilities which are the envy of every grade club in Sydney. Perhaps most importantly, the club has always been able to attract top groundsmen and to produce good, fast, true batting wickets. Bankstown has hosted interstate matches with great success, including the first Sheffield Shield match played in Sydney at a ground other than the SCG.

Sydney grade cricket has been one of the world's great nurseries for first class cricketers for more than 100 years. Brian Freedman told me that Ben Smith, who played for Bankstown for five years and is now captain of Worcestershire, said that in his time with Bankstown, when they had Steve Small, Wayne Holdsworth and the Waugh twins, Bankstown would have won easily against all but a couple of the English county sides.

One of the Sydney grade competition's enduring records is that of Bill O'Reilly, who in 15 seasons of first grade from 1931 to 1946 took 921 wickets at 10 runs apiece and topped the first grade averages twelve times. After the Second World War O'Reilly captained St George, with young players such as Ray Lindwall and

Arthur Morris in his team. Ray Lindwall told how he came into first grade as a young player who regarded himself as a batsman and also bowled medium pace swingers. In his first game under O'Reilly, Lindwall was surprised to be instructed by O'Reilly to lengthen his run and bowl flat out, and even more surprised the following week when St George were batting: 'I went to have a look at the order to see where I was going in and there I was, one before the roller'. Arthur Morris was playing grade as a left-arm wrist spinner until one of the opening batsmen was late one week and O'Reilly took the opportunity to promote him to the top of the order, where Morris went on to make 3533 runs for Australia at 46.49 in 46 Tests. Bradman, after he came to Sydney, made 3022 runs at 91.57 in seven seasons for St George, before he went to live in Adelaide.

Brian Freedman, who has been president of the Bankstown club for 22 years and is now on the Board of Cricket Australia, remarked on one particular change in recent years: 'The thing that intrigues me is the way the Australians play cricket these days. When I first got involved, I reckon 40 per cent of all grade games were draws. There was a mentality that you'd never let the opposition win. Last season [2002–03], except for complete washouts, there was only one draw in Sydney first grade cricket, and I believe the attitude of AB, Mark Taylor and Steve Waugh has rubbed off on Australian cricket, where people don't even think of playing for a draw. There's no encouragement to have a draw in Australian cricket'.

In a foreword to Mick Stephenson's history of the club, Steve Waugh wrote:

> To me the secret of the ongoing success of the Bankstown Cricket Club is the quality of work carried out by the volunteers, who are the heartbeat and soul of the organisation. People like Brian Freedman, Marty Klumpp and Eris Dignam and their wives Ro, Maureen and Margaret are the people in my time who make this club so special.

Bankstown is one of 20 clubs in the Sydney Cricket Association, and it is the hours of work every week of the summer (and many in the winter) over many years that the Sid Boddys and Dion

Bournes and Brian Freedmans and Mick Stephensons of the clubs in Sydney—and around the cricket world—put in that give young cricketers the opportunity to get promoted to the highest level, and, even if they don't, to experience the pleasure and friendships that the game brings.

Stephen and Mark Waugh have done everything they can to repay the opportunity which Bankstown gave them. Brian Freedman says, 'They have been impeccably loyal to the club.' The club's history says of Steve:

> From a Bulldog perspective it is extremely pleasing that, despite reaching the pinnacle of world cricket, he has never forgotten his Bankstown upbringing. Steve has always played for the Bulldogs whenever he was available and gives the distinct impression that he is almost as proud of his Bulldog cap as he is of his treasured baggy green Australian cap.

Bankstown takes pride in its reputation for providing the best lunches and afternoon teas in the Sydney grade competition. Sid Boddy, who was either Secretary or President for more than twenty years during the 1950s, 1960s and 1970s, is remembered for his call: 'Stand back please boys and allow our visitors first choice at the table'.

Flanked by chairman of selectors Trevor Hohns and Board chief executive James Sutherland, at the SCG press conference announcing that Waugh was not selected in the one day squad for South Africa and Zimbabwe, 13 February 2002. *(Chris McGrath/Getty Images)*

A photo opportunity at the SCG with Lynette and children Lily, Rosalie and Austin, after the final day of his last Test match, 6 January 2004. *(Hamish Blair/Getty Images)*

Australian of the Year: Steve Waugh on the ABC's 7.30 Report, Australia Day 2004. *(Australian Broadcasting Corporation Content Sales)*

The last slog sweep: Steve Waugh holes out to Sachin Tendulkar off the bowling of Anil Kumble, for 80, in his last Test innings, SCG, 6 January 2004. *(Chris McGrath/Getty Images)*

With Mark in front of Bankstown Oval's Stephen and Mark Waugh Pavilion in September 2003, at the start of the 2003–04 Sydney Grade season. *(Jack Egan)*

18

ARJUNA'S REVENGE

The changing world order

In February 1995, Phil Wilkins broke the story in the *Sydney Morning Herald* of the allegations that Salim Malik had offered bribes to Mark Waugh, Shane Warne and Tim May in Pakistan in 1994. Soon after, the Cricket Board's media manager and sometime tour manager, Ian McDonald, was told by a journalist of the payments to Mark Waugh and Shane Warne during the Singer World Series in Sri Lanka in September 1994 for information about pitch and weather conditions and the Australian team's tactics and selections. McDonald reported the matter to the Board's CEO and, following an investigation—which was not made public at the time—Waugh and Warne admitted what they had done and were fined $10 000 and $8000 respectively.

Later in the year, the allegations against Salim Malik were investigated by a former judge of Pakistan's Supreme Court. Mark Waugh, Warne and May gave sworn statements to the inquiry, but on the advice of the Australian Cricket Board did not attend. The Judge criticised the Board for not allowing the players to attend the inquiry and found that 'The allegations made against Salim Malik cannot be believed and appear to have been concocted for reasons best known to the accusers'.

It was in this atmosphere that Pakistan arrived for three Tests at the start of the 1995–96 season. Pakistan were coming off a 1–2 loss to Sri Lanka—further evidence of the shift in the balance of power in world cricket. Salim Malik was in the team, but had been replaced as captain by Wasim Akram.

Malik attracted plenty of attention at the start of the tour, not least for his claim that Warne could 'bowl only three different deliveries and has a completely different action for each one—the angle of his hand is different for each ball—I pick each one as it leaves the hand'. As it happened, Malik had injured a hand in the field and did not bat in Pakistan's first innings of the Test series, but in the second innings, batting at number 8 in an effort to avoid defeat, he played three balls from Warne before skying the fourth to McDermott at mid-off to be out for a duck. In James Knight's biography of Mark Waugh, Mark said, 'We all wanted him out really badly. The fact that Warney got him made it pretty sweet.'

Steve Waugh had continued his good form, and his good luck. Early in his innings he completely mistimed an attempted back-foot drive off a ball a metre wide of the off stump, and hit a return catch to Wasim Akram, who juggled and dropped it at the third attempt. It was one of five catches dropped during the day; as Richie said, 'That was a particularly inept fielding performance by the Pakistanis.' Waugh went on to 112 not out, top score in a total of 463. Pakistan made 97 and 240, Shane Warne taking 7 for 23 and 4 for 54.

Waugh drives during his 131 not out in the second Test against Sri Lanka, MCG, 1995-96. (Cricket Australia/Channel 9)

Warne was not able to bowl in the second Test, after having a toe broken by a yorker from Waqar Younis, but Australia still won, this time by 155 runs. Pakistan took something from the tour by winning the toss in the third Test, played in Sydney, and keeping their noses in front throughout a tight match. A century by Ijaz Ahmed set up Pakistan's win. For Australia, 116 in the first innings by Mark Waugh brought him back to level pegging with his brother at nine Test centuries each.

Sri Lanka followed Pakistan, but it was an unhappy tour for the rising stars of international cricket. Australia declared at 5 for 617 in the first Test, at 6 for 500 in the second and at 9 for 502 in the first innings of the third Test. A groin injury, sustained in a Sheffield Shield match, kept Steve Waugh out of the first Test, where his brother made 111 after Slater had powered to 219, and Ricky Ponting made 96 in his Test debut.

Steve made 131 not out in the second Test, finishing his innings with Ricky Ponting as runner. It was during this innings, in front of a crowd of 55,000 people, that Muttiah Muralitharan, regarded by some as the best off-spinner in the world, was called seven times by Darrell Hair for throwing. For most Australian cricket followers, the wonder was that Muralitharan had got this far in his career without someone or some organisation in the game's hierarchy taking steps to correct what seemed to be an obviously illegal action.

The one-day series, which included the West Indies, was sandwiched between Tests. In a one-day game between West Indies and Sri Lanka in Brisbane, Muralitharan was again repeatedly no-balled, this time by Ross Emerson. These incidents stoked the fires of Sri Lankan captain Arjuna Ranatunga's considerable capacity for resentment, with unfortunate consequences soon after.

With the West Indies putting in a lacklustre performance, Sri Lanka qualified for the final series, which was played before the third Test. Australia won the first final comfortably and with 273 from 50 overs again looked set to win the second. But rain reduced the target to 165 from 25 overs and at 5 for 135, needing 31 with 5 overs left and Arjuna Ranatunga scoring freely, a Sri Lankan win seemed likely.

Ranatunga, as Mark Waugh says, 'pushes the rules of the game to the limit'. Early in his innings, Ranatunga said he had a cramp and called for a runner. In *Hands and Heals*, Ian Healy recounts: 'I thought his behaviour was ridiculous, we all did, and told the portly Sri Lankan captain so'.

'Mate, you can't have a runner just because you're unfit,' Healy said.

'It's nothing to do with you. I have cramp,' Ranataunga replied.

'Have a look at yourself, Porky. That's why you've got cramp,' said Healy. 'Ranataunga spun round and gave it to me, pointing a menacing finger as he did so. I didn't say another word,' Healy wrote. 'I'd made my point, and Mark Taylor was in my ear, telling me to shut up.'

Ranatunga got his runner, but when Shane Warne dismissed him and Dharmasena in successive overs, the Sri Lankans lost their momentum and Australia won by 9 runs. Mark Taylor went over to the Sri Lankans after the game to shake hands, but they refused. There is a photograph in Steve Waugh's 1996 *Diary* of Taylor with his hand out and the Sri Lankans standing round looking at him with their hands behind their backs. Waugh wrote: 'The whole episode was an absolute disgrace . . . all I could think of was how little I had enjoyed being involved'.

Steve Waugh had missed the early part of the one-day series because of his injury. In his second game back he scored 102 against Sri Lanka in Melbourne, his first century in 187 one-day internationals.

Waugh's good form continued, with top scores of 170 and 61 not out in both innings of the third Test against Sri Lanka—played in Adelaide—for a series average of 362.00. McDermott, McGrath and Warne shared most of the wickets in the second and third Tests, although Waugh followed his top scores with the bat with best bowling figures of 4 for 34 in Sri Lanka's second innings. His bowling successes are often the result of his clever use of the conditions: if it's keeping low, he finds the right spot; if it's swinging, he pitches up; if there's cut, he pitches a bit shorter and tries to find the gap. In this game, the ball was swinging and he bowled Kaluwitharana with a big in-swinger—something I hadn't seen from him before. Richie said, 'It was quite beautifully bowled. We're into the 68th over with this ball and there's reverse swing there and Steve Waugh has got it. He's swung that old ball back inside that forward stroke from Kaluwitharana.' Later Waugh got rid of Sanjeeva Ranatunga from round the wicket with a ball that cut sharply away for Healy to take the catch.

With Arjuna Ranatunga unavailable for this Test, the captaincy had been handed over to Aravinda da Silva and the match was played in a good spirit. After the game the Australians took some beers into the Sri Lankan dressing room and friendly relations were reestablished. Mark Taylor, typically, expressed regret that they hadn't done this earlier in the tour and blamed himself: 'We took the time in the Adelaide Test match to go in and have a beer with the Sri Lankans. Probably the only mistake I made this summer, I'd say, is that I didn't do it two weeks earlier. It's my fault. I made a mistake with that'.

Australian teams had been visiting Sri Lanka (formerly Ceylon) since 1884, when Billy Murdoch's side, on the way to England, played against Eighteen of Ceylon (who, at that time, were all Englishmen living there). It was a regular port-of-call for Australian teams on the way to England—Bradman played there twice—and Bill Lawry's team played the initial first class game there in 1969. Australian officials lobbied hard on their behalf when Sri Lanka was granted Test match status at the International Cricket Conference in 1981. In 1992, after the civil war which wracked the island through the 1980s, Border's team had played the first home series in Sri Lanka for five years—Steve Waugh was not selected for this tour. Australia won the three-Test series 1–0, despite lbw decisions favouring the home side 16–4. (Border commented calmly that 'the five year lay-off had an adverse effect on the umpiring'.)

The Muralitharan saga is the muddiest chapter in modern cricket. So much has been written and said about it, but it is hard to find out what actually happened after Murali was no-balled in Australia in December 1995.

In *Run Out*, Graeme Halbish wrote:

The matter was referred back by the world's governing body, the ICC, to the home body in Sri Lanka. I was aware from discussions earlier that year that there was little chance the Sri Lankan Board would take action against Muralitharan. As I was told at the time, he was the only Tamil in the team, and the political reality of the day was that he was virtually untouchable.

Over the years, I must have spoken to at least 50 cricketers about Murali's action, and virtually every one of them thinks he throws, yet in Sri Lanka he is universally defended. Wisden has named him as one of the top two Test players in history—Don Bradman was the other—yet, as Murali and Shane Warne raced towards Courtney Walsh's record of 519 Test wickets, the controversy continued. Surprisingly, I haven't heard any of the senior commentators defend Murali's action, so presumably they think it is suspect.

However, two well-respected observers of the game have recently had their say: In *Wisden Cricket Asia* magazine, Bishan Bedi, who took 266 wickets for India, described Muralitharan's action as 'grossly unfair' and 'more like a javelin thrower than a bowler'. Bedi was supported by one of the great West Indian fast bowlers, Michael Holding, a member of the ICC advisory panel on illegal deliveries, who said he was in '110% agreement' with Bedi's comments.

Murali was said to have been cleared by an ICC bowling review group and various orthopaedic and sports institutes on the grounds that he has a permanently bent elbow, but something seems to have got lost in the fog of commentary, panels of experts and administrative dithering. Law 24.2 says: 'A ball shall be deemed to have been thrown if, in the opinion of either umpire, the process of straightening the bowling arm, whether it be partial or complete, takes place during that part of the delivery swing which directly precedes the ball leaving the hand'. In other words, you can't straighten your arm as you are letting the ball go.

During the Australian tour of Sri Lanka at the end of the 2003–04 season, Muralitharan was again the subject of an umpire's report; this time for his 'doosra', which is said to be a new delivery.

Let the pictures tell the story. Anyone who has a video or DVD that lets you watch the action frame by frame can study the images shown here—and we're looking not just at one selected ball, but at just about any ball bowled by Muralitharan.

'More like a javelin thrower than a bowler,' said Bishan Bedi: Muralitharan in action during the 2003 World Cup. *(United Cricket Board of South Africa)*

On their tour of Australia in 1995–96, the Sri Lankans had been let down by their fielding: their backing up in the field was poor throughout and they dropped a lot of catches. Steve Waugh should have been run out early in his innings of 170 in the third Test; instead, he got 5 runs through overthrows.

Nevertheless, Sri Lanka had players of courage and class; as co-host with India and Pakistan of the 1996 World Cup, and with their Australian coach, Dav Whatmore, working on their fielding skills, they were considered one of the chances. But with the country still plagued by terrorists, the arrangements for the tournament were thrown into doubt when a bomb exploded at the Central Bank in Colombo, killing more than 50 people and injuring hundreds more.

Australia's first match was scheduled to be played against Sri Lanka in Colombo seventeen days later. Given that the blast took place only a few minutes walk from where the Australian team was booked to stay, and that following the feuding between the teams in Australia several members of the Australian team had received death threats, and that at least two of the Australians—Ian Healy and Steve Waugh—had wives who were expecting babies, it was not surprising that the Australians were not anxious to play there. Sensibly, the Board did not leave the decision to the players; the executive of the Board announced that the Australian team would not play in Colombo. The West Indies, whose match was scheduled eight days later, made the same decision. Both teams were required to forfeit their matches, giving Sri Lanka an easy 4 points.

Despite the forfeit, the Australians left as originally scheduled on 9 February. At the first team meeting, held in Calcutta on February 10, Steve Waugh, who had by now equipped himself with an IBM ThinkPad on which to produce his diary, wrote:

> Col Egar, the team manager, informed us that, as things presently stood, we were a team without a game, venue or schedule, as well as being devoid of uniforms or friends. Good start! The one positive of the whole meeting came when our liaison manager, Sona, stormed into the room and announced that he had brought with him the official World Cup chewing gum sponsor's product, and that each player was to receive two boxes.

Their first match was against Kenya, on 23 February, by which time they had had a night in Bangkok, four nights in Calcutta, five nights in Bombay, a night in Madras and three nights in Visakhapatnam, on India's eastern coast, the venue for the match. They won by 97, Mark Waugh making 130, Steve 82—the twins putting on 207 for the third wicket, the highest partnership for any wicket in World Cup games to that time. Although Kenya were lowly ranked, they were big improvers and were to defeat the West Indies by 73 runs in Pune six days later. In a topsy-turvy tournament, West Indies would defeat Australia by 4 wickets in Jaipur on March 4, and these two teams would meet again in a semi-final played in Chandigarh, north of New Delhi, on March 13.

Australia's quarter-final game had been a confidence-boosting win against New Zealand in Madras. Chasing 286, they won with 3 overs and 6 wickets in hand. Mark Waugh's 110 (from 112 balls) was his third century of the tournament, and Steve Waugh (59 from 68 balls) and Stuart Law (42 from 30 balls) had shredded the New Zealand bowling in an undefeated 76-run partnership for the fifth wicket.

Three days later, in the semi-final against the West Indies, Australia was 4 for 15 after the first ball of the tenth over, with Mark Waugh, Mark Taylor, Ricky Ponting and Steve Waugh back in the pavilion. Stuart Law (72 from 105 balls) and Michael Bevan (69 from 110) rescued Australia with a stand of 138 for the fifth wicket,

In conference during the 1996 World Cup semi-final against the West Indies. (*Board of Control for Cricket in India/TWI*)

Celebrating with Ian Healy, Damien Fleming and Mark Waugh after their 5-run semi-final win against the West Indies in the 1996 World Cup. (*Board of Control for Cricket in India/TWI*)

but the total of 207 looked inadequate when Australia took the field, and even more so 41 overs later when West Indies were 2 for 165, needing 43 from 9 overs.

However, the Australian bowlers managed to keep the pressure on. Ian Chappell said, 'The Australians have turned their 207 into quite a few more with some good fielding.' Eventually, tight bowling and brilliant saves in the field made the West Indies play rash shots. McGrath made the breakthrough; Chanderpaul lost patience and was caught trying to hit over the top. Then Roger Harper came in to get quick runs and was lbw trying to force a straight ball to leg. Warne came back on and in quick succession had Otis Gibson caught behind and Jimmy Adams lbw. West Indies were 6 for 183 and, despite a brave innings from Richie Richardson, they never recovered. Australia won by 5 runs.

In the other semi-final, played in Calcutta, Sri Lanka had humiliated India, scoring 251 and then bowling India out for 120. The final was played in Lahore. Mark Taylor won the toss and Australia had raced to 1 for 134 in the first 25 overs when the Sri Lankan spinners tightened their grip on the game and, with the help of much-improved fielding, restricted the total to 241.

Although Sri Lanka lost Jayasuriya and Kaluwitharana early, they never looked like losing. Australia had the worst of the conditions, with heavy dew making the ball hard to handle. Shane Warne, in particular, already troubled with an injured spinning finger, had trouble gripping the damp ball. But the deciding factor in Sri Lanka's win was a masterful undefeated 107 from 124 balls by Aravinda da Silva. This time, it was the Australian fielding that faltered, and Arjuna Ranatunga hammered the final nail into their coffin with 47 from 37 balls to win the game with 7 wickets and 3.4 overs to spare.

Shane Warne had been having finger trouble since the West Indies tour in 1995. His spinning finger, the middle finger of his right hand, had deteriorated steadily and during the 1995–96 season he was having cortisone injections into the knuckle. It got worse with the constant wear during the World Cup, and at practice before the quarter final against New Zealand the veins started coming out through the knuckle. He had it operated on after the 1996 World Cup, although there was no certainty that the operation would be effective—there was a possibility that the finger would be stiff and therefore no use for bowling.

Constant cricket is hard on its leading players. In Pakistan in 1995, Warne had a toe broken by a yorker from Waqar Younis. Later, in May 1998, after the tour of India, he had a shoulder reconstruction to repair ligaments and wear and tear from constant bowling. In January 2000, he tore a muscle in his side during the one-day series against India and Pakistan and missed five games. In October, in a Victoria–NSW Pura Cup match, Mark Waugh skied a catch off Colin Miller and Warne took it at slip, but the ball landed on the top of the ring finger of his right hand and he missed the series against the West Indies with a broken finger. In March 2002, after bowling 70 overs in the second Test, he missed the first two one-day games against South Africa with a hamstring strain. Then, on 15 December 2002, diving for a catch off his own bowling in a one-day game against England at the MCG, he dislocated his right shoulder.

He recovered from this injury remarkably quickly, playing for

Victoria in an ING Cup match less than a month later. But in January 2003 he announced that in order to prolong his Test career, he would be retiring from one-day internationals after the 2003 World Cup. 'My number one priority after the World Cup is playing Test cricket for Australia, and I will not be doing anything to jeopardise that,' he said. (This, of course, was before the one-year ban after testing positive to a diuretic.)

Steve Waugh suffered from back strain, eventually diagnosed as stress fractures, throughout the 1989 tour of England, and did not fully recover until late in 1991. He suffered a groin strain early in the one-day series with Pakistan and West Indies in 1989–99, but with treatment from Errol Alcott continued to play. Another groin strain kept him out of the first Test against Sri Lanka in 1995–96. In September 1999, he broke his nose when he collided with Jason Gillespie during the first Test against Sri Lanka. He was back for the second Test, but missed two games in the one-day series in 2000–01 with another groin injury. In England in August 2001, he suffered a double tear in his left calf muscle during the third Test. He had to go off the field on a stretcher and missed the fourth Test, but was back for the fifth and, despite an injury to his right hip early in his innings and a recurrence of the damage in his left calf, he made 157 not out, putting the game out of England's reach. His struggle to overcome the injury, as documented in his *Ashes Diary*, seems to be almost literally a triumph of mind over matter. Later in the year, Waugh missed games in the early part of the season due to a bout of deep vein thrombosis, possibly resulting from frequent air travel. In May 2002, he had minor surgery on the bones in his left ankle to prevent discomfort caused by a heavy workload and training schedule. In January 2003, in the Sydney Test where he scored his celebrated hundred, he suffered another groin strain while bowling and missed the Bradman XI v England fixture.

19

STILL THE ONE

Life at the top

Steve and Lynette Waugh's daughter, Rosalie, was born in August 1996. In the same month, the Australian team had their next international outing in, of all places, Colombo, where they had declined to play the first game of the World Cup six months earlier. The Singer World Series, between India, Zimbabwe, Sri Lanka and Australia, produced another final against Sri Lanka, with the same result—Australia lost by 50 runs. Bob Simpson had been replaced by Geoff Marsh as coach, and with Mark Taylor injured—he hurt his back lifting weights trying to keep fit—Ian Healy captained the Australian team.

Taylor was back for a one-off Test against India in October 1996 in New Delhi, the inaugural Test for the Border-Gavaskar trophy. After a duck in the first innings, Steve Waugh played what is regarded as one of the game's great defensive innings. In a heavy, smog-filled atmosphere, on a wicket described by Geoff Boycott as being 'like crazy paving', he defied Kumble,

Dravid caught Healy bowled Waugh for 40 in the one-off Delhi Test in 1996. *(Board of Control for India/TWI)*

Kapoor and Prasad for four and a half hours and made 67 not out. But it was to no avail; India took the trophy, winning by 7 wickets.

Australia stayed in India for the Titan Cup Series against India and South Africa; the loss of six consecutive games here saw Mark Taylor's captaincy in one-day internationals under threat for the first time.

A summer at home against the West Indies followed. With Ambrose, Walsh and Ian Bishop, West Indies were still not much fun to face, but their batting lacked depth and, with Warne back after finger surgery and Jason Gillespie joining Glenn McGrath, Australia looked likely winners, unless the genius of the often flaky Brian Lara came to the fore. It did, but too late. McGrath got him for less than 10 four times in the first three Tests, and he did not pass 50 until the second innings of the fourth Test. Australia won comfortably in Brisbane and then in Sydney; then West Indies won on a lively wicket in Melbourne, before Taylor's team sealed the series with an innings win in Adelaide.

The final Test, played in Perth, was Curtly Ambrose's last game in Australia. Bowling on his favourite pitch, he departed after what can only be called a vicious display of short-pitched bowling. His 9 overs in the second innings included 20 no-balls. Shane Warne described his last over:

> That over lasted 15 deliveries. There were 9 no-balls and some of them were over the line by at least half a metre. I was batting with Andrew Bichel at the time and Australia was about to be beaten heavily. Ambrose was charging in as he knew it was his last chance to inflict some damage on an Australian team. Everything was short and lifting on a difficult, cracked pitch.

West Indies won by 10 wickets. Glenn McGrath's 26 wickets at 17.42 earned him man-of-the-series. Warne took 22 at 27.00, and the surprise packet was Michael Bevan with 15 at 17.67. Ian Healy topped the batting with 356 runs at 59.33, including a match-winning 161 not out in the first Test. Mark Waugh made 370 at 41.11. Steve Waugh, who missed the second Test with another groin strain and was targeted throughout with bouncers, made 188 at

Waugh cuts Jimmy Adams for 4 during his 58, third Test v West Indies, MCG, 1996–97. (Cricket Australia/Channel 9)

31.33. In the Melbourne Test, coming in at 3 for 26, he made a typically courageous 58, and in the second innings, with 37, he was the only Australian to get more than 20. Nevertheless, by his standards, it was a disappointing series. More worrying was Mark Taylor's form: in 9 innings he had made 153 at 17.00. Australia failed to qualify for the finals of the triangular series with Pakistan and the West Indies.

In recent Test series, Australia had defeated West Indies 3–2 in Australia in 1996–97 and 2–1 in the West Indies in 1994–95, lost a one-off away Test to India in 1996, defeated Sri Lanka 3–0 and Pakistan at home 2–1 in 1995–96, defeated England 3–1 at home and lost to Pakistan 1–0 away in 1994–95. Their last encounter with South Africa had been in 1993–94, when two three-Test series, one at home and one away, had both produced 1-all results. It rankled with the Australians that *Wisden Cricket Monthly's* ratings still listed South Africa as the world's number one Test side. The 1996–97 series, on the Protea's home grounds, would settle the issue.

The first Test was at Wanderers Stadium in Johannesburg. Hansie Cronje won the toss and South Africa made 302, McGrath taking 4 wickets and Gillespie, Warne and Bevan 2 each. Taylor's poor form continued, bowled by Pollock for 16. Hayden made 40, Matthew Elliot a forceful 85 and Mark Waugh 26. Greg Blewett joined Steve Waugh when the score was 174, and at the end of the second day Waugh was not out 14, Blewett not out 3.

Waugh gave a half chance on 45 when he ducked under a bouncer from Klusener that kept low and deflected off the bat to keeper Richardson, who jumped high and got a glove to it but could

With Greg Blewett during their 385-run partnership, first Test v South Africa, Wanderers Stadium, Johannesburg, March 1997. (*United Cricket Board of South Africa*)

not pull it in. Waugh and Blewett batted throughout the third day, taking the score to 4 for 479. They put on another 80 on the fourth day, before Waugh, on 160 scored from 366 balls, edged Kallis to Richardson. The 385-run partnership—against an attack including Donald, Pollock, Klusener, Kallis, Cronje and Adams —was the highest for any team against South Africa. Blewett went on to 214 and the total of 628 gave Australia a lead of 326.

This was the first time Daryl Cullinan had faced the Australians in Tests since the 1993–94 series in Australia, when the promising young batsman had flopped spectacularly, making 26 in five innings for an average of 5.20. The Australians gave him a hard time, although the sledging lacked the vicious edge of later years under Steve Waugh's captaincy. When Cullinan came to the wicket, the Australians would ask: 'You got the shower running Daryl?' David Boon recounts that when Warne came on to bowl to him, they would say, 'It's going to be third ball, Daryl, make sure you come forward . . . Oh, bad luck mate, you're out.' It wasn't all one-way traffic: at the start of one series, Cullinan came in and when Warne, who had put on some weight since they last met, said, 'I've been waiting a long time for this', Cullinan replied, 'Hello Shane, looks like you've spent most of it eating'. (Behind the scenes, the pair got on quite well—Warne was guest-of-honour at a benefit dinner for Cullinan in South Africa in 2003.)

In South Africa's second innings, Kirsten went at 36 and, when Hudson was run out with the score at 2 for 41, it became imperative for South Africa that Cullinan should prove his potential, but Warne tormented him for an over or so before having him caught behind for 0. On a wearing wicket, the only batsman who looked comfortable against Warne was Cronje, and when Steve Waugh, with his third ball, persuaded him to follow a ball going down leg and glance a catch to Healy, the rest of the side capitulated to be all out 130, Warne and Bevan taking 4 wickets each.

In the second Test, played in Port Elizabeth, east of Cape Town, it was Australia's turn to collapse. On a very grassy wicket, after Taylor sent South Africa in and they were bowled out for 209, Australia was all out for 108. South Africa's second innings of 168 gave them a lead of 269, which looked to be more than enough. Mark Waugh then played perhaps the best innings of his distinguished career—always composed and correct, chanceless until he had passed his hundred, and taking Australia to within a dozen runs of victory. Even then, the win was not assured; Bevan was out on the same score and when Warne was lbw to the first ball of Kallis's sixteenth over 7 runs later, Australia was 8 for 265, with Gillespie on strike. Gillespie played out the five remaining balls of the over, and Healy broke the tension by hitting the third ball of Cronje's next over for six over mid wicket.

Mark Waugh's 116 gave the twins consecutive man-of-the-match awards in a series being played for the title of the best Test team in the world. As often happens, the last Test was won by the side that had lost the series, proof perhaps that victory goes to those who want it most. Steve Waugh top-scored in both Australian innings with 67 and 60 not out, and Glenn McGrath took 6 for 86 from 41 overs in South Africa's first innings. The other notable event from Australia's point of view was that the vice-captain, Ian Healy, after being given out caught down the leg side from a ball that only brushed his pad, gave a very public display of dissent, showing his displeasure to the umpire, then hurling his bat into the dressing room, which earned him a suspension for two one-day games.

Taylor had made 80 in five innings and averaged 16 in the Test series. After scores of 7 and 17 in the first two one-day games, he was dropped on the votes of himself and coach Geoff Marsh; Ian Healy, the third selector, who thought Taylor should stay, took over the captaincy.

With the one-day series in the balance in the sixth match, chasing a South African total of 284, Michael Bevan joined Steve

Waugh with the score at 3 for 58, and the pair put on 189, Bevan 103 from 95 balls and Waugh 89 from 102 balls. Australia won with an over to spare.

With 301 at 50.16 in the one-day series and 313 runs at 78.25 in the Tests, Waugh was man-of-the-series in both events. He retained his Coopers & Lybrand ranking as the world's Number 1 batsman, and his brother Mark moved ahead of Brian Lara to Number 2 in the rankings.

Steve Waugh was made vice-captain for the 1997 tour to England—his third tour—replacing Ian Healy, who had done himself no favours with his tantrum after he had been given out in the third Test against South Africa. Taylor retained the captaincy, but the selectors felt that if his poor form continued he might have to be dropped from the Test side during the tour—this was an indication that the selectors' long-term choice of replacement for Taylor was going to be Stephen Waugh.

Healy says he was upset by the decision, and also resentful that, apart from chairman of selectors Trevor Hohns, who called to deliver the news, none of the Australian selectors or officials contacted him to discuss the decision, or commiserate with him, or thank him for the job he had done. But Healy wrote: 'One person who did call on that miserable morning was Steve Waugh. Tugga wasn't sure what to say, but for me the important thing was that he made the call. He had my support and I knew he'd do a good job'.

Waugh's opportunity to captain Australia came sooner than he expected. After losing the first two of three scheduled one-day internationals, Taylor stood himself down for the third match. It made no difference; at Lord's, despite a respectable Australian total of 269 (Mark Waugh 95 from 96 balls) England achieved their third consecutive six-wicket victory, with an over to spare. Interviewed after the match, a nervous looking Steve Waugh, wearing his baggy green cap, said, 'We didn't expect to lose 3-nil—we didn't expect to lose—so in that regard it is a bit of a surprise. We probably deserved to lose 3-nil . . . but it's crunch time now, we really have to pull our finger out and play some good cricket.'

Worse was to follow. Ten days later at Edgbaston—the first Test—Taylor won the toss, chose to bat, and 18 overs later Michael Kasprowicz joined Shane Warne, with Australia 8 wickets down for 54. Australia struggled to 118 after Warne (47) and Kasprowicz (17) put on 56. Although Gough, Malcolm and Caddick (5 for 50) had done the damage for

Glenn McGrath gestures to the crowd during Australia's 0-3 one-day Texaco series loss to England in 1997. *(England Cricket Board)*

England, the Australian fast bowlers could not produce the same result. Hussain made 207 and Thorpe 138 in a total of 478 for 9 wickets, a lead of 360. There was some good news for Australia, as Mark Taylor found his form with 129 in the second innings and, with Greg Blewett (125), took Australia to 477, but England lost only one wicket in making the necessary runs.

Of course, the British press went loony, but the Australians had their turn at Lord's, where, after the first day and most of the second day were rained out, Glenn McGrath, with 8 for 38 from 20.3 overs, had the best ever bowling figures in an Ashes Test at the home of cricket. England made only 77 and Australia replied with 7 for 213 (Elliott 112), but by then the wicket had become slow and easy and England comfortably played out a draw.

Steve Waugh's contribution in three innings to this point had been 12, 33 and 0. England captain, Mike Atherton, in his auto-biography, *Opening Up*, wrote: 'By the time the 1997 series came around I had realised that while Waugh may have looked uncom-fortable against the short ball, and didn't score off it, it rarely got him out. I told all our seamers they had to attack Waugh full and straight when he first came in. He often moved back and across as if he was expecting a bouncer, leaving him vulnerable to the full ball'. Although Waugh had failed to date in the series, this was not necessarily because Atherton's plan was working. In the first innings of the first Test, having belted three boundaries as Australia collapsed, Waugh was out caught behind to a shortish ball from Caddick. In the second innings he was lbw to Gough from a ball which kept low. It's possible that the English plan paid off in the second Test, where Waugh tried to turn a full-length ball to leg and was out lbw.

The third Test was at Old Trafford, Manchester. Atherton wrote: 'We also decided at Old Trafford not to sledge Waugh or engage him in any way. We felt he revelled in a hostile atmosphere and sledging merely fuelled his adrenalin. He arrived at the crease and soon realised this: "Okay, you're not talking to me, are you? Well I'll talk to myself then". And he did for 240 minutes in the first innings and 382 minutes in the second'. On a seaming wicket, with plenty of bounce, Waugh made 108 in an Australian total of 235 in the first innings and 116 in the second, when Australia's total was 395. England made 162 and 200, McGrath, Gillespie and Warne sharing the credit.

It was the 45th time a player had scored a century in each innings of a Test—Arthur Morris was the only surviving player who had made a century in each innings of an Ashes Test. Waugh had made more than twice as many as any of his team-mates in both innings and, like the 200 in the West Indies two years before, it was done in difficult conditions and at a crucial time in the series.

When he reached the first hundred, square driving Croft for 4, Tony Greig said, 'That's a very good hundred—I reckon this is going to go down as one of his best. He's made the century in tough conditions, when most of the batsmen around him have failed.' Bill Lawrie said, 'Yes, I don't think any batsman in the world could play better than that.' When he was out after the second hundred he got a standing ovation. The English team clapped him as he left the field.

Video coverage of his two hundreds shows that he made less use of the cut than usual, taking most of his runs in the V or off his legs. There is a crashing front-foot drive through extra cover, almost down on one knee—an unusual shot for Steve, looking more like Mark.

His century in the first innings came at a cost, with his right thumb hit more than once and badly bruised. In his diary of the tour, Waugh wrote: 'The pain gradually worsened to a point where I couldn't force the ball through the field at all. I was basically defending one-handed as I tried to minimise the pain that was going through my thumb joint and the space between thumb and forefinger'. Atherton called him 'Australia's mentally toughest player' and says Waugh 'has the quickest hands in the modern game and allows bowlers no margin for error. Any width is flayed through the covers, while his iron wrists and low back-lift pick off the leg-side ball with clinical efficiency. He isn't the prettiest player of my generation, but he is the most effective'.

Steve and Mark had brought Beverley over to see the first three Tests of this series. She left after this Test, having seen Steve's twin hundreds and a bright partnership of 92 between the brothers in the second innings of the third Test, Mark scoring 55 from only 81 balls.

On this tour, wives and families were allowed to stay with the team in their hotel. This was welcomed by Steve, although it brought its own problems—as Lynette points out in her foreword to Steve's diary, the rooms are usually small and Steve is famous for being untidy. During the fourth Test, Rosalie couldn't sleep, which kept Steve awake. The problem was solved by tour manager Alan Crompton, who gave them the manager's suite, which had an extra room.

Lynette had arrived in mid-June, planning to stay for three months. Her parents came too, to watch the cricket and to help with the travel and looking after ten-month-old Rosalie. Steve, who has been described by team-mate Gavin Robertson as 'a nappy-changing sort of Dad', hated being away from his family, and Lynette, who had been on the England tours in 1989 and 1993, enjoyed being with Steve and the team and the other wives and children. But the constant moving was difficult for Rosalie, who was not well in the latter part of the tour. On July 9, Steve wrote in his diary: 'It's becoming increasingly noticeable that she is not coping well with the constantly changing routine, with different hotels, long car trips and noisy rooms. She isn't able to shake the slight bout of flu she's been carrying around, and I'm beginning to think that she's better off at home with Lynette, even though I love having them touring with me'. Lynette wrote: 'I had probably been a bit too ambitious to think I could survive three months in hotels with a baby'. She came home a month early.

In his diaries, Waugh is frequently critical of tour arrangements and functions. After being presented with the Variety Club of Australia's award for the cricket personality of the year, he wrote: 'As usual the function went on far too long and, to make matters worse, the food trays were too hard to track down for our liking. After two hours of small talk we dashed for the bus, the mood of the team best summed up by a comment that was heard more than once: "We're outta here!"'. On arrival in Nottingham: 'Our new hotel proved to be a major disappointment, with the rooms being nothing short of abysmal. My particular "kennel" had only enough room for one piece of luggage before the "house full" sign needed to be put up, but this was only a minor irritation compared to the "one temperature for all" air-conditioning system that left us Aussies sweltering while the locals soaked up the warmth'. Of a match after the third Test: 'To have to front up to this politically correct fixture against the Minor Counties XI the day after a Test win and and after two and a half hours on the motorway is so ridiculous it defies logic'.

During the tour, Waugh visited his bat sponsor, Gunn and Moore, to have some bats made up. He prefers a bat weight around 2lb 10ozs with an oval handle and a slight bow in the face.

The fourth Test, at Headingley, was won for Australia by Jason Gillespie (7 for 37 from 13.4 overs), Matthew Elliott (199) and Ricky Ponting (127, his first Test hundred) in Australia's innings of 9 declared for 501, and Paul Reiffel, with 5 for 49 in England's second innings. Australia won by an innings and 61, to lead the series 2–1.

In the fifth Test, played at Trent Bridge, Australia's top five batsmen shared the honours in the first innings. Elliott made 69,

Taylor 76, Blewett 50, Mark Waugh 68 and Steve Waugh 75, in a total of 427. England replied with 313, McGrath and Warne 4 wickets each. Australia then made 336, the runs again being spread amongst the batsmen, excluding, this time, the Waugh twins. Needing 451, England fell 264 runs short, McGrath, Gillespie and Warne taking 3 wickets each.

With the Ashes retained, the final Test was dominated by the bowlers. McGrath took 7 for 76 in England's first innings of 180, Tufnell took 7 for 66 in Australia's 220-run reply, and Kasprowicz outdid them both with 7 for 36 in England's second innings of only 163. Tufnell (4 for 27) and Caddick (5 for 42) then shot Australia out for 104, 19 runs short. Steve Waugh—not at his best when not much is at stake— had a disappointing end to the series, with 22 in the first innings and 6 in the second.

Bowled by Devon Malcolm for 75, fifth Test v England, Trent Bridge, 1997. (England Cricket Board)

20

FAIRY BREAD

Money and the ACA

Towards the end of the 1997 England tour, during the match against Kent in mid-August, Steve Waugh and former Australian off-spin bowler Tim May organised a meeting of the newly formed Australian Cricketers' Association (ACA) in the team's hotel in Canterbury. Waugh was secretary of the association and May, a Chartered Accountant by training, was its president.

I spoke to May in November 2003. 'The ACA was incorporated in February 1997,' he told me, 'and Stephen took a lead role in making sure that communication to players was clear and that the Association was representing the wishes of the player base. That year we had a very public battle with the Australian Cricket Board, as it was called then [it is now Cricket Australia], including threatened strike action, and Stephen had a pivotal role in keeping the players together.'

They were concerned about a number of issues: whether they were getting their fair share of the game's revenue; whether the game's revenue was being maximised by effective marketing, superannuation and insurance arrangements; and the need to secure the game's future by seeing that players at State level were well paid.

Tim May said: 'We came into being because the players in the Australian cricket team took a stance on where cricket was compared to other professional sports, and realised that the number one

163

sport in Australia was well down the pecking order in terms of conditions of employment. The players thought it was very important that players at the State level should have the comfort and security of contracts—if you don't attract young players at the State level, then you won't get your Test players. The strength of Australian cricket has always been said to be its domestic level, and if that domestic level becomes unaffordable, cricket in Australia will suffer significantly; there's no use developing cricket, creating an appetite, and not being prepared to feed it when it needs to be fed.

'We also thought it was very important that cricket showed itself to be very professional, so we could attract elite athletes to our game rather than those athletes going and playing Australian Rules football, or Rugby Union or Rugby League, which had terms far in excess of what we had'.

There had been a great breakthrough in cricketers' incomes in the late 1970s, when nearly all the world's top players abandoned the established cricket boards and signed up with Kerry Packer's World Series Cricket. The boards were lucky that when Packer got what he wanted—television rights—he virtually gave the game back to them. Since then there had been some progress, and certainly Test players were making a good income from the game, but the Australian players believed that they should be sharing the game's increasing prosperity, and that the low level of payment to Sheffield Shield players was not fair to them and not good for the game. A third issue was the fact that the Australian Cricket Board insisted on dealing with the players individually and had resisted efforts to deal with the association that represented them.

Previous captains, including Greg Chappell and Allan Border, had worked towards a better deal, but with limited success. To some extent, the paternal attitude of the pre-Packer days remained. Ian Healy, while acknowledging that 'most of the Board officials are good people who have the best interests of the game at heart', also wrote:

> It always annoyed me that when the Board's senior officials addressed the players it was usually in a hotel room, with the players

strewn like disobedient schoolboys around the room, lying on the floor, perched in a corner, hidden behind a bed or a lounge . . . Why weren't we seated around a table, business-like, maybe even with an agenda where there were a number of issues to be discussed?

The appointment of May, with his business background, and the recruitment of Graham Halbish, recently resigned as chief executive of the ACB, and James Erskine, described by Ian Healy as 'a slick, no-nonsense marketing executive who'd first come to prominence in Australian sports business with the IMG sports management group', gave the Australian Cricketers' Association a professional impetus and a hard edge that the ACB found it could no longer deny, try as it might.

In *Run Out*, Graham Halbish wrote: 'The ACB had known for a couple of years that the players were expecting, and were entitled to, a major share of the new fortune that had filled the Board's coffers. After the lean times in the 1980s and improvements in the mid-1990s, there was no reason whatsoever to deprive the players of their entitlements by 1997'.

Following the August 1997 meeting in Canterbury, in November, on the eve of a Sheffield Shield match between NSW and Victoria at North Sydney Oval, the Association, through Tim May and their 'bargaining agent' James Erskine, presented their proposal to the ACB. It included player input into tour scheduling, representation at the Board's meetings and, most importantly, creation of a fund based on the Board's revenues which would enable greater distribution of the Board's income to the players.

The Board rejected the proposal, and the next morning at North Sydney Oval the players from both teams lined up shoulder-to-shoulder for a brief period in an 'act of solidarity'. Strike action was threatened and the coming tour by New Zealand was targeted. (The Association's affairs did not affect its secretary's concentration, or his view of the emphasis of the media; Steve Waugh was 113 not out at the close of play; then, at a packed press conference where the only questions were about the threatened strike action, Waugh said, 'It's good to see you all at a Shield game. Who said Shield cricket was dead?' He went on to be 202 not out when Taylor declared.)

The Board struck back by releasing the earnings of leading players, showing that Mark Taylor had received $485,000 from the Board in 1996–97; Steve Waugh, Ian Healy, Shane Warne and Glenn McGrath had received $440,000; and Mark Waugh, Matthew Elliott, Greg Blewett, Jason Gillespie and Paul Reiffel had each received $275,000.

With public sympathy shifting from the players to the Board, the players' emphasis changed to getting a better deal for State cricketers. But this too attracted criticism from the press. Malcolm Knox, former cricket writer for the *Sydney Morning Herald*, wrote: 'Few people think entertainers who play to near-empty stadia in loss-making matches should earn double the national wage. If cricketers want to be part of the entertainment industry, they should consider themselves lucky they are not actors, singers, artists or writers'. While Knox's point is valid to an extent, it could also be said that the support that Australia's senior cricketers gave to the less famous members of their craft in 1997 and 1998 might set an example for the actors, singers, artists and writers who make it to the big time.

The negotiations between the Board and the players were lengthy and at times acrimonious. The players didn't want to go on strike: they emphasised it was a last resort. At one stage there was a rumour that another rebel cricket competition was being organised—this was quickly put to rest when Channel 9 quizzed four of the senior players (Taylor, Steve Waugh, Warne and Healy) who were appearing on the network. Private discussions between Taylor and ACB chairman Denis Rogers produced a compromise proposal which was rejected by the players.

Eventually the Board had to go to the table with Tim May and the ACA, and by March 1998, most of their differences had been settled. In September 1998 an agreement was signed. It set out the method of remuneration for all first class cricketers, based on a 'players payment pool' derived from a percentage of the Board's revenue, and it included a standard contract for all State players.

Tim May says, 'It was very important that we tie a percentage to cricket revenue, because we were very much aware that cricket was enjoying and would continue to enjoy a period of increasing profit . . . there will come a time when that curve will flatten out, but we stand behind the principle that we are a partner of Australian cricket, and the health of the game and the health of the players should basically run in parallel.'

The agreement also set out arrangements covering injury; players injured while 'fulfilling their contract' can receive retainer and match payments for up to two years.

Perhaps most importantly, as Ian Healy points out, the players had established that the Board would have to deal with the Association, which gave the players a position of strength. Ian Healy is now president of the Australian Cricketers' Association. Tim May remains CEO, the secretary is Greg Matthews and the Treasurer is Damien Fleming.

Halbish and Erskine are no longer involved; bargaining is now done 'in house' by the ACA. It's also significant that seven countries now have player associations. Bangladesh and Pakistan do not yet have effective associations, but Tim May says, 'England, South Africa and New Zealand are very strong. Sri Lanka's player association has shown that it is able to stand up for its principles and negotiate with its cricket board. West Indies has finally got a strong association enjoying strong support from the players. In Zimbabwe the player association is in the background for the moment—there are more significant issues there.' Together they form the Federation of International Cricket Associations (FICA) which has Barry Richards as president, and vice-presidents including Courtney Walsh, Greg Chappell, Martin Crowe and Majid Khan.

Graham Halbish wrote: 'The ugly fight that took place between the ACB and the players' association in 1997 need never have happened. The money was there to accommodate the players' demands, of that there was never any doubt. The whole issue, unfortunately, was about power'.

In fact, the senior players made a sacrifice, at least in the short term, for the benefit of their State colleagues. In James Knight's book *Mark Waugh: The Biography*, Mark says:

> The first couple of years, the actual contracts went down. I remember Greg Matthews saying at the time that no one would be worse off, then the next year our contracts are cut. We went through all that drama for what? For the life of me I couldn't work out how the hell I'd lost money. But the bottom line was that everyone else was better off. But it's all turned around now . . . it wasn't only about the money—we wanted to have a voice, have a foot in the door with the decisions made by the ACB.

Under the deal negotiated with the ACB by the Australian Cricketers' Association, 25 per cent of Cricket Australia's revenue goes to the player payment pool. This amount was expected to be $26 million in 2003–04. The pool is then split, with 55 per cent going to the 25 international players contracted to Cricket Australia and 45 per cent going to State players.

At the State level, top players get $85,000 each and that scales down to $32,500 at the lowest level, for players who are in the squad but might not play a match. There are also three rookie players on $12,500 each. Match payments—$3200 for Pura cup and $1100 for ING Cup—are on top of this, so a State player who plays a full season of ten Pura Cup and ten ING Cup matches would be earning close to $130,000 in a season.

In 2003–04, of the 25 players contracted to the ACB, those on the lowest scale receive $125,000, scaling up to $484,000 for the top-line players. Match fees are $12,100 for a Test and $4850 for a one-day international, plus an extra 40 per cent on overseas tours.

In a season with, say, a dozen Test matches and twenty one-day internationals, the top players would receive in the vicinity of $700,000 in contract and match fees. The captain (or captains) get an additional retainer, negotiated with Cricket Australia.

The Australian team's prize-money for winning the 2003 World Cup was $3.4 million, allocated 'according to how many days each player served with the squad, rather than how many matches they played'. So top players such as Ponting, McGrath, Lee, Hayden and Gilchrist received almost $250,000—no wonder Steve Waugh was upset at being dropped from the one-day side—while Nathan Bracken and Nathan Hauritz, neither of whom played in a match, each received more than $100,000. Second prize was worth $1.35 million to the Indian team.

In the 2004–04 Test series against India, prize-money was $20,000 per Test and in the VB series, the top team of the preliminary series received $70,000 and the winner of the final series got a further $50,000.

Brian Freedman, Bankstown president and a board member of Cricket Australia, points out that on top of the payments received by the players, there is a lot of money spent on support. For example, a touring party of fourteen players has a support staff of ten. Freedman also believes that the big rises in revenues to the bodies that run cricket are coming to an end. 'It's still a wealthy game,' he says, 'but the bidding wars for media rights are over, the big rises are tapering off . . . I think we're getting close to a stage where one-day cricket has peaked in its appeal, it's plateauing. I know we have to encourage the new players—Bangladesh, and now Kenya want Test status because they get a bigger share of the money—but in the entertainment business I was told you've always got to leave the audience wanting a bit more, never over-supply your market, and I think we've got to be careful there. You know, you can turn Fox on any time and see cricket being played somewhere, can't you. There's an awful lot of one-day cricket and I worry that it's becoming very predictable, so I think we've got some hard thinking to do about how we reinvigorate that game—I think that's an issue we should really put our minds to.'

In 2002, I was involved in a proposal to make a coaching CD featuring Bradman and Sachin Tendulkar. It was to be put together by an Indian/Australian syndicate, made in Australia with money from an

Indian sponsor. My involvement was due to my knowledge of archival film—I had no interest in the business side of it—but I was aware that Tendulkar's management were asking a fee for what would have been about a week's work—three or four days filming and three or four days travelling—of $US1 million. The syndicate was apparently prepared to pay the fee—the Indian market is that big—but in the end it was logistics that stopped the project from going ahead.

Steve Waugh's bat contract with MRF was reported to be worth $250,000 a year for three years. With Cricket Australia's maximum scale payments, prize-money, the captain's retainer, and all the other endorsements, Waugh's income from cricket would have been well over the $1 million mark, perhaps closer to $2 million. Most of the team have been together for some time now and are a tight-knit bunch. They discuss their various deals and the advice they get and they are pretty savvy when it comes to financial matters.

They call Steve 'fairy bread'—he only deals in hundreds of thousands.

21

A BIT OF STICK

The one-day captaincy

Before the tour by New Zealand at the start of the 1997–98 season, it was announced that Mark Taylor had been replaced by Steve Waugh as captain of the Australian one-day side for the series with New Zealand and South Africa, after the Tests.

Australia won the first two Tests comfortably and was the better team in the third Test, which was drawn. With the individual honours fairly evenly spread, Mark Taylor confirmed his return to form and was man-of-the-series. Steve Waugh's scores were 2 and 23 in the first Test, 96 in the second Test, then 7 and 2 not out. His 96 took him past 6000 runs in Tests—the seventh Australian to reach that mark. Appropriately, he did it with his trademark square drive off the back foot past point. The innings won him man-of-the-match and included a partnership of 153 with his brother; Mark was at his languid best while Steve clubbed through covers and played some powerful front-foot straight drives.

Following the series he dropped to number 2 in Coopers & Lybrands world ratings, replaced by Inzamam-ul-Haq.

One of the first things Waugh had to do as one-day captain was to tell Ian Healy that he had been dropped, which he said was 'probably the hardest thing I've ever had to do'. Healy was replaced by Adam Gilchrist, who played a match-winning hand in the second final with 100 from 104 balls.

Waugh had an unimpressive start in the job—Australia lost five preliminary games and his seven innings produced only 57 runs. Australia was lucky to make the final, but typically, with the final series level 1-each, Waugh made 71 from 88 balls and with Ponting (76 from 96) and Bevan (36 not out from 30 balls) took Australia to a total of 7 for 247. Three run outs (two by Ponting) and some tight bowling kept the South Africans in check and they were all out for 233 in the 49th over.

So he won his first series as one-day captain. After the final he said, 'It was a great performance, one of the best one-day wins I've been involved with and obviously one of the sweetest because we've copped a bit of stick over the last couple of weeks . . . you've really got to dig deep when you're struggling and you've got to believe in yourself and have faith and think back to the times when you're doing well and just stay positive; there's no point in dwelling on negative things, otherwise you're going to go nowhere.'

South Africa, with Donald and Pollock, backed up by Symcox, McMillan, Klusener and Cronje, and with batting down to Klusener at number 9, promised the most competitive Test series for some time. In Melbourne, needing 381 in the second innings with four sessions left, South Africa looked likely to lose, but fine innings by Kallis (101 in 279 minutes) and Cronje (70 in 170 minutes) saw them through to a draw with 3 wickets left.

The second Test, played at the Sydney Cricket Ground, was Steve Waugh's hundredth. After South Africa had made 287 (Warne 5 for 75), Steve joined Mark with Australia 3 for 103 and, against Donald at his bruising best, the twins set up an Australian win with a partnership of 116. Mark made an even 100 and Steve (85), Ponting (62) and Healy (46) contributed to a total of 421. Then Paul Reiffel (3 for 14 from 12 overs) strangled the South Africans, and Shane Warne (6 for 34 from 21 overs) skittled them—Australia won by an innings and 21 runs.

In Adelaide it was Australia's turn to defend. South Africa made 517 and Australia replied with 350. South Africa was without

Donald, but Pollock took 7 for 87. Mark Taylor batted through the Australian innings for an undefeated 169. Needing 361 in its second innings, Australia was 2 for 32 at stumps on the fourth day, with both openers out. South Africa had its chances, dropping Mark Waugh four times, but he stayed there all day and his 115 not out in 404 minutes enabled Australia to survive with 3 wickets left and take the series 1-nil. Steve was the best of the rest of the batsmen, with 34 scored in 110 minutes.

A one-day series in New Zealand in February 1998 was split 2–2 before a three-Test tour of India to be followed by a triangular series including Zimbabwe. In India, with McGrath and Gillespie injured and with Warne's shoulder beginning to trouble him, Australia's bowling was below strength and India took full advantage. Despite trailing by 71 on the first innings in Chennai (formerly Madras) India won by 179 after Sachin Tendulkar hit 155 not out from 191 balls in its second innings.

Batting first in Calcutta, Australia made 233, and India's top six all got runs, Azharuddin 163 and still batting when they declared at 5 for 633. Then India bowled Australia out for 181, to win by an innings and 219 runs and claim the Border-Gavaskar Trophy. Steve Waugh had top-scored with a patient 80 in Australia's first innings, but had suffered a painful groin strain and had to call for a runner—Greg Blewett—and was run out soon after. He made 33 in the second innings without a runner, hobbling between wickets for a few minutes less than three hours. His injury kept him out of the third Test, which Australia won, Mark Waugh confirming his reputation as a tougher, more reliable batsman who could be turned to when a big innings was needed, leading the way with 153 not out.

Steve Waugh was back in action for the tri-series with India and Zimbabwe. Australia defeated India in the final, played in Delhi, winning by 4 wickets with 8 balls to spare.

22

STEVE WHO?

Shamlu Dudeja and the Udayan Home

In March 1998, during the second Test in India, played in Calcutta, Waugh had received a letter from Shamlu Dudeja, chairperson of a registered charity called the Calcutta Foundation. I spoke to her in October 2003.

'My son had died and my husband, with grief and a heart condition, was very ill and was in the nursing home. I had promised Udayan that I would help them make a girls' wing. Udayan then was a boy's home for children of leprosy sufferers and I wanted to add on a girls' wing. I had in fact gone to England to try and raise funds, but it was at that time that my husband suddenly fell ill and I had to come back in a hurry.

'Sitting with my husband in the nursing home, Steve Waugh was playing a cricket match in Calcutta at that time. I'm not much of a cricket fan, but my husband was and I was with him and watching cricket all the time. I didn't know anybody else, but I knew Steve, and for some reason his face seemed to crop up on the screen more than anybody else's.

'And then on the fourth day, which was Saturday, I sat down to have my lunch and we have a lot of domestic staff at home and they were sitting and watching cricket at that time, so I sat down behind them with a tray on my lap, just eating my lunch, when Steve got out just at that moment—it was a run out, I remember. Normally, people who get run out challenge the umpire's decision or fume and abuse or whatever, but Steve just turned around and walked away, so I thought, "Gosh, you know, this is a good man, he hasn't challenged anybody's decision," and just as I was thinking these thoughts, I had that particular day's newspaper in my hand which carried an interview with Steve by a local sports journalist and the interview said—I can't remember the whole thing but one of the things that stuck in my mind was that Steve said he liked to work with children's charities. The reporter had asked him what were the qualities he liked in a person, and Steve had said that what he liked was honesty, integrity, sincerity, things like that.

'So I quickly finished my lunch. I happened to have a computer at home, and I was very miserable because I had not been able to fulfil my promise to Udayan for a girls' wing—I had not been able to raise any funds—so I said to myself, "Here's my chance," and I sat down at the computer and wrote off a letter to Steve. I said, "Steve, you lost this match, but I think that there is some hand of God in it because that gives you tomorrow, Sunday, free, and if you mean what you say in the *Telegraph* of today—that you like to do children's charity work, instead of drinking beer with your team-mates at the Tolleygunge club—come with me and visit one of my projects.

'So, after having delivered the letter, I went off to my husband—you know, I used to spend the nights there because he was so ill—and the following morning I came home and the telephone was ringing. I picked up the phone and heard "May I speak to Shamlu Dudeja?"—you know, in the Australian accent—and I said, "Speaking. Who's that?" He said, "This is Steve", and I said, "Steve who?" and he said "Aren't you the person who wrote me the letter about your charity", and I said, "Yes I am. Does that mean that you are Steve Waugh?" and he said, "I'm ringing because you offered to take me to your charity", so I said, "When?" and he said, "Now".'

In *Cricket Beyond the Bazaar*, published in 1990, Mike Coward wrote:

With boys at a Foster Parents Plan slum resettlement in Madras, 1989.

During their 1984 sojourn, Kim Hughes' party walked into the terminal of Indore Airport and into the midst of a group of limbless children propelling themselves towards a viewing area on rough-hewn wooden wheel-carts. Spontaneously and quietly, the party donated to the Apang Manav Marden Crippled Children's Home most of the 25,000 rupees they had won for their six-wicket victory over India.

During the World Cup in 1987, team manager Alan Crompton, Mark Taylor, Steve Waugh and Tim May supported work being done in the slums of Madras by international aid organisation Foster Parents' Plan. Mike Coward wrote: 'With the ready assistance of selfless, enquiring Stephen Waugh and his ilk, Alan Crompton endeavoured to demystify the Indian experience and blaze the trail for more relaxed visits by Australian teams'.

There are about 5 million leprosy sufferers in India. The Udayan Home at Barrackpore, 35 km north of Calcutta, is for the children of leprosy sufferers. Only a few of the children—about 5 per cent—

actually have the disease, but even those who are free of the disease are treated as outcasts. Founded in 1970, Udayan allows them to escape the constraints and stigma of leprosy and gives them an education which enables them to live normal lives and support their families, most of whom would otherwise survive by begging. It also treats and usually cures the 5 per cent who have the disease. In Bengali, Udayan means 'dawn' or 'new beginning'.

Shamlu Dudeja: 'Steve took with him a reporter, who was Michael Coward, and a photographer from London, and we went to Udayan and it was there the boys saw him and they loved him and he loved them and he said, "Would you like to play cricket?" and they said, "Yes" and they went and got out some broken bats and some battered balls and they started playing cricket.

'And Steve had two wonderful hours with the boys and there were some beautiful pictures of him taken by the photographer with the boys and after that he told me he would like to go to the colonies where these children come from, so I said, "Steve, you do not know what these places are, they are like hovels, they are sub-human, they are not the kind of places you have been to before." He said, "Don't you want me to go?" I said, "I'd like you to go, but I don't know whether you'll be able to stand it," and he said, "I'd like to give it a try. Do you think I could catch the infection?" I said, "No, these people do not have the kind of leprosy which is infectious, so the chances are you will not, but in any case when you go back to the hotel I'll give you an antiseptic and you can have a shower or bath with it."

'So that's how it went. Steve was visibly impressed and I said, "What do we do next?" and he said, "Well, I'll get in touch with you".

'So I thought, "Well, a lot of good people talk like that—I'll get in touch with you—he's not the first", but sure enough, his next match was in Delhi and he called from there and said, "I've met Sourav Ganguly and he's going to be bringing you back some old t-shirts and shoes and things like that. Just keep them for a few weeks and

I'll come back for an auction". And I thought, "My God, this man means business".'

The Calcutta Test was played 18–21 March 1998. On July 22, an Indian news service reported:

On Tuesday, Steve Waugh laid the foundation stone for Nivedita Bhavan, the branch of Calcutta-based charity Udayan that caters to the children of leprosy-affected parents.

Nivedita Bhavan, at Udayangram, to raise funds for which Steve Waugh is in Calcutta, will be for girl children. Udayan is run by the Oxford mission, and already maintains a home for 250 male children. The foundation stone was laid amid the chanting of Sanskrit hymns and blowing of conch shells. The building, when completed, is slated to house around 150 female children of different ages.

Nivedita Bhavan will provide its inmates with boarding, lodging and tuitions, besides providing vocational training aimed at making them self-sufficient, and able to take care of their own lives in adulthood.

Waugh became interested when he, as part of the Australian team touring India earlier this year, accepted an invitation to visit a leper colony at Titagarh, near Udayan, and also checked out the work the charity was doing. Much moved, Waugh offered his services towards raising funds for a separate home for girl children.

'I got an opportunity to see the boys and found them to be very happy,' Waugh recalled. 'I felt the need for a similar facility for girls and I thought I should do something for them. I'll be happier once the construction of the girls' wing is completed . . . All of us have a social responsibility,' said Waugh, while laying the stone, 'especially sportspersons, who are in the public eye and who have a following. We have got to involve those who have more money than what is needed to live, try and change things, reach out to those not as fortunate as we are.'

Waugh gently hinted that India's own cricketing superstars should come forward to do their bit as well. The Aussie star said that, already, Sourav Ganguly, whose home is in Calcutta, and Rahul Dravid had both expressed their willingness to spare their time and energies towards helping with the project . . . Waugh, who has already collected $25,000 from friends in Australia for the charity, later moved on to a fund-raising charity dinner at a Calcutta hotel, and spoke of the need for corporate houses to come forward.

During the 'Foster a Girl' charity dinner, Waugh auctioned a bat autographed by the legendary Sir Donald Bradman, and another one with the autographs of the entire Australian cricket team, besides other cricket memorabilia.

With Waugh driving the auction, the sale, held at the Taj Bengal, raised a remarkable Rs 1.1 million [about $A30,000]. The biggest bid, naturally enough, was for the Bradman bat, eventually bought by TIL chairman Avijit 'Bobby' Majumdar for Rs 500,000. A bat autographed by Waugh himself fetched Rs 5,000, while a bat signed by the entire Australian team that toured India earlier this year went for Rs 110,000. A Kookaburra cricket ball bearing the signatures of the Waugh brothers, Steve and Mark, and ace spinner Shane Warne, fetched Rs 50,000.

Among the corporate houses that attended and helped drive up the prices were Tata Tea, Cathay Pacific and Fosters.

Shamlu Dudeja continued: 'People in Calcutta loved Steve—they couldn't believe he was going to be involved in a project like this—and they gave him a lot of money and with that money we were able to build one girls' wing in Udayan which was ready within a year, and Steve came back after 15 months to inaugurate the building'.

The first wing, opened in August 1999, houses 80 girls. Since then, says Shamlu Dudeja, 'Steve has been sending beds and medicine. Every time he is here he tries to go to Udayan, but now Udayan is full they can not take on more children, so what we hope to do—it has been my dream for a long time that the numbers should be equal—is put another 200 girls into Udayan, you know, more buildings, with a school and a dining room and entire facilities. Steve wants to form a new board and that board will then look after this new home which we hope to call Ashray, which means 'shelter'.

'We are talking in terms of a school residential home, a school premises and a corpus out of which we can draw the interest every month to feed the children and pay for their education. Basically this will be money which will keep Ashray going under its own steam. Steve is a major part of this. I can't see that I could have been able to do it without him, because he showed the same kind of dedication that I have myself towards this project, and now Lynette his wife seems to be so wonderfully involved. She just loves the project and she was here with Steve two months ago. So that's how it happened.'

23

O'REILLY'S COLLIE DOG

The captaincy

After the Indian tour in February–March 1998, there was a one-day series in Sharjah. Playing India in the final, Australia made 272, but another onslaught from Tendulkar (134 from 131 balls) saw his side home with an over-and-a-half to spare.

Most of the Australian team had been playing almost non-stop for more than eighteen months. The last break from cricket of more than a month had been after the 1996 World Cup. In the eighteen months since October 1996, Steve Waugh had played 22 Tests and 45 one-day internationals. It had been especially hard on the bowlers, and the absence of McGrath and Gillespie, and the huge workload on Warne, had affected Australia's chances in India. When Warne got back to Australia he was found to have rotator cuff and shoulder ligament and cartilage damage. He needed an operation and was told there was no certainty that he would recover the full use of his shoulder. McGrath also had an operation that winter in an attempt to deaden the nerve system which caused him frequent pain in his groin.

They were due for a break. In the winter of 1998, one of Steve Waugh's few cricket-related duties was to attend a civic reception in Bankstown to celebrate his 100th Test match and his appointment as Australia's one-day captain.

In September 1998 Waugh had another unexpected experience: captaining the cricket team that represented Australia at the 1998 Commonwealth games.

It was different; they weren't paid, they stayed four to a room in the athletes' village, ate in the mess hall, did their own washing; and they made the most of it, going to a lot of events—talking their way in when they didn't have passes—and getting to meet and know many of the other athletes. Steve Waugh wrote: 'The other occupants in the dormitory I was part of were Tom Moody, whose bed was about half a metre too short for him, Gavin Robertson, who became like a mother hen to all of us, and Mark Waugh, who in regard to domestic duties was, it must be said, probably our weak link'.

The gold medal would have completed the experience. In the final against South Africa, Shaun Pollock broke through early and Australia were all out for 183 in the last over, Steve Waugh not out 90. The Australians had to settle for silver—South Africa made the runs with 4 wickets in hand. Waugh was disappointed with the final—'There were a lot of soft dismissals, a lot of poor shots today, not up to the standards we are used to'—but not with the event: 'I can honestly say that our Commonwealth Games cricket experience was as good a two weeks as I've ever had in sport'.

In Pakistan in 1959, Richie Benaud's side had won two Tests with one drawn. Australia had lost each of the four series in Pakistan since then, without winning a single Test. In 1998, Taylor's team was without Shane Warne who was recovering from surgery to his damaged shoulder, but Glenn McGrath was back for his first Test in nine months. Taylor himself had a new, slimmer look after a rigorous fitness campaign leading up to the tour.

The first Test was played in Rawalpindi. Aamer Sohail won the toss and Pakistan made 269, MacGill 5 for 66. It was a spinner's wicket and with Saqlain Mushtaq and Mushtaq Ahmed, Pakistan was well-equipped. Wasim Akram did the early damage, getting rid of Taylor and Langer for 3 and 0. Steve Waugh joined Slater with

Australia 3 for 28. They put on 198, with Slater making 108 and Waugh, dropped at slip on 81, going on to 157 scored in six and a half hours. Allan Border, commentating on Foxtel, said: 'They would have all survived on the Titanic if Steve Waugh had been there'.

Trailing by 244, Pakistan were bowled out for 145. MacGill took 4 more wickets, Ian Healy took his total of dismissals to 356—one more than Rod Marsh—and Australia had its first win in Pakistan for 39 years.

After this match, Mark Waugh, Mark Taylor, and ACB chief executive Malcolm Speed (who had replaced Graham Halbish) flew with an armed guard to Lahore to give credibility to their written statements by testifying to the judicial enquiry into the bribery allegations against Salim Malik. As a result of this enquiry, the allegations were dismissed for 'lack of evidence' (although that was not the end of that particular story).

The second Test was played in Peshawar, in Pakistan's far north. Taylor, dropped twice before he was 30, found his form with a vengeance and with his personal tally 334—equal with Don Bradman as the highest score in Tests by an Australian—declared the Australian innings closed at 4 for 599. Pakistan replied with 9 for 580 in a game that was always going to be a draw. With a second draw in Karachi, Australia won the Test series 1–0, then won all three one-day games before flying home.

On paper, England and Australia should have been evenly matched in Australia in 1998–99. With Gough, Fraser, Croft, Mullally, Such and Headley, England had reasonable bowling to choose from and their batting looked strong: with Butcher, Atherton, Hussain, Stewart, Thorpe, Ramprakash and Hick, they should have made a lot of runs, especially as Australia was still without Shane Warne,

Steve Waugh began the series with 112 not out in the first Test, which was interrupted by rain and drawn in Australia's favour. Fleming, McGrath and Gillespie overwhelmed England on Perth's lively wicket in the second Test. Australia won by 7 wickets there and by 205 runs in Adelaide, where Justin Langer's 179 not out in Australia's first innings total of 391 was the decisive innings of the match. Australia, leading the series 2–nil with two to play, had retained the Ashes.

In the fourth Test, played in Melbourne, England made 270 and Australia followed with 340, Steve Waugh not out 122, an innings which he describes in his diary for the year as 'just about the best innings I've played in Test cricket'. England then made 244 to lead by only 174 and Australia looked safe at 3 for 130, but lost the last 6 wickets for only 32, to lose by 12 runs. Steve Waugh was not out 30 at the end and was criticised for not shielding the tail-enders from the strike, in particular for taking a single from the first ball of an over from Darren Gough, exposing MacGill, who was yet to score, to the strike, with 2 wickets in hand and 13 runs needed for a win. As MacGill had made 43 of an 88-run partnership with Waugh in the first innings, the criticism seems harsh, although, as it happened, within the space of a few balls, Gough bowled both MacGill and McGrath, and England had won the match.

This Test was also notable for one of Glenn McGrath's outbursts. Towards the end of England's second innings, Mullally smacked a few fours off McGrath, who retaliated by walking into his line when he was running and mouthing obscenities at point blank range. Match referee John Reid fined him $2500 for using abusive language, suspended depending on good behaviour.

In the final Test, Mark Waugh made 121, Steve made 96 and their fourth wicket partnership of 190, with two fine spells from Stuart MacGill (5 for 57 and 7 for 50), were the deciding factors. Australia won by 98 to take the series 3–1.

Steve Waugh missed most of the one-day series with England and Sri Lanka with a hamstring injury. Captained by Shane Warne in Waugh's absence, Australia won the series comfortably. By the time it was over, Mark Taylor had announced his retirement and Waugh was preparing to lead his first series as Australia's Test captain. Asked, at the press conference to announce his appointment, where he had been when he got the call, he told the media he had been watching 'Sesame Street' with his daughter, Rosalie.

Bill O'Reilly, who had recognised Steve Waugh's talent in 1984 and 'implored' the selectors to send him to England in 1985—they didn't—also wrote: 'I have never placed great importance on the choice of a captain. There is nothing in the job more than the skill to write down the batting order legibly and to walk in front of the team as it takes the field. The rest is rule-of-thumb stuff that any well-trained collie dog can perform'.

Former national selector John Benaud's criteria for a captain, quoted in his book *Matters of Choice*, were that he should be:

- hell bent on winning, but not to the detriment of the game;
- a sportsman, someone who respects the game's spirit and traditions;
- an entertainer, so spectators want to come to the next match;
- a good man manager who knows how to get the best out of his players;
- a leader by example, with high-rating personal performances;
- a prophet, able to react to the game and anticipate outcomes;
- lucky, prepared to gamble and likely to win.

O'Reilly's theory is a source of debate among cricketers. So much of cricket hangs on individual performance that some say there is limited scope for a captain to influence the game. On the other hand, even at school or park level, the right word at the right time can give heart to a flagging bowler, or shore up the concentration of a tiring batsman. At the professional level today, some of what passes for good captaincy is the result of hours of study by coaching and support staff, or at team meetings, to suss out the weakness in opposition players, or to develop game plans to limit your opponents' scoring opportunities, or maximise your own.

Waugh would rate quite highly on John Benaud's criteria. A criticism might be that he was so hell bent on winning that he didn't always respect the spirit of the game, but he was entertaining to watch because his nature was to play attacking cricket. Early in his captaincy he may have had something to learn about man management, but he certainly led by example. As to luck: he won the toss in all four Tests of his first series as captain, in the West Indies, and in six of the seven one-day matches.

Ian Healy wrote that Waugh:

> struggled a little bit when he first became Test captain . . . the atmosphere at team meetings was a little stiff as Tugga attempted to stamp his mark on the team by imposing his team plans and goals. By doing this he unwittingly denied the ranks any ownership of those plans and goals, which reduced their value. In a team environment, the best way to achieve success is to get everyone involved in the development of objectives and the execution of battle plans.

Later, Healy wrote, Waugh 'learnt a lot from his early captaincy disappointments, and his leadership blossomed through the World Cup and on into the 1999–2000 season . . . Stephen learnt to lead with his actions and inspire with his words and is now able to fill his charges with pride and confidence'.

Waugh's first series as Test captain and first tour as captain of both the Test and one-day teams was one of the most dramatic, exciting and evenly matched of the game's history.

In 1999 the West Indies were trying to rebuild—they had just lost five Tests in a row in South Africa— but they still had Ambrose, Walsh and Lara, each capable of turning a Test. On paper, with a batting line up including Slater, Langer, the two Waughs, Blewett and Healy, and with Warne back, as well as McGrath, Gillespie and MacGill, Australia looked the stronger side. They won the first Test by 312 when the West Indies were all out for 51 in the second innings, their lowest total ever. McGrath (5 for 28) and Gillespie (4 for 18) were the only bowlers used.

In Kingston, Jamaica, the Waugh twins put on 112 for the fourth wicket—Steve made an even hundred. Australia's total was 256 and with West Indies 4 for 37 at stumps on the first day it looked like more of the same. However, at stumps on the second day West Indies were 4 for 377 with Lara on 212 and Jimmy Adams, 88. They went on to 431, then the Jamaican pair Courtney Walsh (3 for 52) and off-spinner Nehemiah Perry (5 for 70), in front of their home crowd, skittled Australia for 177, leaving West Indies needing only 3 runs for victory.

Steve Waugh played another of his great innings in Bridgetown. This time his partner was Ricky Ponting—Mark had been bowled second ball by Ambrose for 0. Ponting came in with Australia 4 for 144 and left at 5 for 425. He made 104 and Waugh went on to 199, made in eight and a half hours. It was perhaps not as great an innings as his 200 in Jamaica in 1995—Curtly Ambrose was four years older and the Bridgetown wicket was much better—but any big innings against a team including Ambrose is an achievement. Waugh paid tribute to the tall Antiguan, acknowledging that he was too good for him in the morning session, but Waugh kept his concentration and dominated the bowling later in the innings.

He was sometimes uncomfortable early, but once he settled he showed the combination of power and economy of movement which characterise his best innings: the trademark square cuts, deft placement on the leg side, powerful straight drives off the fast bowlers, off both front foot and back foot. After one such shot, commentator David Hookes said, 'That's called the full face of the bat'; after another, 'No need to run for that, sunshine'. Ponting's batting, with its swivelling, controlled but powerful pull shots, was an interesting contrast.

Good as Waugh's innings was, it wasn't the innings of the match. West Indies made 329, then Courtney Walsh took 5 for 39 from 17 overs and Australia was all out 146. The West Indies needed 308 to go 1-up in the series. Campbell and Griffith started well, then wickets fell at 72, 77, 78, 91 and 105, when Jimmy Adams joined Brian Lara. They took the score to 238, then two more wickets fell at 248,

The batsman's view of Curtly Ambrose, first Test v West Indies, Port-of-Spain, 1999. (West Indies Cricket Board)

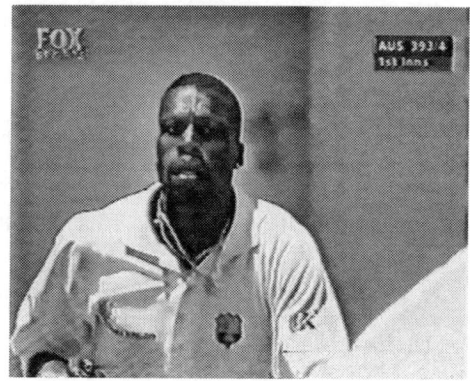

leaving 60 runs to get with only Ambrose and Walsh left to bat with Lara. Steve Waugh freely acknowledges Lara's genius and wrote in his diary of the tour that Lara 'played the knock of his life, guiding and cajoling the tail-enders as he steered his team to a one-wicket victory after all seemed lost. His 153 not out was a masterpiece'. Mark Waugh described Lara's innings as 'the best batting I've ever seen'—high praise indeed.

Lara played another extraordinary innings in the fourth Test, making an even 100 from only 84 balls, against an Australian attack without Shane Warne, who had been dropped for lack of form. Steve Waugh's 72 not out was top score in Australia's first innings total of 303. West Indies replied with 222, including Lara's speedy gem; then Justin Langer, with a well-crafted 127 in 308 minutes, took Australia to 306, a lead of 387. The West Indies lost any chance they might have had when Glenn McGrath had Lara lbw for only 7. Australia won by 176 runs and the four-Test series was tied 2-each.

Colin 'Funky' Miller, who made a valuable 43 in the first innings in a 53-run partnership with Steve Waugh for the ninth wicket, tells a story in *Inside Edge* which seems to show that captaincy isn't rocket science: 'As I reached the middle Steve walked up, looked me in the eye and simply said, "Good luck Funk, if it's in your area have a go"—not exactly the "I'll take the strike and look after you" I was expecting. Hell, I wasn't even sure what my area was'. Miller took Waugh's advice and hit Ambrose for two big sixes over square leg before Ambrose let fly with a bouncer which almost went for 6 byes. Miller claims that the West Indies were so impressed with his big hitting that they gave him a single to get him off strike.

In a less amusing incident, Glenn McGrath was accused of spitting at West Indies' opener Adrian Griffith, and the $2000 fine, suspended from his sledging of Mullaly in Australia the previous summer, was imposed. McGrath also injured a foot, kicking the fence in anger after Lara had been dropped off his bowling, and missed all but one of the one-day matches. However, in a series where Warne had not come back to his best and had in fact been dropped for the fourth Test, McGrath was probably the difference between the teams. The West Indies had seven innings; McGrath took 3 wickets twice, 4 wickets once, and 5 wickets —the bowlers' century—on four occasions. His 30 wickets in the series was only 4 less than all the rest of the bowlers put together and he took them at an average of 16.93.

With 409 runs at 58.43 Steve Waugh topped the Test aggregates and the averages.

In *Hands and Heals*, after the Test series in the West Indies, Ian Healy wrote:

> Stephen puts great importance on the efforts of the Australian one-day team. Whereas Tubby [Taylor] would never have taken one-day slumps as seriously as Test match setbacks, Stephen wants to win it all. He's one very hungry cricketer and captain, destined to be recognised as one of the giants of the game's history.

Honours had been even in the Test series against the West Indies. The seven-match one day series which followed was every bit as dramatic and exciting.

Game 1	St Vincent	West Indies by 44 runs
Game 2	Grenada	Australia by 46 runs
Game 3	Trinidad	West Indies by 5 wickets
Game 4	Trinidad	Australia by 20 runs
Game 5	Guyana	Tied
Game 6	Barbados	Australia by 4 wickets
Game 7	Barbados	West Indies by 8 wickets

For the Australians, Fleming was always economical and Warne returned to better form. Darren Lehmann made the only century but all the batsmen contributed at some stage.

With the series very tight, the later games produced the drama. In Guyana, with the series tied 2-each, the game was reduced by rain to 30 overs and after the West Indies made 173, Australia needed 3 runs off the last ball to tie the match. Keith Arthurton tried a quicker ball but Waugh pulled it high towards mid-on and the crowd started to run onto the field.

Waugh wrote: 'Warney and I tried desparately to scramble a match-tying third run off the last ball of the game. As I raced towards the bowling end, the Windies' Keith Arthurton was trying to find a stump to dislodge the bails and win the game'.

That's not what the video shows; Waugh is just starting in his third run when the return comes in to Arthurton at the bowlers' end, where the stumps are intact, and Arthurton takes the bails off. Waugh was clearly run out before he was impeded by the crowd.

But if there was chaos in the middle, there was confusion amongst the commentators and umpires. David Hookes spoke to match referee Raman Subba Row:

Hookes   What an amazing last over and we don't know the result. Nearly an hour after the last ball was bowled, and with me [is] the match referee Raman Subba Row. Raman, an amazing game. Before we actually get to it, what is the actual result of the match?

Subba Row Well, we have decided now that the match has been tied. The two sides tied the match and therefore they'll go to Barbados all square. It was a chaotic finish, as everyone will have seen.

Hookes   Well, talking about a chaotic finish, we'll take you through the last ball. With one ball to go, Australia needed 3 to tie and 4 to win. Take us through the last delivery, Raman.

Subba Row The last delivery was pulled away to the mid wicket area and they ran one and then they turned and ran the second one. A third really would have been very difficult, but as you can see Steve is fighting his way down the wicket to get the third with all those people around him. The situation had become really quite impossible. But they had started on the third run and that's something that actually influenced me considerably.

Hookes   And the other thing is, Raman, that Keith Arthurton went to take the stumps out of the ground but there were no stumps there—they were all out of the ground and well on their way to somewhere in Georgetown.

Subba Row   They'd all disappeared at the speed of light. It's a great shame when we get situations like that, but I believe that when we do cricket has got to be the winner and we can't go off with any rancour that such-and-such a thing might have happened or might not have happened. I think that when you get chaos like that you've got to make sure that commonsense prevails, and I personally think that a tie is the right answer.

Perhaps they didn't have replay facilities available at the ground, but it doesn't look like commonsense to me. The video coverage clearly shows that the stumps were intact at the bowlers' end when the ball came back to Arthurton, and as Arthurton took the bails off Steve Waugh was just starting the third run and had not yet been impeded by the crowd. There were never 3 runs in the shot; it was quick thinking by Waugh to go for the third, probably anticipating that with the crowd on the way something might happen and he would get away with it, as he did.

Australia went 1-up in the series with a 4-wicket win in the sixth and second last match of the series, played in Bridgetown, Barbados. If Australia had been lucky to achieve a tie in the fifth game, the balance was redressed in the final match, also played in Bridgetown, where the officials got it wrong again.

The end of the fifth game of the one-day series v West Indies, Guyana, 1999. Arthurton takes off the bails as Waugh starts on his third run. Clearly, the stumps are still there and Waugh has not yet been impeded by the crowd. (West Indies Cricket Board/TWI)

Waugh was almost hit by a bottle during the final game of the 1999 one-day series in the West Indies, Bridgetown, Barbados. (West Indies Cricket Board/TWI)

Australia was 9 for 252 at the end of 50 overs. With the West Indies 1 for 138 in the 29th over, Chanderpaul played a ball from Julian down on the leg side and took off for a run. Julian continued on his follow-through to get to the ball but when he saw Bevan coming in from mid wicket he stopped and Sherwin Campbell ran into him, fell over and lay in the middle of the pitch while he was run out. Tony Cozier said: 'He bumped into the bowler, he'll have to go . . . the crowd doesn't like it but that is the law'. Michael Holding agreed: 'It's always unfortunate when things like this happen, but the bowler is within his rights to try and get to the ball'. Campbell was out.

The crowd started to throw things onto the ground and several of the Australian players left the field. A bottle thrown from the top of a stand went within inches of Steve Waugh's head. The game was held up for three quarters of an hour, and they had to get Garry Sobers to announce that the Australians had decided to recall Campbell to get the crowd to calm down. The West Indies' target was recalculated from 253 from 50 overs to 196 from 40 overs, so they needed only 58 runs from 60 balls, with 8 wickets left. They won by 8 wickets, tying the series 3–all.

In an interview after the game, Waugh was asked if he had enjoyed the tour. He was obviously tense and upset. Never one to mince his words, he shook his head and said, 'Yes and no. There was some good cricket but obviously there were some things that spoilt the game and hopefully they'll be addressed because, from a player's point of view, it's not satisfactory.' Later he said, 'I'm sort of lost for words because I'm just so disappointed at what's happened in the last couple of games. It makes you wonder what are you playing cricket for . . . it's only a matter of time before someone gets killed— it'll happen. They said they couldn't guarantee our safety if the game was called off—it'd be a much worse situation if you don't go out and play, so we had no choice in the matter.'

As Waugh made clear, the Australians had a gun at their heads; if they didn't accept the reinstatement of Campbell and the reduced runs and overs, there might have been a full-scale riot.

Ironically, 3–3 may have been the right result as each team suffered a wrong decision. In another irony, Sherwin Campbell, who, if he had known the rules and played by them, should have left the field without demur instead of lying on the pitch gesticulating to the umpire, was voted player-of-the-match and of the series and smilingly took possession of a red Rover car.

24

TWO MIRACLES

The 1999 World Cup

The last one-day match in the West Indies was played on 25 April.
On May 1 the Australians flew to London, where they faced ten
functions in the first week. On top of this, Waugh, as captain, had
to meet his many obligations to the press. After a team meeting,
Waugh wrote:

> It's going to be difficult to fit in the cricket, even though that should
> be our priority. The importance of prioritising effectively was empha-
> sised before the meeting, when we had a chat with our sports psych,
> Sandy Gordon . . . he gave us what should be some good advice on
> how to stay focused and alert while effectively handling our off-field
> obligations.

After warm-up matches against Glamorgan, Worcestershire and
Somerset, Australia played its first World Cup game on 16 May,
defeating Scotland at Worcester. On 20 May, at Cardiff, the
Australians lost to New Zealand, and on 23 May they lost to
Pakistan at Leeds. They were then in the situation of having to win
the next two games—against Bangladesh and the West Indies—to
qualify for the 'Super Six', and would probably need to win the next
three matches—making it five straight—to make the semi-finals.
This they did.

```
27 May v Bangladesh          Won by 7 wickets
30 May v West Indies         Won by 6 wickets
4 June v India               Won by 77 runs
9 June v Zimbabwe            Won by 44 runs
13 June v South Africa       Won by 5 wickets
```

The 13 June game against South Africa, the game that got Australia into the semi-finals, was a see-sawing affair. South Africa was 1 for 140 before Warne bowled Cullinan (50) and had Cronje lbw for 0 in the space of a few balls. Herschelle Gibbs made 101 from 134 balls, then late in the innings Rhodes took 39 from 36 and Klusener crunched 36 from only 21 balls. South Africa's 271-run total looked

'The catch that wasn't': Herschelle Gibbs celebrates too early and loses control of the ball. Waugh, on 56 at the time, went on to a match-winning 120 not out to take Australia into the 1999 World Cup semi-final. (*England Cricket Board*)

like enough to win. Mark Waugh, Gilchrist and Martyn were out before Australia had reached 50, but Ponting steadied the ship and Steve Waugh started to take the South African attack apart. They had taken the score to 152 when Waugh clipped Klusener waist high to mid wicket where Gibbs moved a couple of paces to his right and caught it comfortably, ran a pace and a half with the ball in his right hand, and then, as he went to throw it in the air in celebration, lost control of it and watched in horror as it fell in front of him.

In his *Captain's Diary*, Waugh reveals that he didn't say anything about 'dropping the World Cup', as is commonly believed. He and

Gibbs had been 'chipping away at each other', Waugh says, 'engaged in friendly banter'. What he actually said was 'I hope you realise you've just lost the game for your team'—even Waugh probably didn't believe it at the time. He was 56 when he was dropped; he went on to 120 from 110 balls and Australia won with 5 wickets in hand and 2 balls remaining.

So they played South Africa again in the semi-final, at Edgbaston, six days later. Australia lost early wickets, Bevan joined Steve Waugh at 4 for 68 and they put on 90, but with Pollock and Donald at their best and Kallis bowling well, runs were hard to come by and when the last Australian wicket fell with 4 balls left and a total of only 213, the momentum was definitely with South Africa. South

Africa started well but with the score at 48 Warne bowled Gibbs for 30.

Tom Moody said later in an interview: 'Until Shane Warne grabbed the ball we were in all sorts of trouble and I think Shane Warne really decided that today was the day, that it was one of the days that he had to really rip it, because I think when he really goes hard at it and does try to rip it hard it can take a couple of days for him to recover from it. And he let go and you could see that he was so determined. I remember fielding at mid on and he was walking back to his mark and he was just yelling to himself, you know, to spur himself on, to get himself revved up, and he just, well, he bowled Herschelle Gibbs with a similar delivery to what Mike Gatting copped six or seven years ago'.

The video coverage shows a very pumped up Shane Warne yelling encouragement to his team-mates. After Gibbs's dismissal, Kirsten tried to hit Warne out of the ground and was bowled. With the momentum swinging away from South Africa, Cronje put himself up the order, only to have another perfect leg spinner dip, bite and fly from the edge of his bat into the safe hands of Mark

Waugh at first slip. Bevan then hit the stumps from mid-off to run out Cullinan and, at 4 for 61, South Africa was in trouble.

Rhodes and Kallis put on 84. Rhodes went for 43 but Pollock came in and smashed Warne for 6 and 4 in the same over before Kallis was caught by Steve Waugh at cover, chipping at Warne. Klusener and Pollock took the score to 183 before Pollock played on to Fleming.

McGrath began his final over with South Africa needing 18 from 12 balls. After a dot ball, he bowled a rather nervous Mark Boucher with a perfect yorker which removed his middle stump. Elworthy edged a single from the third ball, bringing Klusener onto strike. He drove the fourth ball hard to Fleming at deep mid on and set out for two, but Reiffel's throw from just inside the boundary then beat Elworthy back to the bowler's end where McGrath cleverly palmed it onto the stumps. Sixteen to win with 8 balls left and the last pair at the wicket—virtually impossible against McGrath and Fleming— except that Klusener was still there.

Reiffel went from rooster to feather duster in the space of two balls when Klusener smashed a full toss from McGrath straight at him. At full stretch over his head, he got both hands to it, but couldn't pull it in. It bounced off his hands and over the fence for six. A single off McGrath's last ball, 9 needed from six balls to win, and as Australia had finished higher on the table, South Africa had to win to move into the finals.

The first ball of the last over, from Fleming, was on a good length but outside off stump. Klusener smashed it two metres to the right of Steve Waugh at cover for four. The next ball was on a good length on the off stump and Klusener hit it two metres to Waugh's left. Scores tied, 4 balls left, game over, but . . .

Steve Waugh brought the field in. Fleming bowled short, Klusener got a bottom edge to Fleming's next ball which went to Lehmann at mid-on. Donald, at the bowler's end, started to run and Lehmann's throw from about six metres would have run him out if it had hit. It missed by inches. Moody at short cover neatly backed up, stopping overthrows. One chance missed. Lehmann looked furious; Donald looked embarrassed.

The next ball was full, outside off stump. Klusener clubbed it towards Mark Waugh at mid-off and ran. If Waugh hit, he was out; if he missed, South Africa was in the final. Waugh had to move quickly to his left, grab the ball and backhand it from about three metres. He missed the stumps and Klusener made his ground at the bowlers' end . . . only to find that, this time, Donald had stayed home. Fleming, who had stopped in the middle of the pitch, picked up Mark Waugh's backhand flick and rolled it along the ground to Gilchrist. It was a tie. Australia was in the final.

Bevan made 65, Steve Waugh, 56. Warne (whose form a couple of months before had been so poor that he had been dropped from the fourth Test against the West Indies) took 4 for 29 from his 10 overs. Given what was at stake, it was one of the greatest games of cricket ever played.

The final, played at Lord's, was a non-event; Pakistan was a very good side, but they were crushed by a brilliant and totally professional performance from the Australians. Pakistan were all out after 39 overs for 132. McGrath took 2 for 13 from 9 overs and Warne 4 for 44 from 9. By the time Gilchrist was out for 54 from 36 balls with the score at 75, the result was a foregone conclusion. Australia reached the target with 29 overs to spare and 8 wickets in hand.

Early in the tournament, Waugh's 'Captain's Notes', published in his *Captain's Diary*, seemed to reflect a belligerent, unsettled mood. Against the West Indies: 'Make them feel unwanted—it's 11 v 2 when we're in the field'. Before the India game he wrote: 'Our effort v West Indies was great . . . we had urgency, aggression, hustle, intimidation, desire—must do the same'. Before the final he seemed more relaxed: 'The key tomorrow is to enjoy the game— the result will look after itself. Back yourself, be decisive' and 'If the pressure is on us—enjoy it. Go forward, take on the challenge'.

In interviews after the final, Waugh was thoughtful and inclusive. To Ian Chappell, he said, 'We've talked about taking half chances— which we haven't done most of the tournament—today we pulled

Australia v South Africa, World Cup semi-final, Edgbaston, Birmingham, 17 June 1999

Result: Match tied. Australia advances to final

AUSTRALIA	R	M	B	4	6
+AC Gilchrist c Donald b Kallis.................20	70	39	1	1	
ME Waugh c Boucher b Pollock.....................0	3	4	0	0	
RT Ponting c Kirsten b Donald..................37	49	48	3	1	
DS Lehmann c Boucher b Donald...................1	4	4	0	0	
*SR Waugh c Boucher b Pollock..................56	108	76	6	1	
MG Bevan c Boucher b Pollock...................65	151	101	6	0	
TM Moody lbw b Pollock..........................0	2	3	0	0	
SK Warne c Cronje b Pollock....................18	36	24	1	0	
PR Reiffel b Donald.............................0	2	1	0	0	
DW Fleming b Donald.............................0	2	2	0	0	
GD McGrath not out..............................0	4	1	0	0	
Extras...16					
Total (all out, 49.2 overs)...................213					

FoW 3 54 58 68 158 158 207 207 207 213

Bowling	O	M	R	W
Pollock 9.2	1	36	5	
Elworthy 10	0	59	0	
Kallis 10	2	27	1	
Donald 10	1	32	4	
Klusener 9	1	50	0	
Cronje 1	0	2	0	

SOUTH AFRICA	R	M	B	4	6
G Kirsten b Warne..............................18	59	42	1	0	
HH Gibbs b Warne...............................30	51	36	6	0	
DJ Cullinan run out (Bevan).....................6	39	30	0	0	
*WJ Cronje c ME Waugh b Warne...................0	2	2	0	0	
JH Kallis c SR Waugh b Warne...................53	119	92	3	0	
JN Rhodes c Bevan b Reiffel....................43	70	55	2	1	
SM Pollock b Fleming...........................20	27	14	1	1	
L Klusener not out 31	32	16	4	1	
+MV Boucher b McGrath...........................5	13	10	0	0	
S Elworthy run out (Reiffel/McGrath)............1	3	1	0	0	
AA Donald run out (ME Waugh/Fleming/Gilchrist) ...0	7	0	0	0	
Extras..6					
Total (all out, 49.4 overs)...................213					

FoW 48 53 53 61 145 175 183 196 198 213

Bowling	O	M	R	W
McGrath 10	0	51	1	
Fleming 8.4	1	40	1	
Reiffel 8	0	28	1	
Warne 10	4	29	4	
ME Waugh 8	0	37	0	
Moody 5	0	27	0	

The return of the ball from hell, World Cup semi-final 1999: like Gatting in 1993, Gibbs was bowled by Warne with a ball that pitched outside leg stump and hit the off stump. *(England Cricket Board)*

them off, you know, we hit the stumps, we took some great catches, that was what it was all about.'

Chappell said, 'Glenn McGrath and Shane Warne did a terrific job', and Waugh replied, 'Yeah, they certainly bowled superbly, but you can't take anything away from guys like Paul Reiffel and Tom Moody and Damien Fleming. I thought they were great today as well, and, you know, they probably don't quite get the credit the top-line bowlers do, but it really was a great team effort.'

Later, to Mike Munro, he said, 'The feeling today was as good as I've ever had, if not better, just for the way we came back in this

Umpire Venkat signals 4 and the scores are tied. *(England Cricket Board)*

With the scores tied, and Donald well out of his ground, Gilchrist is about to take the bails off and give Australia a place in the 1999 World Cup Final. *(England Cricket Board)*

The Australians celebrate their 1999 World Cup semi-final victory over South Africa. (*England Cricket Board*)

Winning captain Steve Waugh being interviewed by Ian Chappell after the 1999 World Cup Final. (*England Cricket Board*)

competition. We were written off, the guys showed a lot of character, they dug deep, and when you win in those circumstances it makes it even more special. So for me this is as good as it's ever got playing for Australia.'

Munro asked, 'What does all this say about your new captaincy?'

Waugh replied, 'I'm not really sure, mate, you'll have to ask the other guys, but I know that I've committed myself to the Australian captaincy and I've given it 100 per cent from the word go. Sometimes I'm going to make wrong decisions but I back my gut feelings and today I guess was vindication. I think I've come a fair way with the captaincy and it's nice to win today, but, you know, it was a great team effort, not only eleven guys on the field but the fifteen guys in the squad, the guys who haven't played a lot of cricket, they've been tremendous off the field, their practice has been inspirational and they've led the way.'

Mark Waugh said, 'Critics say one-day cricket isn't proper cricket, but those two games against South Africa showed they can be as good as anything anywhere. They were two miracle performances.'

They came home to another tickertape parade. Two months later they were in Sri Lanka for the three-way Aiwa Cup one-day tournament with Sri Lanka and India, followed by three Tests against Sri

Lanka. After winning all four lead up matches, in the Aiwa Cup final Australia made only 202 and Sri Lanka reached the target in less than 40 overs.

The first Test was played in Kandy. Batting first, Australia was 7 for 60 before Ponting (96) and Gillespie (41) put on 107 for the eighth wicket. The total was 188 and on the second day Sri Lanka had reached 3 for 139 when Jayawardena top-edged a sweep high behind square leg and Steve Waugh set off after it from backward square leg. Jason Gillespie, on the fence at square leg, also started to run for it. They were running full speed towards each other, both looking up at the ball, and they didn't see each other until they were a few metres apart.

Waugh's head collided with Gillespie's left arm, breaking Waugh's nose. Gillespie's right leg, which collided with Waugh's chest and shoulder, was broken below the knee and his right wrist was injured. Waugh had two hours of surgery in hospital in Colombo. Gillespie was flown home to have a pin inserted in his

Waugh and Gillespie have seen each other, but it's too late to avoid the collision. First Test v Sri Lanka, Kandy, September 1999. (Board of Control for Cricket in Sri Lanka)

fractured right tibia. A rather shattered Australian side, with only nine men to bat in the second innings, lost the Test by 6 wickets. Waugh recovered in time for the second Test, which was ruined by rain, as was the third Test, so the series was lost 0–1.

25

OUTSIDE THE SQUARE

Modern coaching

During the tour of Sri Lanka in 1999, Geoff Marsh told Steve Waugh that he was resigning after three years as Australian coach, saying that he had been affected by the death of a close friend and that he thought he should be spending more time with his family. Marsh, who had taken over from former Test player and Australian captain Bob Simpson three years earlier, was replaced by John Buchanan, who had played seven games for Queensland in the late 1970s and had coached Queensland to their first Sheffield Shield title in 1994–95.

Bob Simpson told me that when he became NSW coach in 1984–85, he had no coaching qualifications: 'I'd never been officially a coach although I had been coaching at Western Suburbs for about ten years after I'd stopped playing Test cricket. I was asked if I'd be interested in coaching NSW, and I wasn't particularly, because I was running my own businesses and we were doing well and I was very busy, but they prevailed on me, and we did well— we won one of the one-day comps and we won the Sheffield Shield two years in a row—and then Freddie Bennett asked me if I'd be interested in coaching Australia.

'What I did was to implement the ideas and ways I used to practise with my mates when I was young, and later at Wests. They were routines which were based on speed, agility, pressure and enjoyment—things to keep everyone involved—and the boys used to enjoy it. In the end the crowds used to come early to watch us train before the Test matches on the day of the game, so we used to put on a bit of an exhibition for them—we'd go round different sections each day, and the crowds would be yelling, and everyone enjoyed it.

'I don't believe you should do drills that don't have any resemblance to what's happening in match conditions, so everything we did was based on what the players would be required to do in a match. With fielding, there was heavy concentration on technique, and on using both hands, because, while I'm very flexible about bowling and batting, I'm very very strict on catching; you've got to catch properly and field properly to be successful at it—the margin of error is just too great if you don't do it right. So in our competitions a one-handed catch didn't count, unless I gave approval to it, and then it had to be an absolute ripper.

'It was that sort of competitive stuff all the time—practice and practice and know what you're doing—and by doing that we got match fit. It's all right to do the gym work and all that sort of fitness stuff, but you can't neglect the basic fundamentals.'

On Steve Waugh, Simpson said, 'When I first saw Stephen and Mark, they were obviously two talented boys. Steve in those days was a wonderful, wonderful striker of the ball, but his footwork wasn't that great and, like a lot of people, he didn't bend his knees—when Steve went forward he always had a straight left leg and his head was up. It took him nearly three years to totally master that, and it finally came into place in England in 1989—if you look at some of the old videos, you'll see that Steve's back knee is almost on the ground because he's getting so low—as he should—into the shot.'

'That's why Mark looks so lovely: he's got this lovely flex in his knees, and even catching and fielding you'll see his knees are very bent, which they have to be.' Simpson says that, although he insisted on particular techniques for fielding, this was not the case with batting and bowling: 'My attitude with the Australian side was don't change anything unless it's necessary and when you think of change, think again and think again, to make sure'.

Simpson became coach in 1985, when Australia's cricket reputation was close to rock bottom. Of the previous 21 Tests, Australia had lost 10, won 3, and 8 had been drawn. Ten years later, when Geoff Marsh, who had played most of his cricket for Australia under Simpson as coach, took over, Australia was regarded as the strongest Test side in the world. Marsh's three-year stay built on Simpson's techniques and success and was capped with the triumph of the 1999 World Cup.

If Bob Simpson's approach had brought new techniques to the job, John Buchanan brought to it a new dimension. In James Knight's book, *Mark Waugh: The Biography*, Mark Waugh said:

> Buchanan was a keen supporter of statistical analysis and thinking outside the square. Together, he and Steve not only thought outside the square, but were moulding entirely new shapes. Buchanan introduced report cards, euphemistically referred to as Player Feedback Sheets, which he handed out after every Test. Innings are broken down into scoring rates, the percentage of singles and boundaries, the number of partnerships, the times a batsman plays and misses, and how many appeals he survives. Bowling is addressed in a similar fashion and fielding is a matter of touches, dive-stops, assists, throws, poor throws, miss-fields and errors. This is the era of the dressing room contract in which players pledge support for each other and their individual goals. Personal development is highly regarded to the extent that team-mates are encouraged to express their feelings and thoughts on pieces of paper stuck to dressing-room walls.

Ian Healy first came across Buchanan as coach of Colts in the Brisbane grade competition:

> Buck is very organised, as am I, and big on goal-setting, the effectiveness of which is something I've always reckoned is very under-rated in the cricket community. Before each club round, we'd scrutinise every scorecard and article about our upcoming opponents, to ensure that we knew exactly what we were up against. I thrived on such detail—some didn't . . . Mark Waugh is the type of player who would love to play without too much detail,

Greg Blewett, Damien Fleming and Andrew Symonds are probably in the same boat, but Buck is smart enough to recognise that not everyone is alike, that too much analysis can bog some people down, and is happy to meet such cricketers half-way.

Mark Waugh's attitude to Buchanan's methods is mixed: 'You've got to change, otherwise you'll get left behind. In some ways it's refreshing, in other ways it's hard to change . . . I think you can get carried away with making it too complex . . . I think we still try to keep it simple'.

I didn't get to speak to John Buchanan; however, a piece he wrote in *Wisden Cricket Monthly* (now *The Wisden Cricketer*) in June 2003 is revealing:

> To take the game to a new level requires us to rethink all our technical, physical, tactical and mental skills to determine what can be done differently, more effectively and within reasonable boundaries of time and resources.
>
> The concept had its origins in a lecture I attended in Brisbane in the late 1980s by Dr Edward de Bono titled 'The Process of Thinking'. De Bono enthralled the audience with his theories and examples of how to think differently or 'laterally' and demonstrated how our thinking is constrained by history. In order to solve problems he devised a range of strategies to challenge conventional approaches.
>
> Stephen Waugh and I visited him during the 2001 Ashes tour to discuss some of his ideas and he met a small group of players and administrators during the following domestic season in Sydney. I am not skilled in De Bono's techniques but I subscribe to his process. 'If it ain't broke, don't fix it!' should be amended to 'If it ain't broke, break it!' The 'Fred Flintstone principle' is one that many organisations, particularly sporting ones, adhere to. Why would Fred want to change anything? Everything works, so Fred is satisfied.
>
> It is at this point—actually it is probably long before, due to the presiding culture or an individual's lack of ambition—that an ever increasing decline begins.
>
> We must question everything we do—things that are not working

and things that are. We must constantly seek ways of improving. 'Can we improve?' The answer is obvious. I wanted to improve our fielding at the [2003] World Cup as I believed the best defence— bowling and fielding—would win the tournament. So I employed Mike Young, a baseball coach whom I had worked with at Queensland Cricket. Young brought new skills and drills to improve our on-field performance but also a new culture to the team.

Before the final I used a quote from Sun Tzu. 'Invincibility comes from defence; attack gives you the opportunity for success.' Young's work with us, together with our planning strategies and player skills, gave us additional confidence in our ability to contain teams with the ball or defend totals. Our attack through our top four batsmen gave us the opportunity for success. It was then left to our defence to seal the World Cup.

Buchanan's 'If it ain't broke, break it' seems an odd contrast to Simpson's 'Don't change anything unless it's necessary, and when you think of change, think again and think again', yet both coached teams that won World Cups. As someone who watches cricket, it's hard to tell whether a new approach really makes a difference. You could argue that Australia won the World Cup in 1999 because of a single act of stupidity by Herschelle Gibbs. Mark Waugh's catch in the final to dismiss Wasti off McGrath, and start the rot for Pakistan, was pure Picnic Point Road, Panania; nothing from Sun Tzu or Mike Young could have made any difference. For all the talk of motivation and analysis, the basic skills are immutable. An Australian coach's —and an Australian captain's—greatest assets are a climate and a culture that encourage people to play cricket, and an infrastructure, from the clubs through to Cricket Australia, that sustains it and enables it to flourish.

Buchanan himself acknowledges this. At the 2004 Wisden International Awards, where he was presented with a special achievement award by none other than Bishan Singh Bedi, he said of the Australian team: 'I think probably in years to come people will look back and realise that in this group of players we've got five, six, maybe even seven of the great players of all time'.

26

SIXTEEN STRAIGHT

The winning streak

Between October 1999, when they played Zimbabwe at the Harare Sports Club, and March 2001, against India in Mumbai, Australia played sixteen Test matches and won every one. Steve Waugh was captain in all but one match—the third Test against the West Indies in December 2000, when he was out with a strained left buttock muscle and the team was led by Adam Gilchrist. The previous sequence without a draw or a loss was achieved by Clive Lloyd's West Indies juggernaut of the 1980s—for my money, the best side ever—who defeated Australia six times and England five times between March and December 1984.

Australia had depth in batting and bowling; Shane Warne made 86 batting at number 8 against India and Brett Lee made 62 at nine against the West Indies. Adam Gilchrist, who would be in any other team in the world as a batsman, had replaced Ian Healy as wicket-keeper. Eight bowlers—Fleming, Warne, Lee, McGrath, Miller, Bichel, Gillespie and MacGill—took five or more wickets in an innings during this sequence. With Shane Warne out with a broken finger for the 2000–01 series against the West Indies, MacGill and Miller took 36 wickets between them. Apart from the three Tests against Pakistan, where his highest score was 38, Steve Waugh's personal contributions were significant, with five centuries, three of which went on to 150 or more. Langer made 223 in the third Test against India and two centuries against Pakistan; Ponting made three centuries including 197 against Pakistan; Mark Waugh made three centuries; Slater made 169 in the first Test against Pakistan in an opening stand of 269 with Greg Blewett; and Gilchrist made two hundreds, including 149 not out (from 163 balls) in Hobart in the 238-run stand for the sixth wicket which won the second Test against Pakistan after Australia had needed 242 with only 5 wickets left.

October 1999 v Zimbabwe in Zimbabwe

1 Only Test, Harare Sports Club, won by 10 wickets

November 1999 v Pakistan in Australia

2 First Test, Brisbane, won by 10 wickets

3 Second Test, Hobart, won by 4 wickets

4 Third Test, Perth, won by an innings and 20 runs

December 1999–January 2000 v India in Australia

5 First Test, Adelaide, won by 285 runs

6 Second Test, Melbourne, won by 180 runs

7 Third Test, Sydney, won by an innings and 141 runs

March–April 2000 v New Zealand in New Zealand

8 First Test, Auckland, won by 62 runs

9 Second Test, Wellington, won by 6 wickets

10 Third Test, Hamilton, won by 6 wickets

November 2000–January 2001 v West Indies in Australia

11 First Test, Brisbane, won by an innings and 126 runs

12 Second Test, Perth, won by an innings and 27 runs

13 Third Test, Adelaide, won by 5 wickets

14 Fourth Test, Melbourne, won by 352 runs

15 Fifth Test, Sydney, won by 6 wickets

February–March 2001 v India in India

16 First Test, Mumbai, won by 10 wickets

Their record in one-day series was almost as impressive. They lost a series in South Africa 1–2 and halved a series against the same opponents played in Australia, under cover in the Colonial

Stadium, but otherwise they hardly lost a game and at one stage had a record fourteen-game winning streak, thirteen of them under Waugh's captaincy. In the series with Zimbabwe and West Indies in 2000–01 they didn't lose a game, and in the second final, played against the West Indies in Melbourne, Mark Waugh scored 173 off 148 balls with 16 fours and 3 sixes, the highest one-day international score by an Australian. Australia made 6 for 338 to win the match and series. When player-of-the-series was presented after this game, from votes by the media, it was assumed Mark would get it, but somehow he missed by one vote. Brian Lara, who won it, said, 'I don't deserve this award. One of the Australians should get it.' Waugh's comment was 'Only the media could have been so far off the mark'.

In November 1999 Stephen and Lynette Waugh's second child, a son named Austin, was born.

In February the next year the twins were honoured with the opening of the 'Stephen and Mark Waugh Pavilion' at Bankstown Oval, part of a $1.3 million upgrade which meant the ground was capable of hosting first-class cricket.

It had been a dramatic period for international cricket. Early in April 2000, South African captain Hansie Cronje and three other South African players were charged by Delhi police with match-fixing. They denied the charges, but on April 11, the day before the one-day series against South Africa was to begin, Cronje was sacked as captain and dropped from the team. A senior judge, a well-known advocate in political trials during the time of apartheid, was appointed to conduct a one-month investigation.

Early in May 2000 the ICC announced the formation of an anti-corruption unit headed by the former Commissioner of London Metropolitan Police, Sir Paul Condon, to investigate match-fixing and bribery allegations.

Meanwhile, another judicial commission was being held in

Pakistan, which among other things reexamined the bribery allegations against Salim Malik. In *Run Out*, Graham Halbish wrote: 'The issue became so big, so involved, with other allegations coming to light, that the Pakistan government eventually stepped in . . . Justice Qayyam said the inquiry was left with no doubt that the Australians' testimony was true'. In late May 2000 the bribery charges against Malik were found to be proved and the Pakistan Cricket Board banned him for life.

In October 2000 an announcement came from the United Cricket Board of South Africa that Hansie Cronje had also been banned. It was reported that Cronje 'admitted to the King Commission that he received thousands of dollars from gamblers and bookmakers on five separate occasions between 1996 and 2000. He confessed that he offered team-mates money in exchange for under-performing in Test matches'.

It was also reported that 'former president Nelson Mandela met Cronje and urged him to rise above the match-fixing scandal that cost him the captaincy of the national side'. 'I am saying to him, without excusing in any way what he has done, if the allegations are proven to be right, that he can be a role model and turn this tragedy into triumph,' Mandela was reported to have said.

On 3 November 2000, a few weeks before the start of a series against the West Indies, as the Australian team were in training on Queensland's Sunshine Coast, the story broke that an Indian bookmaker claimed he had paid Mark Waugh $US20,000 for information on teams and weather and pitch conditions. Others named included Cronje, Alec Stewart, Brian Lara, Arjuna Ranatunga, Martin Crowe and Salim Malik. Mark denied the allegations. This issue came to a head over the summer with bitter dealings between Mark, his lawyers and advisers and the Board. Mark said, 'I had a good talk with Stephen in Adelaide. He was right behind me.'

On 10 February 2001, the day after Mark Waugh's record-breaking 173 in the one-day final against the West Indies, he had to appear before Greg Melick, a special investigator appointed by the ACB, and the ICC investigators, concerning the allegations. When Melick's findings were made public in August, while the team was in England for the Ashes series, he said he had been 'unable to locate any credible evidence' concerning the allegations that had been made against Mark Waugh.

Australia's 10-wicket win in the first Test of the 2000–01 series in India was its sixteenth consecutive Test victory. After the first two days of the second Test, played in Kolkata, it was long odds on that Australia would extend its winning streak to seventeen. Batting first, Australia's total was 445 (Steve Waugh 110, Harbhajan Singh 7 for 123 including a hat trick) and at stumps on the second day India were 8 for 128. Steve Waugh wrote in his *Diary*: 'For us, it was almost the perfect day of Test match cricket. Our collective will and hunger for victory reached a new level. We were "on fire", nothing seemed out of reach, blinding catches were taken, bowling changes and field placements came off at the right time and the togetherness of the team was breathtaking'.

The following day India were all out for 171 and, made to follow on, they were 4 for 254 at the end of the third day, V.V.S. Laxman 109, Rahul Dravid 7. At the end of the fourth day, these two were not out 275 and 155 respectively, and India batted on to 7 for 657 on the last day of the Test, leaving Australia with an impossible 384 to win in less than a day; they had two options—lose or draw.

They started well enough; Slater and Hayden had put on 74 when Slater went for 43. Langer was out with the total 106 and Mark Waugh when it was 116, then Steve Waugh and Hayden put on 50.

In an echo of the 1999 World Cup, Sourav Ganguly wrote:

Just before tea on the final day when they were only three wickets down, I dropped a sharp chance off Steve Waugh at backward short leg. Maybe if he had said nothing the game would have drifted to a draw, the result that appeared to be its natural conclusion. But Waugh could not resist the chirp, 'You just dropped the Test, mate'. Sometimes sledging can work against you and, on this occasion, it had the effect of geeing up the Indians. Immediately after tea, Harbhajan Singh got Waugh out

and Rahul Dravid gave him a send-off from slip asking who had
given away the Test match now.

Waugh went at 166 and Ponting, Gilchrist, Hayden and Warne
had gone with the addition of only another 8 runs. Australia was all
out 212; Harbhajan took 6 for 74 and Tendulkar, who had failed
twice with the bat, 3 for 31. The series was square, with one Test to
play.

In Chennai, Waugh won the toss and Australia's total was 391.
Honours were even: Matthew Hayden made 203, Harbhajan Singh
took 7 for 133 from 38.2 overs. Mark Waugh was second top score
with 70 and Steve Waugh, when he was 47, attempted a sweep, but
saw the ball bounce off his pads and spin back towards the stumps;
he became the sixth batsman in Test history to be given out
handled the ball.

India was all out for 501 (Tendulkar 126) early on the fourth day
and the final two days must have reminded Steve Waugh of the
heat, tension and exhaustion of the tied Test that he had played in
on this ground fifteen years before.

Trailing by 110, Australia made 82 before Hayden went, then lost
wickets at 84, 93 and 141. The Waugh brothers put on 50 to take
Australia 80 runs ahead, and a lead of 200 plus seemed likely. But
Harbhajan had got his second wind, as Steve Waugh wrote:

> Intriguingly, our batsmen always scored off Harbhajan when he
> first came on to bowl, but then he'd come back to produce some
> lethal spells . . . A lot has been said about how the Australians
> were unable to read Harbhajan's straighter ball, but I think it was
> his subtle changes in line and pace that made things difficult for
> us . . . he bowled beautifully, with an excellent line, always on a
> length and always getting bounce through his unusual, high
> delivery.

Mark Waugh, top score with 57, went at 193 and Australia was all
out 264, Harbhajan 8 for 84. India needed only 155; the odds were
against Australia.

Still, India had to get them. Laxman played fluently, but when

Colin Miller had him caught by Mark Waugh for 66 from 82 balls, India was 6 for 135, and when Miller also claimed the Test newcomer Sairaj Bahutule on the same score, suddenly it seemed like even money. Another newcomer, Mumbai wicket-keeper Sameer Dighe, kept his head, the 8th wicket fell at 151 and, appropriately, Harbhajan hit the winning runs. India had won the Test by 2 wickets and the series 2–1.

That the Australians, after six months of almost constant cricket, were able to match India in the first four one-day matches, says much for their determination, and their depth. The rotation system had helped, and although Matthew Hayden, with three innings for scores of 99, 57 and 111, was the star turn, Ian Harvey, Michael Bevan and Nathan Bracken had done much more than relieve tired Test players. It had been a strange, see-sawing contest: India won by 60 in Bangalore; Australia by 8 wickets with 5 overs left at Poona; at Indore India won easily, by 118; and Australia won by 93 at Visakhapatnam.

So they came to the Nehru Stadium, in Margao, Goa, level at 2-each. Australia lost the toss and saw India forge to 265 on a wicket that was holding up a little, Laxman giving another master-class with 101 from 107 balls and Ganguly helping with 74 from 83 balls. Bracken (1 for 37 from 10 overs) and Harvey (2 for 49 from 10) were the best of the bowlers. Shane Warne, who had a disappointing tour, went for 62 runs from his 8 overs, without a wicket.

Hayden had an off day, with only 36 and Gilchrist made the early running with 76 from 60 balls, including 10 fours and a six. Bevan (87 not out from 113 balls) then took over in his accomplished fashion, earning high praise from his captain: 'He once again proved that he is the best one-day batsman in the world. Others, especially openers, may score more runs, but Bevo is invariably obliged to craft his runs towards the end of the innings, when the pressure is on'. Ian Harvey also withstood the late pressure, making 25 not out from 26 balls and, with Bevan, guiding Australia to a 4-wicket win with 2 overs in hand.

27

BODY LANGUAGE

Steve Waugh's tour diaries

Many years ago, before I was reduced to golf, I went on a cricket tour to India, with a team organised by the redoubtable 'HA', Hartley Anderson, still a stalwart of the Sydney University Cricket Club. We were known as the Grey Kangaroos, a reference to the colour of our hair—our average age was about 40—and we discovered that anyone in India with any sense gives up cricket after about age 30; it's just too hot. The tour started in Bangalore, where we lost (Chandrasekhar 2 for 38) and we lost again in Hyderabad, first to Hyderabad Union CC then to Hyderabad Blues. Ranga Reddy, who was looking after us in Hyderabad and who has taken the Blues overseas many times and knows it is important for touring teams to have a win, arranged a third game for us in Hyderabad against a team of schoolboys. It emerged later that they were the State under-16 champions and when, during the afternoon, it seemed that they might defeat us, Ranga Reddy put a consoling hand on HA's shoulder and said, 'Do not be worrying, Grey Kangaroos, if the schoolboys are beating you this afternoon, I am organising another game tomorrow—against their sisters.' The tour was an experience I will never forget, and the memory of a ride home after midnight on the back of someone's motor scooter through the streets of Hyderabad, full of people and cattle and with a huge moon rising, still fills me with wonder. Did I do that?

Steve Waugh's *Ashes Diary 2001* was his eighth diary and his ninth book, the odd one out being *Images of Waugh*, a book of his off-field photographs, almost all on overseas tours, published in 1998. His first two diaries, which covered the 1993 Ashes tour and the 1994 tour of South Africa, were published by Pan Macmillan under their Ironbark imprint. The rest are published by Harper Sports, a division of Harper Collins.

Waugh's 1996 *World Cup Diary*—his first covering a tour of the sub-continent—is distinguished by its many interesting photographs of subjects other than cricket (and not so many of the mess in the Australian dressing room). His fifth diary returns to England for a comprehensive coverage of the 1997 Ashes tour, and the next book, *No Regrets*, starts with the Commonwealth Games in September 1998 and covers the series in Pakistan, then England in Australia and West Indies away, ending with the 1999 World Cup. His seventh book, *Never Satisfied*, covers the several series that took place in 1999 and 2000.

The *Ashes Diary 2001*, which also includes coverage of the Tests and one-day internationals in India from February to April that year and the visit to Gallipoli on the way to England, is, to my mind, the most interesting and revealing. The 'Captain's notes' for the first team meeting in India are a mixture of the inspirational and the practical.

> I want us to be:
> * the hungriest and most uncompromising side they've ever seen. Never give them an inch. If we get a sniff, we go in for the kill.
> * a side with the strongest body language and most intimidating aura they've encountered.
> If you haven't a solution to a problem, don't bring it up.
> Our tour motto: 'Attitudes are contagious, is yours worth catching?'

The trip to Gallipoli arose from a conversation Waugh had with Lieutenant-General Peter Cosgrove, the Chief of Australia's Defence Forces, when they compared 'cricket and the army—especially things that are important in both endeavours, such as camaraderie, discipline, commitment and the importance of following a plan'. Waugh described the visit as 'a daunting but wonderful experience. The camaraderie of our team was clearly evident as we learnt and appreciated the lessons learnt together. We will all grow as individuals because of the insights and knowledge we have gained and we now admire and respect even more these true heroes who helped forge and shape our nation'.

Waugh is always prepared to deal, in his diaries, with the current issues involving the tour and the world of cricket. On the subject of age:

> Some critics have argued that our average age, which is over 30, may be our downfall, either here or in the near future. I must say I totally disagree, as youth does not inevitably mean intensity, hunger, desire and skill . . . to me it makes no sense to drop someone simply because of their age, especially as they have spent many years working on their techniques, practising their skills, knowing their own game and becoming stronger mentally. Why automatically discard them for someone who is yet to go through this process?

On speculation about the end of his own career:

> I truthfully don't know when I'll give it away. Money isn't an issue; if the desire isn't there I'll get out straight away . . . At the moment, however, while I'm still enjoying the challenge and discovering new things about the game and myself, I see no specific end in sight. Age is irrelevant to me.

Early in the Ashes tour Waugh made a public statement about player behaviour, partly as 'a reaction to the flak we received following the incident involving Michael Slater during the first Test of our recent India tour'. (Slater had remonstrated with the umpire and the batsman when his claim for a catch was refused.)

> We've made a conscious decision for this series that we'll endeavour to accept every decision. Disputes never look good on TV and they replay it many times. Sometimes you don't realise how bad it looks. The Australian team will be trying to accept every decision in the

best way possible . . . We've stepped out of line a couple of times. I don't think we've been worse than anyone else, but we want to be the best at what we're doing and that's all part of it.

Safety was a significant issue during the triangular one-day series with England and Pakistan which preceded the Tests. Children were injured in a crowd invasion at the end of a one-day game in Cardiff, and in a game between England and Pakistan at Headingley, a section of the crowd surged onto the field with Pakistan 4 runs short of victory. Alec Stewart had to concede the game and a ground steward's injuries included broken ribs. Of a press conference later, Waugh wrote:

Every question was loaded, with the journos clearly wanting me to bag the officials, the spectators, anyone. The safety problem was one that I raised many years ago and ever since, whenever there is a problem, the journos come straight to me for a comment . . . I stopped the continuous, repetitive questions with one final statement: 'I'm not going to give you guys a headline, write the facts yourself'.

As the first Test approached, the selectors (Waugh and Gilchrist on tour and the third selector, Trevor Hohns, via a phone hook-up) made the decison to replace Justin Langer with Damien Martyn. Waugh had to break the news to Langer:

Knocking on Lang's door and seeing his expression when I said, 'Can I have a couple of minutes of your time?' wasn't easy . . . I must admit I was somewhat shattered by the experience. A hollow feeling in the pit of my stomach developed almost immediately, as I thought about what was going through Lang's mind right now and the utter confusion we selectors have just created for him.

(Martyn justified the selectors' decision with a century in the first Test.)

It was a few days before the second Test that coach John Buchanan arranged the meeting with Edward de Bono. Unfortunately for Waugh, he had developed a migraine headache before the meeting. 'This was a stimulating experience to say the least', he wrote,

> and the nature of the challenging conversation turned my migraine into the 'vice-like' category, with dizzy spells coming rather too frequently to take in all the concepts. One observation [de Bono] did have about one-day cricket, after we explained that the aim is to restrict the opposition scoring by either taking wickets or stemming the flow of runs, was quite simple and commonsense. He enquired, 'If someone is not scoring quickly and struggling, why wouldn't you want to keep him in?'.

A few weeks later the English press somehow got hold of a set of Buchanan's team notes, which drew heavily on the Chinese philosopher Sun Tzu's *The Art of War*, written in the fifth century BC and described as 'the oldest military treatise in the world'. Waugh wrote:

> All Buck's scribbled comments are designed to do is to instigate comment and thoughts among our team . . . Despite what some papers are shouting, it's hardly dramatic stuff, and it is for each individual within the team to use it as he wants. If you want to take it on board then you do, if you get something out of it, great, but I know brother Mark, for one, read four words and said it was rubbish so he threw it out.

Waugh's family was in England for much of the tour, but went home late in July. 'Winning a Test match is special', Waugh wrote,

> but so is playing with the kids in the park, and just watching their zest and love of life is both invigorating and infectious. The days over the past few weeks when we have been a family together —which doesn't happen too often on a cricket tour—have been fantastic. The 26th was our last day as a family before we went our separate ways and a sadness came over all of us because this may be the last time we come to England together under these circumstances.

The diaries go a bit over over the top with photos of players in the dressing room—singing or sleeping or drinking or wearing ice packs, amongst other things—but something they do convey is that touring with a team is fun: getting to know people, the casual meals, the time on the bus, the banter and in-jokes as the tour progresses, the friendly heckling as you get to know each other's eccentricities and habits. When it's going well, being with a team of people with the same aims, achieving those aims (as they usually did), meeting people, having an itinerary but not necessarily knowing what's around the next corner, being met and feted—all this can be truly stimulating and enjoyable.

As captain of a national team, achieving the success that our cricket team has over the years, to sit in the dressing room after making a hundred or taking vital wickets, or after the team has won a Test—how good must that be? You get a sense of it in Steve Waugh's diaries.

The Ashes tour in England in 2001—and the English press— promised a competitive series. England had defeated the West Indies 3–1 in England in 2000 and at the end of the year had toured Pakistan and won the three-Test series 1–nil. Early in 2001 they won a series in Sri Lanka 2–1, and before the Ashes tour had tied a series in England against Pakistan 1-each.

Steve Waugh wrote:

> The vision and planning of coach Duncan Fletcher and captain Nasser Hussain have clearly inspired the team to not only back themselves but also to fight every centimetre of the way . . . you don't win two series on the Indian sub-continent unless you're a 'together' team; any series win in these countries requires a steeliness of not only the body but also the mind. They're going to be a lot tougher than they have been in the recent past.

England might have had an improved attitude, but Australia played McGrath, Gillespie and Warne in every Test and had Gilchrist, who averaged 90.66, coming in at number 7. They had won the three-way one-day series with England and Pakistan with ridiculous ease, losing only one game in the preliminaries and winning the final, against Pakistan, by 9 wickets.

After the first three Tests, England had lost 60 wickets and not one English batsman had made a century. Australia had lost 35 wickets and both Waughs, Damien Martyn and Adam Gilchrist had made hundreds. Gilchrist's 152 from 143 balls including 20 fours and 5 sixes—this was in a Test match—had earned him man-of-the-match in the first Test. McGrath (5 for 54 and 3 for 60) took the honours in the second Test, and Warne got the award in the third Test with 2 for 37 and 6 for 33—this despite the fact that the captain thought that Jason Gillespie had been the pick of the bowlers.

The only hiccup from Australia's point of view was that Steve Waugh had seriously injured his left calf muscle in the third Test and could not play in the fourth. In his absence, Adam Gilchrist declared Australia's second innings leaving England 315 to make in a little more than a day, which they did, Mark Butcher coming in at 1 for 8 and batting 5 hours and 15 minutes for 173 not out. Waugh makes no comment on the declaration in his diary.

Before the fifth Test, Waugh again had the unpleasant task of telling a team-mate that he had been dropped. Waugh wrote that Michael Slater was left 'in shock . . . clearly devastated by his demotion', while Waugh himself felt 'sick in the stomach and drained both physically and mentally'. However, he wrote: 'This is by no means the end of his career. In fact, I see it as a career-enhancing moment that will eventually bring out the best in him'. Sadly, Waugh's optimism was not justified—Slater has not regained his place in the Test team.

Waugh's injury at Trent Bridge in the third Test had been so severe that he could not walk off the field—he had to be taken off on a stretcher. The odds were very much against him playing in the fifth Test, which started less than three weeks later. However, he set his mind to it, and with the help of Errol Alcott and a routine, detailed in his *Diary*, that included ice packs, stationary bike riding, running in the pool, deep friction massage, balance work, hamstring curls, hot and cold therapy, a heat vibration pad, a leg press machine, electric current through the calf and boxing, he took his place in the team.

Batting first, Hayden went at 158; Langer wore a bouncer from Caddick and retired hurt with the score at 1 for 236; and Steve Waugh joined his brother with the score at 2 for 292. Mark made 120; Steve 157 not out, despite straining his right hip and a recurrence of the damage in his left calf. Australia declared at 4 for 641 and bowled England out for 432 and 184.

28

THE UTMOST RESPECT

Time for a change

In the *West Australian* in July 2001, cricket writer John Townsend wrote:

> When Steve Waugh held his cleanskin bat aloft after scoring a century at Edgbaston, it was a blade made by Fremantle podshaver Paul Bradbury . . . Steve Waugh's bare bat indicates he does not have a bat contract as he waits to see if the rules are relaxed to allow non-manufacturers to advertise . . . Brian Lara has already used a gambling company's logo on his bat while Sachin Tendulkar, who has a lucrative sponsorship with the Madras Rubber Factory, can use bats with their emblem because they set up a bat making arm simply to meet the ICC rules. Waugh knows that his potential market value is enormous and is prepared to [play] a series without a sponsor in a bid to sign a bigger deal in the future.

Waugh had played the 2001 Ashes series in England with a 'cleanskin' bat. In common with many sports goods companies, his former sponsor Gunn & Moore was reducing spending on sponsorships and Waugh was not able to come to terms with them when his contract expired. Early in the 2001–02 season, Waugh announced that he had joined Sachin Tendulkar in endorsing MRF's bats and other cricket equipment for a reported $A250,000 a year. ICC rules require bat sponsors to actually be makers of commercially available bats. MRF (for Madras Rubber Factory), a

Chennai-based tyre-maker, bought a company which makes bats so it could take advantage of the ever-growing promotional and commercial opportunities from cricket.

Waugh first used an MRF-endorsed bat in the 2001–02 series against New Zealand in Australia, which produced three drawn Tests, with rain playing a part and honours almost even. In a second series at home, Australia dominated a new-look South Africa, winning 3–0. The first Test of this series was the Waugh twins' hundredth Test together, but they had a disappointing summer, with neither making a century. Steve averaged 19.5 against New Zealand and 35.25 against South Africa. Their relatively poor form continued in the one-day contests with South Africa and New Zealand. Mark played seven matches and made only 126 runs at an average of 21.00. Steve played one more match, for 187 runs at 31.16. Australia lost three of its first four matches and failed to reach the finals.

Perhaps it was time for a change.

Steve Waugh's best innings of the summer had been 90 in the second Test against South Africa, which ended when he was run out by a direct hit from Herschelle Gibbs. Replays showed that South African wicket-keeper Mark Boucher may have broken the stumps before Gibbs's throw hit the stumps, but umpire Darrell Hair upheld the appeal and Steve Waugh made it obvious that he disagreed.

He was charged with dissent under the ICC's Code of Conduct by match referee Rajan Madugalle and was fined 50 per cent of his match fee. A statement from the ACB said: 'In handing out his judgement, the match referee reminded Stephen of his responsibilities as a premier Test match captain to represent the game in a good light . . . He also recognised there was no malice in Stephen's actions'.

It was the summer's second charge of misconduct against an Australian player—Brett Lee had been fined 75 per cent of his match fee for using 'crude and abusive language and offensive gestures' during the Perth Test against New Zealand.

The last preliminary game of the one-day series was Australia v South Africa at the WACA, played on 3 February 2002. Australia made 287 but needed to win by more than 60 to earn the bonus point necessary to edge New Zealand out of the final series. South Africa made 5 for 250, losing the game but keeping Australia out of the finals. At a press conference after the match, Waugh was antagonised by repetitive, aggressive questioning about the need for changes to the team:

'Oh well, if there's call for changes, there's call for changes. I mean, that's the selectors' prerogative. That's why they've got the job. If they want to make changes that they think can improve the side, then that's what they've got to do.'

'Do you support that? Do you think changes should be made as captain?'

'I'm not a selector any more'.

'But as captain, you're going to be the one-day captain as well as the Test captain. Do you support changes to the one-day team for the World Cup build-up?'

'I'm not a selector any more.'

'What about as captain?'

'No, it doesn't matter.'

'Don't you have a say?'

'I have a say, but I don't pick the side.'

'If you had a say, what sort of changes would you talk about?'

'I don't have a say.'

It went on in that vein for some time—remember: this was a game that Australia had won comfortably—and as Waugh was leaving after the conference, he said to an accompanying ACB press officer, loudly enough for nearby journalists to hear, 'They're a bunch of cockheads'.

Ten days later he was at another press conference, this time sitting with chairman of selectors Trevor Hohns, and James Sutherland, the Board's recently appointed CEO, who announced that Waugh had been dropped from Australia's one day squad for the coming tour of South Africa.

Hohns said, 'After reflecting on the VB Series, we decided that for the one-day side to continue to be successful and to prepare for the 2003 World Cup, it was time to make this change. There is no ideal time to announce a decision like this, but by making the change now we hope that it will give the new captain a chance to step up and grow into the role well before next February . . . Obviously, no one enjoys making these types of judgements, particularly when it deals with a player such as Steve, for whom we as selectors have the utmost respect—not only as a player but also as a person.'

Waugh had been told of the selectors' decision a couple of days earlier, and perhaps the most surprising thing was his obvious shock and resentment. His place had been widely discussed and many commentators thought it was time for him to go, at least from the one-day side. His form had not been great—he'd had complications following his leg injury in England the previous winter—relief from the constant strain of one-day matches might well enable him to extend his Test career, and there was no shortage of talent to replace him. The selectors also had to look to the future. The World Cup was to be held in South Africa in February–March 2003; Waugh was 36 and if his position was in doubt already, his prospects weren't likely to have improved when he was twelve months older. If Australia was to have a new captain, it was sensible to give the new man time to settle in before the World Cup.

And yet Waugh seemed hardly able to comprehend the fact that he wasn't considered good enough. After Hohns spoke to him, the first thing he did was ring Lynette.

'As had been the case many times in the past', he would write, 'my wife was able to put things into perspective by saying, "Things happen for a reason. It mightn't be clear right now, but it'll work out in the end". I followed this up with a call to my manager, who was both shocked and supportive. The moment I put the phone down I vowed to see this as a setback; it was not to be a career-ending move but a career-enhancing one.'

At the press conference, he said, 'I want to go to the World Cup in 2003. I regard this as a setback and a challenge. I've never shied away from a challenge and I will do everything in my power to get back into the side. If it doesn't happen, I know I have given it my best shot. That's all I can do. My campaign starts today.'

As was often the case when Waugh was asked to depart the scene, he went reluctantly, and the selectors took quite a lot of criticism, but two months later the Australian one-day side led by Ricky Ponting won the one-day series in South Africa 6–1 and went on to win the 2003 World Cup without losing a match. Ponting's contribution of 140 not out from 121 balls is considered one of the classics of modern cricket.

29

HYPE AND THE HUNDRED

'It wasn't about the team anymore'

The day after the press conference at which it was announced that he would no longer be part of Australia's one-day campaign, Waugh was flying with the Australian Test team to South Africa, leaving behind a third child, Lillian, born that summer. 'Saying goodbye is always a gut-wrenching experience', he wrote, 'and with each new addition to the family the anguish is magnified. Looking back through the cab window and seeing Austin, Lillian, Rosalie and Lynette standing between and behind the wrought-iron gates was almost a surreal experience'.

Ten days later Waugh led Australia off the Wanderers ground in Johannesburg after defeating South Africa by an innings and 360 runs, the second-biggest innings defeat in Test match history. Australia had batted first. Hayden, dropped by Kallis at first slip when 0, made 122, and Martyn, in the best form of his life, made 133. Alan Donald couldn't bowl after straining a hamstring in his sixteenth over, and Adam Gilchrist, coming in at 5 for 293, took 204 from 213 balls. Steve Waugh made a dogged 32 from 98 balls. Australia had its full attack on show: McGrath, Gillespie, Warne and Lee. South Africa were skittled for 159 and 133.

The second Test was a better contest. South Africa made 239 and Australia replied with 382, due mainly to another extraordinary performance from Gilchrist—138 from 108 balls. With the wicket becoming easier as the match progressed, the inexperienced South

Africans batted with more confidence and application, most getting runs in a total of 473. Only the stamina and skill of Shane Warne— 6 for 161 from 70 overs in his hundredth Test—saved Australia from being set an unreachable target; as it was, needing 331 to win, they had a difficult task. Langer (58), Hayden (96) and Ponting (100 not out) laid a good foundation and at 2 for 250 it looked assured. Both Waughs and Martyn then fell cheaply, but Gilchrist and then Warne stayed with Ponting, who ended the game and reached his hundred with a six. Steve Waugh made 0 and 14, succumbing both times to the unorthodox spin of Paul Adams.

In his *Captain's Diary* 2002, Waugh mentions an incident in the second Test involving the South African batsman Neil McKenzie, who was run out for 99. McKenzie had an elaborate routine between balls which involved, among other things, not treading on lines at the crease. As he approached his century, Brett Lee called out to him, 'Hey Macca, you just trod on a line.' 'Whether he did or didn't tread on a line was irrelevant', Waugh wrote, 'that little voice in his head was now saying, "Maybe I did, I hope it doesn't jinx me or cause me to get out"'. Waugh continued: 'As I have said many times, in my opinion this is gamesmanship, not sledging. Too often, people confuse the two'.

Waugh does not deal with another incident during the match, which involved 20-year-old South African newcomer Graeme Smith and Australian opener Matthew Hayden, and was picked up by the *Sydney Morning Herald*'s Trevor Marshallsea from the South African edition of *Sports Illustrated*. According to the report, Smith said Hayden 'had greeted him at the crease before his second Test innings in Cape Town with a two-minute tirade'. He said Hayden had followed him to the crease and said, 'You know, you're not f—ing good enough. How the f— are you going to handle Shane Warne when he's bowling in the rough? What the f— are you going to do?'.

'And I hadn't even taken guard yet,' Smith said. 'He stood there right in my face, repeating it over and over. All I could manage was a shocked, nervous smile. I'd taken a bit of banter before but this was something else. Hayden had obviously been told that his job was to attack me.'

Australia lost the third Test by 5 wickets. Waugh made 7 in the first innings and top score of 42 in the second, for a disappointing aggregate for the tour of 95, averaging 19.

However, the series win confirmed the Australians as the best cricket team in the world, an achievement recognised by the award of the Team of the Year by the Laureus Sport for Good Foundation at the award ceremony in Monaco in May 2002. Laureus's founding patrons are Mercedes-Benz and Cartier and their aim is 'To fund and promote the use of sports as a conduit for social change throughout the world'. Steve Waugh, Glenn McGrath, Shane Warne, Ricky Ponting and their wives were invited to the presentation, and they were in good company: other awards went to Michael Schumacher (Sportsman of the Year), Jennifer Capriati (Sportswoman of the Year), and the other nominees for Team of the Year were Ferrari's Formula One racing team, the French Davis Cup team and the LA Lakers basketball team. Nominations for awards are made by an international panel of sports journalists and are voted on by an 'Academy' of 44 former sportsmen and sportswomen which reads like a Who's Who of the greats: Pele, Nadia Comaneci, Dawn Fraser, Michael Jordan, Jack Nicklaus, Mark Spitz, Franz Beckenbauer, Boris Becker, Martina Navratilova—as well as Ian Botham, Sir Vivian Richards, and Kapil Dev, who had caught a nervous Stephen Waugh for 13 off the bowling of Laxman Sivaramakrishnan some seventeen years earlier at the Melbourne Cricket Ground, when the young batsman was playing in his first Test.

In the off-season, the winter of 2002, Waugh spent some time in India, visiting the Udayan home and attending a product launch as 'brand ambassador' for AMP-Sanmar, a new insurance company formed through a joint venture between Australia's AMP and the Chennai-based Sanmar engineering, shipping and chemical group. He also had a month with English county Kent. A press release from his manager, Robert Joske of TEAM-Duet, said: 'We looked at the Australian program and found that Steve would not get any match practice prior to the Pakistan series if he stays in Australia. Steve decided that county cricket would provide him with some valuable time at the crease. The subsequent interest from English clubs has been overwhelming'.

His form in Kent was only fair, with a couple of half centuries, and it took a turn for the worse at the start of the 2002–03 season, in a three-Test series scheduled for Pakistan but moved to Colombo and Sharjah because of political unrest. In the first Test, played in Colombo, Ponting's 141, with support from Langer, Mark Waugh and Gilchrist, took Australia to 467 and Warne (7 for 94) put Australia in a winning position. Pakistan made 279, Australia's lead was 188. But after Langer and Hayden had put on 61, Australia lost all 10 wickets for 66 to the pace of Shoaib Akhtar (5 for 21) and the wiles of Saqlain Mushtaq (4 for 46). Pakistan needed 316 and started well, but Warne again proved a match-winner, taking 4 of the first 5 wickets to fall and leaving McGrath and Gillespie to mop up the tail.

The second Test, played in Sharjah, was a one-sided affair after Pakistan succumbed for 59 in the first innings and 53 in the second, Warne taking 4 wickets on each occasion and giving Australia victory by an innings and 198. Steve Waugh's contribution to this stage had been 31, 0 and 0, the last two innings taking a total of 3 balls; there were obvious doubts about his continued place in the team. The same applied to his brother, whose recent Test scores had been 53, 25, 16, 45 and 30 in South Africa and 55, 0 and 2 against Pakistan. With the series decided, the main interest was in the continued presence of the twins in the Test team—and from the way Pakistan was performing, it was likely they would only get one chance.

And so it proved. Batting first, Australia made 444: Ponting 150,

Steve Waugh 103 not out. Pakistan made 221 and 203—another innings loss—Shane Warne took 8 wickets, Glenn McGrath took 7.

In a piece headlined 'Just for a second, Waugh the hard man cracks', the *Age*'s Martin Blake wrote:

> During his press conference after making an unbeaten 103, Waugh looked ready to let some emotion squeeze through his defences. After a prolonged run drought—his worst in 10 years—he took enormous satisfaction in proving he wasn't ready for the scrapheap just yet. Following his sacking from the one-day side, he had been under a huge amount of pressure as the Test failures mounted during the past year. So when he reached his century, he made a show of pointing his bat to the team area in a gesture of thanks . . .
> 'I just thanked one or two people for their inspiration,' Waugh said of his gesture with the bat. 'I don't want to single out anyone in particular but my wife, when she was here, said one or two things that just helped me along, and a couple of guys in the side have been excellent. This side's got a lot of players who have a lot of depth to them, and they help you out when you're struggling a bit.' At this point Waugh had to gather himself, and there was no mistaking the fact that he was moved by the support he had received.

Mark Waugh had made 23 in what was to be his last Test innings. He had also been dropped from the one-day side. In South Africa, the day after he had scored 110 from 113 balls against South Africa A, the last 50 coming from 24 balls, he had a phone call from Trevor Hohns. In *Mark Waugh: The Biography*, Mark says:

> I immediately thought that he wasn't ringing to say hello. He told me that I hadn't been picked in the one-day squad. He said it was a tough decision but the selectors felt it was time for a change. I thought I was still good enough to perform at that level, but the selectors had their job to do. It was disappointing, but life goes on. I'd had a very good run.

When asked how he and Mark get on, Steve has been known to reply to the effect that he doesn't want to mess up a good story: 'Everyone says we don't like each other and we don't talk. It's a pretty good story, leave it at that'. In the early days, neither of them showed much emotion, acknowledging applause with a half-raised bat, a tilt of the head. When they started playing Test cricket together, I remember reading that when one of them was asked why they didn't show much affection towards each other, he replied that they didn't touch or show emotion because they reckoned it was 'daggy'—many would agree.

Steve has changed in recent years. As Ewen Page wrote in the *Bulletin*:

> The popular view of Mark and Steve Waugh is that the former is a kind of playboy batsman: laid-back, loose of limb and, on occasions, a bit easy-come, easy-go with cricket and life generally. Steve, on the other hand, we see as intense, gritty, dour, colourless, edgy. This doesn't sit so easily with Steve . . .
>
> 'These guys have no idea but it's what they'll always write because it's a tag you get stuck with,' says Waugh. 'Once again, there's a misconception that Mark is the talented one and I'm not. We're equally talented. I was more attacking than Mark in my youth and I was actually not picked in a couple of sides because it was felt I was too loose and too aggressive . . . There was probably a time growing up when we grew apart because there was so much intense debate about who was better and what we did . . . We were almost forced apart. Towards the end of our careers, we've sort of come back together a bit more in our thoughts and probably our feelings. We still don't talk a lot but we certainly feel for each other. We've been under scrutiny all of our lives, really. From being twins to playing for Australia, there has been no real period where we could relax and be ourselves and see each other as just brothers.'

Mark Waugh played 128 Tests, had 209 innings with a highest score 153 not out, and made 8029 runs at an average of 41.81. He took 59 Test wickets at 41.16 and took 173 catches in Tests, 18 more than Mark Taylor, who is second on the list. If his Test batting record puts him just outside the realm of the really greats, there are many who would put him top of the list of players they would want to go to watch.

His one-day record is 244 matches, 236 innings, highest score 173, and 8500 runs at an average of 39.35 with a strike rate of 76.54. At the time he retired he had made more runs in one-day internationals than any other Australian and was fourth on the list of players from all countries, behind only Sachin Tendulkar, Mohommad Azharuddin and Desmond Haynes.

The Australian XI continued its dominance in the 2002–03 Ashes series, winning the first Test by 384, then by an innings and 51 in Adelaide, an innings and 48 at the WACA and by 5 wickets in Melbourne. Hayden's innings were 197, 103, 46, 30, 102 and 1; Ponting had made 123, 3, 154, 68, 21 and 30; Langer had made 250 in Melbourne. All the bowlers had contributed and when Shane Warne missed the fourth Test with a dislocated shoulder, Stuart MacGill took 5 for 152, including both opening batsmen, in England's second innings. Steve Waugh was having a moderate series, averaging 33. His best score was 77 in the first innings of the fourth Test. In the second innings, with Australia needing only 107 to win, he went in at 3 for 58 with England pumped up and sensing they might be able to break through, and after batting for a few minutes he started to suffer from a migraine, feeling dizzy and sick, with blurred vision. He survived for a lucky half-hour— he was caught off a no-ball and feathered a catch for which no one appealed—before being caught in slips for 14. Martin Love and Gilchrist saw the side through to their fourth win of the series.

For England, Michael Vaughan, with innings of 177 in the second Test and 145 in the fourth, looked like a batsman of world class, and when, in the fifth Test, played in Sydney, Lee had him caught by Gilchrist for 0 in the fourth over of England's first innings, a 5–0 series whitewash looked likely. Trescothick went soon after, but then England captain Nasser Hussain (75) and Mark Butcher (124) took the total to 166 and, lower in the order,

Crawley (35) and Stewart (71) provided unaccustomed backbone. England made 362 and Australia replied with 363, Gilchrist 133 from only 121 balls and Waugh (102 from 135 balls) reaching his hundred on the last ball of the second day.

Vaughan then proved his class, his 183, with Hussain again getting into the 70s, taking England to 452, and leaving Australia 452 to make in three and a half sessions. For once, the England bowlers got on top; both openers went early and only the bowlers Bichel (49 after being sent in as night-watchman) and Lee (46 from 32 balls) offered worthwhile resistance. England won by 225.

Much has been made of Steve Waugh's first innings hundred, not least by Waugh himself. A chapter called 'The Hundred' takes up almost a third of his eleventh book, *Never Say Die*, with the sub-title 'The inspiration behind an epic hundred'. The innings marked some big milestones: Waugh became the third person (after Gavaskar and Border) to reach 10,000 runs in Tests, and he joined Bradman with 29 Test centuries, the most by an Australian. 'That is the most special of the records that I've been a part of,' Waugh wrote. 'I'm obviously nowhere near as good a cricketer as Sir Donald Bradman was—it took me exactly three times as many Tests to score the same number of centuries.'

It was a good innings, and the fact that it was made when his place in the team was at stake and he reached it on the last ball of the day made for great drama, but the problem I have with all the hype about 'The Hundred' is that it was made against weak bowling, in a match that didn't matter, in a Test Australia lost.

In 2001, after England had lost the first three Tests, and Mark Butcher's 173 not out at Headingley won the fourth Test for them, Steve Waugh wrote in his *Ashes Diary*: 'A critical part of the jigsaw is missing from a major innings if the team's objective has not been reached . . . Mark Butcher's innings was an Ashes epic, but I know that, deep down, he will one day wish that it was scored in a do-or-die Test match'. Of course, the same could be said of Butcher's 124 in the fifth Test in 2002–03, which underpinned England's first innings in Sydney and set up their win, but the fact that Butcher's innings doesn't rate a single mention in Waugh's

57-page chapter about the Sydney Test does indicate a certain—what to call it?—double standard? Self-centredness?

For all the talk about being an inspiration to his team, a great captain, a leader by example, it seemed as if it wasn't about the team any more, it was about whether or not Steve was in it.

Never Say Die, which covers the 2002–03 series and also the subsequent tour of the West Indies, is a departure from the ten books that went before it. Smaller in content and format, much of it is transcripts from interviews with Adam Gilchrist, Justin Langer, Nasser Hussain, Andrew Denton and Waugh himself. Some of it is adapted from Waugh's columns for various newspapers. It lacks the detail and seems to me to lack—dare I say it?—the commitment of the previous books, which, despite all the photos in the dressing rooms, are straightforward and informative accounts of events, and amount, overall, to quite an impressive body of work.

Significantly, Waugh's managers, Robert Joske and Harley Medcalf of DUET-Group, are thanked more than once in the intro-ductory pages of *Never Say Die*, and, sadly, the book feels more like a marketing exercise than an account of what happened on tour.

It's also unfortunate that the other side of the decision to keep Steve Waugh in the team was that it meant a young player (and there were plenty of them around) was being kept out—and no one had been given more chances than Waugh was when he was young. But having said all that, it's also fair to say that with top cricketers making more than $1 million a year these days—not least because of the influence and the work done by Waugh himself—it's not unreasonable for them to fight tooth and nail to hold their places.

Waugh has said it isn't for the money, but the money comes with the territory; being in the Australian Test team, especially being its captain—who wouldn't want to keep the position while they could?

What we are seeing at the end of Steve Waugh's career is a future in which sport has become entertainment, where manage-ment companies, public relations firms, sponsors and lawyers have more and more influence on what is written and public perception, and where, because of this, the senior players will have more and more power.

Steve Waugh is one of the first Australian sportsmen to use their leverage in this way, although he is not alone: Lleyton Hewitt took the ATP to court over a fine he received for refusing to do an interview, and has been involved in the formation of the International Men's Tennis Association, a breakaway players' union, claiming 'a lack of transparency and under-representation of the players' interests in the ATP's decision-making processes'; boxer Antony Mundine has also made clever use of publicity and the politics of boxing in his rise towards the top.

As Bob Simpson said to me, 'Steve was conscious from early on that cricket could be very lucrative—which is a good thing.'

30

THE HEAT OF
THE MOMENT

Sledging and the 'Spirit of Cricket'

After the Ashes series in Australia in 2002–03, the one-day side, captained now by Ricky Ponting, completed the three-way series with England and Sri Lanka, losing only one match. In February and March they went one better in the World Cup, winning every match on the way to the final and winning the final, against India in Johannesburg, by 125 runs.

In April, the Test team was back together for a four-match series in the West Indies. They were without Warne, who had also missed the World Cup, banned for a year after a positive test for a drug which is used to assist in weight loss but can also be used to mask steroids. Damien Martyn missed the tour after breaking his right index finger during the World Cup. Glenn McGrath, whose wife was receiving treatment for cancer, missed the first two tests.

Andy Bichel had made a place for himself in the team. MacGill replaced Warne, sometimes joined by the left-arm wrist spinner Brad Hogg. Darren Lehmann and Martin Love were vying for places.

It made little difference to the pattern of results: Australia won the first Test by 9 wickets, the second by 188 runs and the third again by 9 wickets.

Despite the relative ease of the victories, the West Indies had not been embarrassed and had sometimes looked as if they could be competitive. Lara had made two hundreds and a ninety and

Chanderpaul had reached 100 from only 69 balls in the first Test. Ganga's first Test century was more orthodox, and like Lara he repeated the feat in the second Test. Their problem was getting Australia out, and they never solved it; Australia had made 489, 1 for 147, 4 for 576, 3 for 238, 9 for 605 and 1 for 8.

Ponting had made hundreds in the first and third Tests and a double hundred in the second. Langer, Lehmann and Gilchrist had also made hundreds and all the bowlers had played a part. Waugh made 25 in the first Test and 115 and 42 in the third. He chose not to bat in the second Test; when the third wicket fell at 3 for 371, he said he 'didn't feel right' and sent Gilchrist in. It did Australia no harm: Gilchrist made 101 from 104 balls and Waugh declared at 4 for 576.

Strangely, again, most of the interest in the series ended up being in the fourth Test, after the series result had been decided. It was played at the Antigua Recreation Ground on a pitch produced by the former West Indies fast bowler Andy Roberts, a pitch that had bounce and turn and held up throughout the match. For once, the West Indies' bowlers had contained Australia's top order; young Jermaine Lawson, in his last Test before being sent for corrective work on his suspect action, rattled the Australians with 7 for 78, limiting them to 240, a score which the West Indies matched exactly. The Australians looked likely to put the game out of reach when Langer (111) and Hayden (177) put on 242, but Gilchrist, Love and Lehmann went cheaply.

Waugh came in at 4 for 330, the blue Travelex logo prominent on his white shirt and the edge of the red rag peeping out of the left trouser pocket. On his first ball there was a confident appeal for lbw. In real time it looked close, but umpire Shepherd said, 'Going down', and the replay showed it was a good decision. Hayden clubbed Omari Banks to the mid wicket boundary with such force that you wondered how the ball could retain its shape, then took a single to deep mid wicket. Waugh got off the mark with a wristy flick to the same area from a full-length ball. Soon after, Waugh played Dillon behind gully and Hayden assumed the single, but Waugh was on the back foot after playing the shot and stayed home; Hayden had to turn around and was run out by 5 metres. It was bad running by Hayden, Australia was 5 for 338, and the tail was knocked over by Mervyn Dillon and Vasbert Drakes.

Waugh, who had made 41 in the first innings, remained not out 45. Australia was all out 417, which meant the West Indies needed 418 to win. The highest fourth innings total to win a Test to that date was India's 4 for 406 against West Indies at Port-of-Spain in 1975–76 but, in West Indies' favour, there were more than two days left to play.

At stumps on the third day West Indies were none for 47, but they lost both openers early in the fourth day and Ganga went not long after. Lara and Sarwan then built a partnership, Lara going after MacGill with three sixes high into the crowd. The leg spinner kept his nerve though, and on 60, Lara went after him once too often; the ball dipped on him, left him short, spun through between bat and pad and clipped the top of middle stump. West Indies 4 for 164.

Sarwan and Chanderpaul continued to go for their shots and when McGrath, who had had 21 runs taken off two overs, taunted Ramnaresh Sarwan, asking, 'What does Brian Lara's cock taste like?', Sarwan gave the standard response: 'Ask your wife', at which McGrath walked up to him, pointing and shouting in his face, 'If you ever fucking mention my wife again I'll fucking rip your fucking throat out'. McGrath continued to snap and snarl for some time afterwards, but later, when Sarwan reached his century, the Australians applauded and Waugh, Hayden and Langer shook his hand.

'A strange way to behave': Glenn McGrath's confrontation with Ramnaresh Sarwan, fourth Test v West Indies, Antigua, May 2003. *(West Indies Cricket Board)*

Sarwan was out for 105, top-edging an attempted hook off Lee for a caught and bowled. Ridley Jacobs went next ball, given out caught behind—a difficult but incorrect decision by David Shepherd, as replays showed the ball came off the elbow. West Indies were 6 for 288, needing 130 with Chanderpaul and the bowlers left. Omari Banks was dropped early off Lee but played steadily, and after Chanderpaul went for 104 at 372—caught by Gilchrist, again off Lee—Banks (47 not out) and Vasbert Drakes (27 not out) calmly saw the West Indies through.

In his coverage of the McGrath–Sarwan incident, Waugh wrote:

> The finger-pointing and angry words picked up by the on-field cameras and microphones offered a negative image that I concede cricket doesn't need. It wasn't pretty and we all wished it hadn't happened, but these things do happen in sport sometimes. It was actually a moment that blew up quickly and was over pretty rapidly too; but the images remained—images that went all over the cricket world and unfortunately gave a false impression about the relationship between the two sides.

Later, Waugh was interviewed by David Hookes, who asked, 'Did the game get out of hand?'

'Oh, it did at moments,' Waugh replied. 'There were some moments where it did, but I think this series has been played in a great spirit. I think this is the best the West Indies and Australian sides have ever got on. We've had a lot of conversations off the field and a lot of friendly stuff. Unfortunately there was some ugly stuff in this Test but that happens occasionally . . . it took a lot out of us in Barbados to win that Test match. I think it probably showed in this match, we were a bit fatigued and in some ways a bit frustrated. I think back-to-back Test matches will bring some more emotions out of the players and I think that's why you saw a few confrontations. It's difficult to play Test match cricket at this level back-to-back.'

Adam Gilchrist backed his captain up: 'Some people may want to make a bigger deal of it but it's something we accept playing international cricket—it's going to happen. But relations between the two sides have been terrific'.

But James Sutherland, CEO of the Australian Cricket Board, made a statement echoing what a lot of people thought: 'It's all very well to be playing the game in the right spirit when things are going your way, but if things are not going your way, that's when the real test is on. If you can't carry yourself in the true spirit of the game at those times, perhaps you need to have a good look at yourself. They are ambassadors for their country and the game of cricket and they need to carry themselves in an appropriate manner. In this circumstance, there's no doubt that what I saw on my television this morning was not what I would have liked to have woken up to'.

The term 'sledging' is usually associated with the Australian teams of the 1970s. It's not true, as some think, that the practice was invented then. Like professionalism and commitment, it goes all the way back to W. G. Grace in the 1800s, and beyond to the 1700s when cricket was played for large sums of money between teams got up by wealthy patrons, some of whom had 'gardeners, grooms and gamekeepers kept to play cricket'.

An early example of sledging is attributed to George Parr, who in 1864 led the second English team to come to Australia. Parr 'played a different game to anyone who went before him' and was noted as a 'leg-hitter'; he 'hit more balls to leg than anyone else' at a time when hitting across the line was considered rather crude, and 'not good form'. In a match against Cambridge, it is said, he took a ball from outside off stump and lofted it sweetly over the fence at mid wicket. The bowler glared at Parr and called down the wicket, 'Do you know where that pitched?' Parr looked across toward the boundary and answered, 'In the hedge, I think'.

But if Chappell's men did not invent the practice, they did give it a name. In an article for an Indian magazine, Chappell wrote that the word came into being in the 1960s

when a New South Wales player swore in front of a team-mate at a party. Normally this wouldn't be cause for concern amongst

Australian cricketers but at the time the team-mate happened to be accompanying a lady. His response was straightforward, 'Mate, you are as subtle as a sledgehammer', and from then on anyone who committed a faux pas in front of a woman was classed as a sledge. It was a term only used in relation to off-field behaviour but a later generation of players, unaware of its origins, began to describe on-field antics as sledging and with the help of the media the meaning of the word was broadened.

Chappell says, 'The amount of abuse on the international cricket field has probably not altered much through the ages apart from an increase in the strength of the language, which is in keeping with changes in society.' But he draws a line between gamesmanship and any attempt to upset a batsman's concentration, and he says the problem is easily solved.

'First of all the batsman is entitled to some peace and quiet out in the middle,' Chappell told me, 'and if the umpire doesn't step in to ensure that he gets that, then I'm going to take the law into my own hands, and I'll tell you exactly what I'd do: if I'm at the bowler's end, I'm going to start talking to the bowler as he's running in, and I know what's going to happen then, the umpire's going to chat me, and I'm going to say, "Well, listen mate, when you stop them yakking while I'm batting, I'll stop talking to their bowler".

'If you're facing, I can't understand why batsmen don't pull away. I've only seen two batsmen pull away, Mark Waugh and Ricky Ponting, but if it happened to me I just pulled away and said, "Listen mate, it's going to be a long game, because I don't face up till you shut up". My point there is, I'm trying to let the umpire know, if he hasn't heard it, to do something about it, and if he's not going to do something about it then I will, I'll just stand there until they shut up.

'You are entitled to your concentration and it's absolute total bullshit that this should be part of the game. I'll give you a good example of what I think is quite reasonable: Shane Warne bowling to Ganguly in Adelaide—he's come around the wicket trying to bowl out in the footmarks, so he's bowling wide of off stump.

Tendulkar's at the other end and going pretty well, Ganguly lets about three go, Shane Warne says to him, "Hey mate, the people didn't come here to watch you let balls go, they came here to see the bloke down the other end play shots". And two overs later Ganguly charged Warne and got stumped off a flipper. Now if you're silly enough as a batsman to fall for that, you get exactly what you deserve. I think that's quite clever gamesmanship, I have no problem with that, but if it's just inane chatter, even if it's not abusive, I still expect the umpire to step in after a while and say, "Now listen, let's have a bit of quiet out here, fellers, and get on with the game."'

I'm told I saw Don Bradman bat at the Sydney Cricket Ground, but unfortunately I have no recollection of it. My father took me, it must have been in 1946 or 1947. I was too young to remember it, I never thought to ask what game it was, and now, of course, it's too late to find out.

In the course of making documentary films about cricket I spent some time with the Don, and have spent many hours watching film of him in his playing days. But it would be nice to have a memory of the real thing, as I have of most of the great players since his time: Miller, Hutton, Benaud, Trueman. I can still hear the thud when Frank Tyson ducked into a short ball from Ray Lindwall, and the reaction from the crowd when they realised Garry Sobers had hit Ian Meckiff for six over mid wicket with what seemed to be a defensive shot off the back foot. A year or so later, after Bradman had persuaded Sobers to have a couple of seasons with South Australia, legend has it that the Western Australian fast bowler Des Hoare surprised Sobers with a short ball and made him look awkward. Next ball was the same but quicker. Sobers smacked it over the square leg boundary, then looked down the wicket and said to Hoare, 'Don't bowl that shit to me, man'. Another time, Sobers told me, he was facing Wes Hall who was playing for Queensland. It was an easy wicket and Hall was at the end of a long spell. Sobers hit consecutive fours and pride demanded that Hall bowl him a bouncer. The wicket meant it would be easy meat, but out of respect for the big man, Sobers went under it and let it go through, only for Hall to call down the wicket, 'I make you duck, you bitch'.

Norm O'Neill and Rohan Kanhai were my favourites. At the wicket, both of them lived on the edge, and the wonderful summer of 1960–61, when Benaud's and Worrell's teams rescued cricket from the drudgery of the late 1950s, was the happiest of 50-odd years of watching cricket. Later there was the majesty of Greg Chappell, the raw excitement of Lillee and Thomson, and I remember watching a young, slim Viv Richards go down the steps and onto the Sydney Cricket Ground for the first time—you just knew that here was something special. As C.L.R. James wrote of Charley Macartney, when someone suggested that he might be as good as Victor Trumper: 'Nobody was ever as good as Vic,' he laughed, 'you only had to see him walk'.

But I digress.

I realised that something had really changed in the spirit in which big cricket was played during the third Test of the 1999–2000 series against India at the SCG, Steve Waugh's fourteenth Test as captain. Tendulkar won the toss and batted and India lost wickets at 10, 27, 58 and 59. Tendulkar at that stage was about 30, seeing the ball well, but running out of partners. He decided to go on the attack and took to McGrath, hitting three or four stunning boundaries with commanding ease. But McGrath then bowled as good a ball as you are ever likely to see, just short so Tendulkar had to play back, and cutting back sharply at the leg stump. Tendulkar tried to turn it to leg and was out plumb, lbw. You couldn't see fifteen minutes of better cricket, but for many at the ground, it was spoilt by McGrath, who rushed at Tendulkar, screaming, eyes wide, apparently consumed by hatred.

It was the ugliest thing I had ever seen on a cricket ground. It was shown on the ABC News that night, and it worried me that it would have been seen by tens, if not hundreds, of millions of people in India, to many of whom Tendulkar was a personal hero. To his credit, the Indian captain gave no visible reaction (unlike

McGrath's send-off for Tendulkar in the third Test v India, 1999–2000.
(Cricket Australia/Channel 9)

the English quick Darren Gough the following year in England: when McGrath made him miss a couple of times, then came down the pitch to eyeball him, Gough lent on his bat, eyeballed him back, and although you couldn't hear it, as the camera moved in close you could see Gough say, 'Fucking wanker').

If McGrath's screaming at Tendulkar had been an isolated incident it might not have mattered much, but the worry with things like this is that the actions of the senior men are copied by the juniors. The following month, in a one-day international against New Zealand, when a good bouncer from the then emerging fast bowler Brett Lee made the New Zealand 'keeper Adam Parore rear backwards and lose his helmet, which fell onto the stumps, Lee, following through, changed course and crossed the wicket to sneer defiance in Parore's face.

There had been incidents like this in the past. In South Africa in 1994, during Allan Border's last series as captain, Shane Warne and Merv Hughes were fined for verbal abuse during the Johannesburg Test. Hughes had reacted to provocation from the crowd around the notorious 'race' which is needed in Johannesburg to protect the players from the crowd. Warne's offence, however, was gratuitous and ugly. He had bowled Andrew Hudson around his legs after Hudson had helped to put South Africa in a winning position. As Hudson left the wicket, Warne walked towards him shouting, 'Fuck off, Hudson. Go on, fuck off out of here'.

In 1997, again in South Africa, this time under Mark Taylor, Ian Healy was suspended for two games for throwing his bat up the steps towards the dressing room.

McGrath's ugly temper had been exposed before in the Melbourne Test of the 1998–99 Ashes series, when late in England's second innings Alan Mullally connected with a series of swipes and

McGrath snapped, shouting at Mullally and moving into his line when he went for a run. McGrath received a $2500 suspended fine, subject to good behaviour.

Under Steve Waugh's captaincy, in India in 2001, on the final day of the first Test, with India on the rack, Rahul Dravid clipped a ball to Michael Slater, who claimed the catch. Dravid stood his ground and when, after reference to the third umpire, Dravid got the benefit of the doubt, Slater remonstrated with umpire Venkat, then with the batsman. In his diary of the tour Steve Waugh wrote:

> Unfortunately for Slats, the combination of the heat of the moment and a green light sparked his uncharacteristic display, which caught me off guard. By the time he had confronted Venkat and Dravid, all I could do was yell out from a distance 'Get out of there Slats'. Unfortunately, Slats either didn't hear me or it didn't sink in.

Slater escaped without a penalty, which Ian Chappell says was 'disgraceful'. Chappell also questions Waugh's version of events: 'Slater was fielding at square leg when he said he caught the ball— I didn't actually think that he caught it anyhow—and Steve Waugh was fielding at mid wicket, so my question is how did Michael Slater ever get to the umpire?

'Some players might catch you by surprise, but at that stage Michael Slater was going through some problems and was in a very tense state, which everyone knew about, and when you know that, as a captain you sort of keep a bit of a wary eye, and particularly someone like Slater, who can be a bit volatile anyhow.

'So if someone says, "Oh, he caught Steve Waugh by surprise", I don't accept he did. But anyway the next question I've got to ask is, having gone to the umpire and remonstrated with Venkat for quite some time, he then got to the batsman at the other end. So how did he get to the batsman? Well, if [Waugh] doesn't get to him before he gets to the umpire, and I don't recall him making any attempt to drag him away from Venkat, it becomes a valid question, how did he get to Rahul Dravid?

'I've seen Steve Waugh's quotes about "We discuss it in the dressing room but when you get out on the field it's up to the players", but that's completely ignoring what it says in the Laws of Cricket, that the captain is responsible for his players.'

It was a year after Slater's encounter with Venkat and Dravid, during the second Test of the series in South Africa early in 2002, that the young South African batsman Graeme Smith, playing in his first series against the Australians, was greeted by a lengthy stream of abuse, mainly from Matthew Hayden. In the past, players had generally adhered to the unwritten code—'Leave what happens out on the field out on the field'—but after the series Smith went public in the South African magazine *Sports Illustrated*. According to Smith, Hayden 'stood on the crease for about two minutes telling me that I wasn't fucking good enough . . . And I hadn't even taken guard yet. He stood there right in my face, repeating it over and over . . . Hayden had obviously been told that his job was to attack me'. Smith said he also copped continual abuse from the fieldsmen close to the bat, including Ponting, Langer, Warne and Mark Waugh. Smith also clashed with Lee after they collided on the pitch: 'I apologised, but he said nothing,' Smith said. 'Then I hooked him for four and then a one and then it was drinks. As he walked past me he told me that he would fucking kill me right there if I ever touched him again.'

McGrath, according to Smith, 'starts off quietly, but the minute you hit him for a boundary he loses the plot and it never stops'. Smith eventually said something back to McGrath, which 'caused a massive fallout. After that he never stopped hurling abuse even when he was fielding at third man'.

Smith said, 'There is never anything funny about the sledging. All Warne does is call you a cunt. When he walked past me he said: "You fucking cunt, what are you doing here?" And I remember looking at [umpire] Rudi Koertzen and he just shrugged his shoulders.'

In January 2003, Hayden, who is said to be deeply religious and generally regarded as a very decent man, was charged with a breach of the ICC Code of Conduct when he smashed the glass in the dressing room door at the SCG after being given out lbw for the second time in the match against England. Match referee Wasim

Raja said, 'Matthew Hayden admitted the offence and apologised for his action. Allowing for Matthew's previously clean record I decided the appropriate punishment is a severe reprimand and a fine of 20 per cent of his match fee.'

Ten days later in Brisbane, after Darren Lehmann was run out during a one-day international against Sri Lanka, he shouted a racist remark in the dressing room. It was heard by the Sri Lankans, who complained to match referee Clive Lloyd. Lehmann apologised and the Sri Lankan management appealed to Lloyd for leniency, but Lehmann was suspended for five one-day matches for breaching the ICC's racial vilification code. Chief Executive of the Australian Cricket Board James Sutherland said, 'I have expressed to Darren the ACB's disappointment in the incident and organised immediate counselling for him. It is clear that he has acted in an undesirable manner and steps will be taken to see that behaviour such as this is not repeated.'

As Lehmann's offence took place during a one-day game, Steve Waugh wasn't involved, but he came under criticism four months later for failing to step in during the fourth Test against the West Indies after McGrath's obscene taunting of Ramnaresh Sarwan and, when Sarwan answered him back, his threats and finger-pointing. Peter Roebuck wrote:

> If victory cannot be achieved without recourse to the sort of antagonism seen in Antigua it is not worth bothering about. Cricket searched for a champion team and found only an unscrupulous aggressor . . . as usual the Australians hunted as a pack with others joining the fray. Not for the first time Steve Waugh comprehensively failed to pour cold water on these tempers.

Perhaps, in this instance, almost anyone but McGrath could be given the benefit of the doubt, but it's hard to avoid the conclusion that, in recent years, the Australian cricket team has used personal abuse as a means of breaking a batsman's concentration. As Graeme Smith said, 'Hayden had obviously been told that his job was to attack me.'

It seems a strange way to behave. It's hard to imagine another walk of life where the use of obscene personal insults or unrestrained anger would be regarded as anything other than loony, laughable or despicable. And demeaning—an admission that you think that winning is so important that it's OK to throw normal standards of behaviour out the window. It's hard to imagine players of previous generations doing it—apart from anything else, they would have had too much pride, they would have considered it beneath them.

I wonder where the idea came from. I would have liked to ask John Buchanan whether it was a strategy that arose from lateral thinking—'not constrained by history' and 'challenging conventional approaches'—perhaps inspired by his and Steve Waugh's meeting with Edward de Bono.

Perhaps there is a clue in Steve Waugh's tour diaries. Early in his captaincy he often included excerpts from his 'Captain's Notes', written for pre-match team meetings. While the notes cover many areas—among other things, not arguing with umpires and respect for the traditions of the game—they are also frequently an exhortation to aggression: 'Let's play aggressively, together as a unit . . . Make them feel unwanted—it's 11 v 2 when we're in the field . . . Keep wearing them down, they'll crack before us . . . Be ruthless'.

No doubt the players get very pumped up in the field, and perhaps the Hayden–Smith incident was just an occasion where it went too far. Perhaps the McGrath–Sarwan incident can be put down to McGrath's super-short fuse. Whatever the case, it didn't play well with the public. The Board received hundreds of phone calls complaining about McGrath's outburst, to the extent that people who worked at the Board were reluctant to answer the phone for fear of being abused. The Board insisted that something should be done to stop it happening again.

In June 2003, the Australian Cricket Board was re-badged as Cricket Australia. In October 2003, at the WACA, in company with Steve Waugh, Ricky Ponting and captain of the Australian women's team Belinda Clark, Cricket Australia's CEO James Sutherland launched the 'Spirit of Cricket' project. Headed 'Spirit of Cricket to be a priority for new Australian cricket season', the press release said:

Australian elite cricketers have defined a set of standards of behaviour and values by which they intend to play the game. The players' definition is part of a broader national Spirit of Cricket project announced today which is designed to ensure all Australian cricketers from school and park cricket up understand their obligations to fair play.

Australia's two international men's team cricket captains, Steve Waugh and Ricky Ponting, announced an elite players' definition of the Spirit of Australian Cricket based on playing the game hard but fair, accepting umpires' decisions and leaving the game in better shape than it was before they arrived. The definition, which documents issues which Cricket Australia-contracted players have been discussing for several years, is designed as a guide to the shared standards of behaviour they expect of themselves, and of the values they hold.

The players' code, finalised during the contract-player camp in Perth last weekend, does not condone on-field abuse or sledging, but accepts that banter between opponents is part of the competitive nature of cricket. Test captain Steve Waugh said Australian players had been discussing the importance of playing the game in a positive way for several years: 'We believe we have made good progress, despite a handful of set backs. But we acknowledge that the intense and increasing scrutiny of Australian international cricketers on and off the field imposes very high standards on us as role models and ambassadors for the game.'

Sutherland avoided any criticism and, like the press release, seemed to be at pains to indicate that the initiative wasn't a reaction to any particular incident, but some of his speech at the launch was to the point:

In recent times we have been spoilt by the performances of our elite cricketers. The current Test team scores its runs at a superior strike rate to any team in the game's history. Batting or bowling, the team plays positive, attacking cricket and wins. This brings and keeps fans in the game. It encourages sponsors into the game. And together, the fans and sponsors provide the dollars to keep the game healthy.

The spirit in which the game is played is just as important—whether it be in the schoolyard, the local suburban oval or at international level. It is not well understood that the official Laws of Cricket recognise this. The preamble to the Laws of Cricket says:

- Cricket is a game that owes much of its appeal to the fact that it is played not just within the laws of the game, but also within the spirit of the game.
- Any action seen as abusing the spirit of cricket causes injury to the game itself.

The official laws . . . require players to respect opponents, umpires and the game's traditions and values. The major responsibility for this rests with captains. All captains, no matter the grade or competition . . . At the top end of Australian cricket, we have sat down on a number of occasions with the leadership group of the men's team to talk through the issues. Our players are under extraordinary and increasing scrutiny, both on and off the field, as role models and ambassadors for the game.

They in turn have privately discussed and developed their own definition of how they want to play the game. It is their definition, they developed it themselves, and a copy has been provided to you in today's media kit.

At international level, Australian players have had a reputation for on-field toughness. But while acknowledging some failures, I honestly think the perception and the reality are a little out of alignment. I have said before that today's Australian teams are victims of their own success, because that success raises the standards expected of them as role models.

The word 'sledging' is often associated with this team. If sledging is personal abuse of an opposition player, why is it that no Australian player has been reported for such an offence in the last couple of years?

The players' 'definition of how they want to play the game'—known as the Players' Pledge—said:

As cricketers who represent Australia we acknowledge and embrace 'The Spirit of Cricket' and the laws of our game. This Players' Spirit of Australian Cricket serves as a guide to the shared standards of behaviour that we expect of ourselves, and of the values we hold.

We play our cricket hard but fair and accept all umpiring decisions as a mark of respect for our opponents, the umpires, ourselves and the game. We view positive play, pressure, body language and banter between opponents and ourselves as legitimate tactics and integral parts of the competitive nature of cricket.

We do not condone or engage in sledging or any other conduct that constitutes personal abuse. We encourage the display of passion and emotion as a sign of our enjoyment and pride in the game, as a celebration of our achievements and as a sign of respect for our opponents.

Subsequent clauses dealt with off-field conduct, the traditions of the game, and respect for the governing bodies of the game.

An editorial in the *Sydney Morning Herald* took up James Sutherland's question: 'If sledging is personal abuse of an opposition player, why is it that no Australian player has been reported for such an offence in the last couple of years?'

What many find highly offensive, elite cricketers and Cricket Australia's chief executive, James Sutherland, see as normal. Well, it's all a matter of definition. This is what Glenn McGrath said to West Indian batsman Ramnaresh Sarwan in May: 'If you ever f—ing mention my wife again I will f—ing rip your f—ing throat out'. He was not reported, presumably because all involved—players, umpires, captains and the ICC's match officials—saw this as banter, as hard but fair, as anything but sledging. Perhaps the Australian players will improve. As leopards age, their spots don't change, but the colours may soften a little. Far more likely, though, is that better behaviour, should it arrive, will come with the next generation of cricketers.

It's hard to imagine that Steve Waugh would have welcomed the initiative, although others might have, and I have been told that the players—who are often dismissive of the critics of sledging—

became more cooperative when they heard the experience of people who answered the phones at the ACB after the McGrath–Sarwan incident. Waugh's comments at the launch were predictably cautious: 'There's always going to be mistakes so I'm not going to say we're going to be perfect from now on because that would be a mistake. We want emotion. We want passion in the game. That's the way we play our cricket and that's why we say banter is part of the game. But now we know the standard expected of each other'.

After that, if Waugh was asked about sledging, he would give a knowing smile and say, 'There's no sledging in Australian cricket.'

Waugh himself, in recent years, was not a sledger—although he had a reputation for being quite vocal in his younger days. The complaint against him has been his inaction as captain, his state-ment that 'Once they step onto the field, they're accountable for their own actions. It's up to each player to know his responsibility', when the rules clearly state that playing within the spirit of the game is the captain's responsibility. To see the video of Richie Richardson pulling Curtly Ambrose away from Steve Waugh in the 1995 confrontation, and compare it with Waugh's inaction in the face of Hayden's verbal assault on Graeme Smith, or Slater's petulant approach to umpire Venkat, or McGrath's bullying rage with Ramnaresh Sarwan, is to understand why the Spirit of Cricket initiative was necessary.

There is another way to look at it. The coverage that prompted the much-publicised phone call from Cricket Australia chief executive James Sutherland to Steve Waugh, telling him that the team needs 'to have a good look at the way they play when things are not going their way', was not the real story—it was the media story. The media story took a minute or so in a seven-hour day when Chan-derpaul scored 105 from 139 balls and Sarwan 104 from 154, as West Indies, needing 418, went from none for 47 to 6 for 371, within striking distance of a record fourth innings total to win a Test. The real story was a great day's cricket between two sides that for the most part got on very well throughout the series, with a brief cameo performance from a great fast bowler who sometimes carries on like a boorish clod. Of course, Sutherland has to react to the media story, because the media story is what nearly all of us see.

Back here in Australia, our version of the day's play was completely dominated by the McGrath–Sarwan incident. In the *Sydney Morning Herald* of Wednesday 14 May the story took up three-quarters of the back page, and in the weekend edition the whole of the front page of the sport section dealt with the sledging issue. The coverage on television news was similar: extensive coverage of the incident followed by a summary of the scores.

In *Hands and Heals*, Ian Healy wrote of Glenn McGrath:

> I reckon when Pigeon's cricket career is over, he'll surprise a lot of people when they discover what a nice bloke he is. Today, everyone sees him as a cranky old sledger—and he is on the field; he'll tee off at any batsman who scores a run off him—but off the field he's a fantastic bloke with a vast knowledge of the game and a very positive, gentlemanly approach to life . . . and—more than most international cricketers—he is a man with many and diverse interests outside the game.

Rob Laurie, who entertained the team in India as Australian High Commissioner and knows his cricket, also spoke highly of McGrath: 'Glenn McGrath and Jason Gillespie were absolutely marvellous blokes to have around at a function. I mean, talk about McGrath as a genial giant, you'd never know it on the field, but off it . . .'

Rob Laurie's brother John, a friend from my cricketing days, can vouch for the fact that the Australians and the West Indies fraternised and got on well off the field during the 2003 West Indies tour. Laurie was staying at the same hotel as both teams during the second Test. He said, 'Over breakfast they had tables set up at different parts of the dining room and they would sit half-and-half with the different team and they were talking while they were getting their orange juice and different things—particularly Lee and Lara, you'd see them every morning with each other. I've got to say that in terms of fraternal attitude off the field, it was good, there was no aggro, they were all able to talk to each other and, you know, Steve Waugh was no different than the rest of them. When there was all this stuff about open warfare and McGrath etcetera etcetera, I got sufficiently irritated to write a letter to the editor because it just wasn't true. The spirit between the teams when I saw them was very very good, just like the cricket we used to play.'

No doubt Healy's and the Lauries' comments about McGrath are accurate, no doubt he is a good bloke—and the same is said of Matthew Hayden by those who know him personally—which makes it more obvious that the personal abuse was used intention-ally to upset batsmen and put them off—to 'make them feel unwanted'.

And, of course, the Australians were not the only team using the mental ploys that win matches: I spoke to Graeme Smith (now South Africa's captain), who stands by what he said but admits to having done his own share of sledging in the past. In *Never Say Die*, Waugh points out that Brian Lara often picks a fight when he is batting, to get himself pumped up; New Zealand wicket-keeper of the 1990s, Adam Parore, was always niggling at the batsman's sub-conscious; some of Sri Lanka's success has been credited to Arjuna Ranatunga's ability to get under an opponent's skin; India's recent record in Tests is said to owe something to Sourav Ganguly's use of Australian methods. England . . . England . . . I can't think of an example—perhaps that's their problem.

So the Australians aren't alone, although in recent times they seem to have been the leaders when it comes to obscene personal abuse.

Does it matter? Yes, for at least a couple of reasons. First, if young people see the players billed as heroes physically intimidat-ing their opponents and using obscene language to try to stop them performing at their best, they might think it's all right to behave like that, on and—even more importantly—off the field.

Second, both David Boon and Ian Healy comment on the fact that relations between teams became much less friendly during their time in cricket, and say the game is the poorer for it. Boon says, 'Gradually this part of the game has deteriorated. And that is just about the only major disappointment of my Test career.' Generations of cricketers made many friends playing cricket, at school, in clubs, around the world. That still goes on, of course, but if the unrestrained use of obscenities became the norm, cricket would have become a much less friendly game.

Fortunately, Cricket Australia have stepped in to make sure that it won't.

31

THE LAST SUMMER

Hype and hoop-la

Two Tests were played against Bangladesh in the winter of 2003. Australia won both by an innings. Waugh made 100 not out in Darwin and his 156 not out in Cairns was to be his last Test century. The 2003–04 season began with Tests against Zimbabwe in Perth, won by an innings, and in Sydney, won by 9 wickets. In the Perth Test, Matthew Hayden made 380, passing Brian Lara's 375, made against England in 1994, as the highest score in Tests.

There are good reasons for bringing new countries into the Test arena—Sri Lanka's success has proved the point most recently—but the downside is that it cheapens the great achievements. Lara is a genius, a man who has won Tests against good bowling off his own bat, challenged only by Tendulkar as the great batsman of his age; I thought it was unfortunate that his record was broken against such weak opposition and I was glad to see Lara regain the record against England in April 2004. That said, to see Hayden being interviewed on Channel Nine's 'Today' show the next morning, while members of the team, including its captain, standing on the balcony above, tossed bits of rubbish and pieces of fruit at him, was to be aware that members of the Australian cricket team won't let their record-breakers get too big-headed.

The Test team wore the grey and red '3' logo in 2003–04, part of a reported $3 billion investment by Hutchison Telecommunications to promote its next generation phone network. Was it only last year

Steve and Lynette Waugh with Waugh's manager, Robert Joske, at the announcement of Waugh's retirement, November 2003. (*Australian Broadcasting Corporation Content Sales*)

that they were wearing the orange patch, promoting Nokia's Orange network, also owned by Hutchison?

Early in the season, playing for NSW in Pura Cup matches against Western Australia, Tasmania and South Australia, Waugh scored two centuries—and made three ducks—then, in late November 2003, a week before the start of the four-Test series against India, he called a press conference to announce that this series would be his last.

Ever the family man, at the press conference almost five years before where his appointment to the captaincy was announced, he mentioned that he had been watching 'Sesame Street' with Rosalie when the call came; when he announced his retirement, he said that one of the reasons he was going was that Rosalie had said she would like him to be at home more often. He wanted to spend more time with his growing children, he said, and also to end the speculation about when he would retire.

But it had been well known for some time in cricket circles that the selectors and executive of Cricket Australia wanted him to go. It was time to bring on younger players, and Waugh's attitude to sledging and umpiring decisions, and possibly his stance on players' rights and contracts, counted against him with the men who ran Australian cricket.

There was talk that a deal had been done, assuring him of selection if he agreed to go at the end of the summer, but I think it's more likely that the reasons Waugh gave were genuine and, on top of that, he and his management saw an ideal opportunity to maximise his sponsorship potential with a final grand tour.

It seemed to be at odds with Waugh's reputation of hating fuss to call a press conference at the SCG and appear there, all suited up, with his wife and manager. Could it have been coincidence that a fax from the Prime Minister arrived as the press conference was about to start? Afterwards, according to the *Sun-Herald*, he and Lynette spent 'an hour doing one-on-one interviews and posing for photographs'.

If it seemed Waugh might be putting himself above the game, the game soon brought him back to earth. The second day of the Brisbane Test was headlined 'Steve Waugh's swansong turns into ugly duck'. He came onto the ground to a standing ovation but was criticised for entering the stage before century-maker Justin Langer had left it, thus depriving Langer of his fair share of the applause. (It should be said that the Australians set a very good example in having the incoming and outgoing batsmen cross after a wicket falls, and Waugh's timing was probably a result of doing it by the book.)

Five balls later Damien Martyn, on 42, drove Zaheer Khan through the covers and after both batsmen had run 2, Martyn went a couple of paces on a third run, but as Harbhajan Singh gathered near the boundary, Martyn stopped and signalled Waugh to go back. Waugh at that stage was only a couple of paces down the wicket but must have missed the call because he put his head down and went flat out. As it happened, Singh's throw was well wide of the stumps—Patel took it a third of the way down the pitch as Waugh completed his run—but with both batsmen at the striker's end Patel lobbed it back to the bowler's end. Martyn was back in his crease and could have stayed there, but Waugh had run well through and Martyn chose to sacrifice his

'Swansong turns into ugly duck': after running out Damian Martyn, Waugh treads on his wicket, first Test v India, Brisbane, December 2003. *(Cricket Australia/Channel 9)*

wicket by trotting to the other end, as Ganguly took the bails off.

Two balls later Waugh went back to try to turn Zaheer to leg, but he slipped on the greasy wicket and bumped the off stump with his left leg. It was his 22nd duck in Tests.

The next week, referring to comment on the run out, Waugh said, 'I think it was personal what was written the next day. I wasn't appreciative of what was written because it was a mistake by both of us, we were both to blame for that run out yet some of the innuendo I read the next day was very disappointing.' On the replay it doesn't look like both made a mistake; Martyn saw that Harbhajan had the ball, then he stopped, then he signalled Waugh to stop. Waugh presumably wasn't watching Harbhajan or Martyn; if he had been watching, it wouldn't have happened. As with the disputed catch of Brian Lara in 1995, Waugh would have been better to say he made a mistake, instead of finding fault with others.

In the second innings Waugh should have been stumped off Harbhajan when he was 8, and went on to 56 not out. Interrupted by rain, the Test was drawn.

In the second Test, played in Adelaide, as Laxman and Dravid, with their 303-run partnership, closed the gap on Australia's first innings total of 556 (Ponting 242) and India surged to a 4-wicket victory, Waugh was looking more and more like the bloke whose lawnmower has broken down, and his team was looking increasingly middle-aged. According to statistics in the *Sydney Morning Herald*, with an average age of 31, it was the oldest Australian team since the 1935–36 season. Waugh's scores in Adelaide were 30 and 42.

Australia got the show back on the rails in Melbourne, thanks to the bowlers and another double century by Ponting. Australia won by 9 wickets, to square the series. Waugh batted once for 19 runs. (Ponting's two double centuries raised comparisons with Bradman, but with so much emphasis on Waugh's farewell, Ponting might have felt more like Arthur Morris, who likes to point out that he was at the other end when Bradman made his famous last-Test duck in 1948; if he is asked whether he made any runs he is able to say, well, yes, he was run out the next day for 194.)

With Harbhajan's throw on the way, Martyn signals Waugh to go back, first Test v India, Brisbane, December 2003. *(Cricket Australia/Channel 9)*

The press coverage of Stephen Waugh's last series reached a crescendo in the lead up to the fourth and deciding Test, played in Sydney, starting on Friday 2 January 2004. On Wednesday the ABC's '7.30 Report' ran a story (picked up from the *Sydney Morning Herald*) about medical students, inspired by Steve Waugh, working during their holidays in the slums of Calcutta. On Thursday, the *SMH*'s back page carried a piece by music writer Bernard Zuel about growing up in Chester Hill (near Bankstown) and playing cricket in the backyard, and another by cricket-writer and statistician Kersi Meher-Homji—'Waugh in exalted company'—about great players, including Victor Trumper, Richie Benaud, Harold Larwood, Clive Lloyd, Greg Chappell and Mark Taylor, who finished their Test careers at the SCG. Meher-Homji's article noted rather pointedly that Greg Chappell announced his retirement on the second day of his last Test (during which he became the first Australian to pass 7000 runs in Tests, overtook Colin Cowdrey's record 120 catches and made 182 in a match which Australia won by 10 wickets). Mark Taylor also claimed the most catches in his last Test—by that time the record was 156 and it was held by Allan Border. Taylor announced his retirement a few weeks *after* the Test.

Under the headline 'East Hills Boys salute star pupil' in the *Daily Telegraph*'s Wave Our Hero Goodbye campaign, Jane Searle wrote: 'When Steve Waugh walks from his beloved SCG for the last time in a Test match, five young cricketers from his old high school will be there to cheer him off'. In the same article former sports master Ron Perrett recalled 'When Steve and Mark came fresh-faced from primary school they had already represented NSW in three sports— cricket, soccer and tennis. Steve was a very likeable young man, always polite, but you could also see that steely determination to succeed'. The *Tele*'s back page had a picture of Waugh at the airport with his daughter Rosalie and the headline 'The man who changed cricket'. Inside there was a double page spread—'Waugh geared up for final battle'—several articles previewing the Test, and the promise of a special Steve Waugh souvenir edition on the Friday, including Waugh's Top 10 SCG moments, his exclusive column, and Paul Kent on the making of a champion.

Thursday's *Australian* restricted its coverage to the sports pages, which carried half a dozen cricket pieces but only one about Waugh, dealing mainly with the logistics of preparing for his final Test—the printing of the red handkerchiefs, extra catering, a large screen behind the members' area for the many members who would not be able to get seats in the stands. It promised a Steve Waugh Special Tribute for the following day.

On Friday, the first day of the Test, *The Australian*, the *Sydney Morning Herald* and the *Daily Telegraph* all had Waugh on the front page, as well as special editions devoted to him. *The Australian* had a 6-page sports special and a lead editorial, 'Waugh's last hurrah looms as a thriller'.

The Australian's Mike Coward, who has on occasions been critical of Waugh, wrote: 'People see in him qualities they greatly admire: his unfailing loyalty to his men and to the game; his courage under fire; his combativeness and tenacity; the fact he is so unpretentious and cannot tolerate fools and is true to his working class roots in Sydney's western suburbs. These are the characteristics that have defined him'.

The *Telegraph* had a brief editorial, ending 'On this historic day, we wish Waugh and his family the very best and thank them for the pleasure and pride his on-field feats have given so many of his countrymen'. In the four-page wraparound, Waugh rated his top ten SCG moments, number 1 being the 102 against England in January 2003.

He wasn't featured in the *Sydney Morning Herald*'s editorial column but was the subject of two flattering letters on the same page. In the *SMH*'s four-page wraparound souvenir edition—'My Magic Moments'—he also dealt with his 102 v England: 'In terms of personal performance, can it get better than this?' he wrote. 'A ton off the last ball of the day in front of my home crowd after all the stress and media debate about my future in the days and weeks that preceded it.' Peter Roebuck wrote: 'Waugh is released in a crisis, drawn from himself and his insecurities so that he becomes an extrovert, a match-player, an actor upon a stage. In a tight spot, he becomes a better person and usually prevails'.

The day began with India winning the toss. It was suggested that the wicket would have early life and that it would not be such a bad toss to lose, but as it turned out, the wicket was made for batsmen and with both teams strong in batting and relatively weak in bowling, to lose the toss was to lose a reasonable chance of winning the Test.

If Australia had a chance to win, it was probably lost when in the seventh over Sehwag hit catches off consecutive balls from Lee, the first a no-ball, the second a straightforward waist-high chance which was inexplicably dropped by Simon Katich in the gully.

A chink of light appeared when Chopra was bowled by Lee for 45 with the score at 123 and Sehwag edged Gillespie to Gilchrist 5 runs later, but it was dimmed by Dravid and Tendulkar who took the score to 194 before Gillespie bowled Dravid off his pads. It was extinguished for good by Tendulkar and V.V.S. Laxman—'Very very sexy', said a sign in the crowd—who batted together for the next seven hours for a 603-ball partnership of 353, the second highest in Tests in Australia, behind only Bradman and Barnes's partnership of 405 against England in 1946–47.

By Saturday, with India 3 for 284, the media's tone had changed: 'India won't toe the party line' said the *Sydney Morning Herald*, and 'As the Iceman goeth, Mum cometh by train', a reference to the fact that, in a train to Sydney from the south coast, crowded with people coming to see her son at the SCG, Beverley Waugh had to stand all the way. India was 5 for 650 at the end of the second day: 'Catch us if you can' said the headlines, along with 'Waugh fans weep into red hankies' and 'It wasn't meant to be like this'.

India batted on into the third day to 7 for 705, Laxman 178, Tendulkar not out 241. It was India's highest Test score ever and the highest score by a touring team in Australia. Australia batted bravely but by the end of the third day it was a wicket that suited Kumble very well—Australia was 6 for 342 and looking likely to lose. Langer made 117 and Simon Katich made his first Test century in Australia's total of 474.

Waugh himself made 40 in 90 minutes with 6 fours. He played a couple of blinding cuts but he didn't look settled, Kumble tucking him up and making him fidget and jab. Eventually he slashed at a ball from Irfan Pathan, who was born two months before Waugh played his first Test innings. It left him, caught an edge and carried through to Parthiv Patel, who was born two months after Waugh's Test debut. The crowd rose again as Waugh trudged off into the shadows.

Despite the record crowds, perfect weather for the first four days, and some of the best batting seen at the ground, there was a feeling of anti-climax from lunch on the first day, as it began to sink in that it was not a foregone conclusion that Australia would win. The Mexican wave lacked its usual exuberance; the green, white and orange flag of India—more strident than the stolid red, white and blue—seemed to be everywhere.

It was as if the popular will had challenged the gods of cricket to deliver a pre-ordained result, but the gods had made it clear they were sticking with their standard marketing slogan—the charm of cricket is its glorious uncertainty.

Brett Lee could have fired the crowd up, but his time out injured counted against him; he had no luck and he lost his rhythm and with it his pace. For all his antics when he takes a wicket—is he pretending to start a lawnmower, and if so is it a reference to Peter Roebuck's description of Steve Waugh?—Lee is now a generous opponent: at the end of the over, after the young Indian wicket-keeper reached 50, Lee went out of his way to say 'Well done'.

Gillespie bowled very well, but has lost that yard of pace which made him really nasty. Then he and Katich breathed a little life into the game on the fourth day with a partnership of 117 when it looked as if Australia might trail by 350, but they never looked to be in a position where they might be able to conjure up a win.

They trailed by 231, but Ganguly did not make them follow on, instead posting a further 211 for the loss of 2 wickets, declaring with Australia needing 443 in 94 overs, with 15 minutes of play left on the fourth day. The highest winning fourth innings total previously at the SCG was 4 for 276, scored by Australia to win the fifth Test against England in 1897–98. But given the depth of Australia's batting, the state of the wicket, and the lack of depth in India's bowling, it was a sporting declaration. The required run rate was 4.7 per over—India's second innings 211 had been made at a rate of 4.9.

Much was at stake: for India a draw would be a win, and a win would be an unexpected triumph; for Steve Waugh and Australia, a win would legitimise the legend, and any other result would justify the doubters.

Langer and Hayden started briskly, but when they went, Anil Kumble and Murali Kartik slowed the tempo, made the Australians dance to their tune. Martyn couldn't get any traction, taking 96 balls to score 40, and even Ponting's fluency wasn't enough to score at a rate of 3 runs an over.

Waugh came to the wicket for the last time in a Test with his team needing 273 at a rate of 6 runs an over. He gradually settled in, all the old habits on display: the hooded eyes, wrinkled now from too many seasons in the sun; the look of mild disdain, as if something disapproved of was happening out there in the middle distance; a few threads of the red rag sticking out of his left pants pocket; talking to himself—'C'mon, c'mon'—you could see the young wicket-keeper watching him with a mixture of admiration and mild amusement

Kumble kept wheeling in over after over, seeming to get his spin, like Bill O'Reilly, as much from the leverage of his long arms as from the work of his wrists. Kartik made amends for the hammering he took in the first innings; the new boy Pathan, looking as if he might have copied his action from Wasim Akram—he could have done worse—seemed a prospect for the future; Sachin Tendulkar bowled his casual, loopy leg breaks, much at odds with the fierce precision of his batting.

Sourav Ganguly, a man whose time has come, was edgy and watchful, always on the move. Watching the video later, the commentators are constantly critical of his field placings, although they don't always agree with each other and sometimes talk as if they had a few extra men on the field.

Waugh, eventually, when it seemed Australia couldn't win, looked more relaxed, happy even, to have a role to play in making sure they didn't lose.

Then it was a lesson in defensive play, the eyes over the ball, the bat right next to the pad, but if it was short or wide the arms were freed and the hands exploded and the ball flashed through off-side field. When a good length ball from Kumble leapt to head height, there was the hint of a wry smile; if he looked a little stiff when hurried or surprised, Simon Katich at the other end was a reminder that young players should be brought on: young limbs are more elastic, young legs are more nimble and young eyes are quicker.

When Waugh swept Sehwag for 4 to bring up his 50, he kept his head down as if to say to the crowd, 'Wait a bit, there's still work to be done here, leave me alone for the moment'.

Then suddenly, with 6 wickets left and 160 runs needed from 18 overs, an Australian win seemed possible again and Waugh needed only 42 runs for another miracle hundred. Fifteen overs have to be bowled in the last hour; when drinks were taken at 5.15, before the last hour started, reducing by one the number of overs to be bowled, there was even a show of the petulance that has made Waugh unpopular with umpires. He shook his head at umpire Billy Bowden, then threw down his bat and gloves as he headed for the drinks tray.

Trying to hit Kumble, he played and missed several times, conceding a maiden over. Katich took 4 and 2 from the first two balls of Agarkar's next over and Ganguly had to spread the field. But Kumble, bowling into the scuff marks outside off stump, kept it to one or two an over, and Ganguly backed his spinners, not taking the new ball and bringing back Kartik, who gathered confidence.

Waugh's manager Robert Joske, Channel 9's Richard Wilkins, Lynette Waugh and Simone Warne watch Steve Waugh's last Test innings at the SCG, 6 January 2004. *(Cricket Australia/Channel 9)*

And eventually it was too much. Australia needed 105 with only 31 balls left. They couldn't win, but Waugh needed only 20 for his hundred. Katich refused an easy single to leave Waugh on strike, facing Kumble. Unfortunately, I thought, in view of the many fine performances during what was easily the most absorbing series in Australia in a decade, the focus had become whether Waugh could score a hundred that didn't matter.

Appropriately, the television coverage cut to a close up in the stands of Waugh's manager, Robert Joske, sitting next to Channel Nine's Richard Wilkins, both applauding enthusiastically. Immediately behind them were Lynette Waugh and Simone Warne— Australian royalty. An Australian flag waved across the bottom of the screen.

The crowd chanted 'Steve Waugh! Steve Waugh!' Ian Chappell said, 'Ganguly has got two men back in the deep on the on side. He really needs to have both of them in off the rope, it's a very long hit there, you've gotta have them in position to catch the miss-hit.'

Waugh blocked one, then connected nicely with a slog-sweep which carried straight to Tendulkar, perfectly positioned on the rope at deep mid wicket. Tendulkar had the wit not to overdo the celebration, and Waugh hurried off with a minimum of fuss, head down, as the crowd rose to him for the last time.

Gilchrist went soon after and the Indians went into their huddle. Katich and Gillespie played out the last few overs, Katich following his first innings century with 77 not out from 96 balls. Waugh's 80 had taken 159 balls.

Australia finished with 6 for 357, 86 runs short. With the series drawn 1-each, India retained the Border–Gavaskar Trophy.

The crowd total for the match was 189,989, the highest at the SCG since the second Test in 1946–47, another echo of Don Bradman and Sid Barnes and their record partnership. The crowd was a tribute to the public's support for Steve Waugh, but by stumps on the second day the wisdom of Bill O'Reilly's comments on captaincy and collie dogs was evident. Lacking his great bowlers, Warne and McGrath, and in the face of strong batting, there is not a great deal a captain can do, for a cricket team is seldom more than the sum of its parts. Australia had been reduced to playing out time to save a series loss, against a side they had expected to defeat.

The articles of praise for Waugh's captaincy talk about commitment, self-belief, owning the wicket, giving 100 per cent, staying positive and outperforming your potential. I guess the great players of the past—Border, the Chappells, Simpson, Benaud and beyond, back into history—might resent the inference that they lacked these attitudes and characteristics. Perhaps the main change has been the willingness to talk about them.

Apart from the coverage in the sports section, Waugh's farewell was on the front page of the *Sydney Morning Herald*, and the second editorial dealt with the importance of cricket in breaking the diplomatic deadlock between India and Pakistan: 'The planned Indian cricket tour of Pakistan in March, then, is an extraordinary breakthrough which cannot—like dull, diplomatic wrangling—be easily overlooked . . . decades of rivalry could then be safely played out on the cricket pitch'.

Page four of the *SMH* also carried a half-page ad featuring Steve

Waugh pretending to steer a yacht, in an advertisement promoting a superannuation retirement fund.

Three days after the hype and hoop-la of the Sydney Test, Steve Waugh was back on the cricket field, this time in Newcastle, captaining NSW in their struggle to reach the Pura Cup final, playing again in the same team as his twin brother and team-mate of 30-odd years. Between them they were not able to prevent Victoria from piling on 455 for 7 wickets for an outright win, thanks to an unbeaten 212 from David Hussey. Steve made 7 and 20, Mark 31 and 13.

A week later in the interstate one-day ING Cup competition, Steve top-scored for NSW with 48, but Queensland passed NSW's total of 246 with two balls to spare. This match was played at the Telstra Stadium at Homebush, the Olympic Stadium. It was the first day–night match played at the former Olympic Stadium and drew a crowd of 26 109, the highest for an interstate one-day game in NSW.

A 127-run Pura Cup loss at the WACA followed, then a 1-run loss leading the Prime Minister's XI against the touring Indians, and another ING Cup match—a 25-run loss to Queensland. In the next Pura cup match, against Queensland, with NSW needing an outright win to have a realistic chance of playing in the final, Waugh dropped Jimmy Maher on 39 and saw him go on to 116 as Queensland amassed 431 for 5 wickets. At the end of the second day NSW were 4 for 96, with both Waughs not out on 2. It was all there to play for—could the twins manage one last miracle? Rain took away most of the third day, NSW struggled to 229 (M. Waugh 90, S. Waugh 8), then Queensland thrashed 124 in less than an hour, leaving NSW 327 to make in a minimum 55 overs. They tried gamely, Phil Jaques made 146 at a run a ball, but they came up 50 short. Steve Waugh made 28 from 21 balls, Mark made 5 from 12.

32

THE SEARCH FOR STEVE WAUGH

It is difficult, of course, to write a biography of someone who won't talk to you. It doesn't make it any easier if his management also asks other people who could help not to talk to you. But it's not impossible—many a good life story has been told a couple of hundred years after the life under consideration has ended.

And the face-to-face interview is of limited use. People tell you what they want you to hear; two or three meetings, in which you get some opinions about particular events and check some facts, might not give you any real insight into whether, say, support for a cause comes from a genuinely-held belief or a wish to improve an image, or both. Not having the subject's cooperation has its advantages; if you haven't had any help you don't feel under any obligation, you feel less inhibited about saying things the subject might not want you to say.

There's plenty of information out there. I spoke to people who knew Steve Waugh. I had video highlights of most of his Test innings and the important moments of his one-day career. I read books by or about his cricket contemporaries—including his brother Mark, Ian Healy, Mark Taylor, and David Boon. I was lucky to be given access to a pile of scrapbooks full of press clippings, pictures, advertisements and interesting odds and ends. The Internet is an amazing source of statistics and other information. And then there are the ten tour diaries; I tried not to use them too much—it didn't seem the right thing to do. I only referred to them if I wanted to check something, or wanted more information, or wanted to know what Steve thought or said about a particular event. Of course, when I did that I often found myself drawn into the detail and would surface half an hour later when the phone rang, and find that the screen had gone black.

When you have done all that, prepared your material and written it all up, there are things that stick in your mind, that seem to have a kernel of truth, or to offer an insight. On their own, they don't make much sense; perhaps together they add up to something.

I spoke to several people who know Steve Waugh well—not personal friends from outside cricket, but those who know him well through cricket—and I formed a distinct impression that those who know him well like him best. People who played in the same teams as Steve Waugh described him as confident of his own ability and able to make people believe in their ability; they described him as thoughtful—someone who rings people up to congratulate or commiserate; as a leader who goes out of his way to be inclusive, to make the newcomers, or those in the squad but not selected, feel part of the team. As Allan Border said: 'He's a very positive bloke. He never believes we're going to lose. He always believes something is going to happen'.

In private, he is not as focused or intense as he may appear to be in public. A paragraph from David Boon's autobiography stuck in my mind (Pip is Boon's wife and Georgina their daughter).

> Pip was Lynette's matron of honour when the Waughs were married and the Boon troop—Georgina was the flower girl at the ceremony—went to Sydney several days before the big event. As per usual in the Waugh household, there were a number of quite important matters which had to be arranged at the last moment. I reckon I made six or seven trips to Bankstown to pick up items for the wedding . . . He's never, ever really late, but it's all down to the last minute. Not perfectly planned, more living on the edge of potential disaster.

Bob Simpson told me that early in Steve's career he organised Steve and Lynette's first trip to Europe: 'We were pretty close and Meg [Simpson's wife] was sort of a mother figure to Lynette at the time. Steve has always been a traveller and always listened to my talk about Italy and places like that and at one stage he was talking about going away and I said, "Do you want me to help you with organising something?" So we set them up with what we thought were the nicer parts of Italy and in many cases recommended hotels to stay at and things to do and we organised to meet up with them half way. I'd sent them south because we were going to end up south. We went north and then we met up on Lake Garda. I gave them the name of the hotel but when we arrived we found it wasn't open. There was one next door so Meg and I went in there and booked our room, as well as one for Steve and Lynette right next to us. We were due to meet them at four o'clock and at quarter to four I said to Meg, "We'd better wander up to see if they're there." Well, I've never seen two young kids so happy to see us. You could see they were nervous, you know, they were thinking, "The hotel's not open, what have we done . . ."'

In his book *Run Out*, Graham Halbish, former CEO of the Cricket Board, who was responsible for getting players to sign their contracts with the Board, wrote: 'Steve Waugh was almost always the last to sign. He was never totally happy with his contract, whether it was the financial terms or the conditions. It was not ill-natured. He just wanted to make the point that he would not sign it just because it was there'.

Bob Simpson says, 'You can easily get the wrong impression about him. I think he's very reserved, he's very shy and I think he's been burnt enough on the way through to be a bit suspicious. He's a great family man, he's very loyal to his players and his team-mates. Yeah, he's got a hard side to him, but then it's probably something that he takes pride in—it's not something he's going to step away from—and that's probably what allowed him to save his career; he's very strong-willed in what he wants to do.'

In an interview for the *Sydney Morning Herald Good Weekend*, Waugh said to John Birmingham:

> I hate it when people treat you as famous—it's one thing that I really can't stand. I'd rather sneak into the background where no one will notice me. The only people I find I can really trust are good friends from school or from cricket when I was young. These days a lot more people want to be your friend and you're not quite sure if they are.

Peter Roebuck, who captained Steve Waugh at Somerset in the late 1980s, described him as 'a steely-wristed fighter, who likes life to be simple, expects it to be tough, and has no time for the shirker'.

In a 1992 interview with Mark Gately quoted in the *Telegraph*, Waugh said of his intensity on the field:

> It's just the way I come across. More than anything it's the way I concentrate, it's not the way I am. I find if I'm out there mucking about and laughing when I'm batting I'll get out. That's the reason I'm like that. Especially with my bowling, I've got to be aggressive. I know if I try and relax and have a bit of a joke when I'm bowling I bowl a heap of garbage. If I try to knock someone's head off I bowl a lot better.

John Faulkner, Labor Senator for NSW, is a regular in the top of the Noble Stand at the Sydney Test. Faulkner is at pains to point out that he is not a cricket tragic: 'I go with my mates,' he told me. 'I've been going with the same guys for 25 or 30 years.' He is interested enough, however, to have gone to the West Indies in 2003 to watch two Tests with his colleague in the Senate, Robert Ray.

Faulkner said of Steve Waugh: 'He strikes me as a person who has some very genuine values about him. He is, I think, a thoughtful person, a person who has, it seems from what I've read and seen, a genuine commitment to people who might be underprivileged or less well off or suffering from disablement or disability or who might be discriminated against in the community. It strikes me that he has some very genuine values in that regard, which I think puts him apart from very many people in the community—it's not just a question of putting him apart from sportsmen, he seems to be able to use his status to shed some light on those sorts of issues of concern. I think that's to his credit. That's the first thing I'd say.

'And the second thing I'd say, and again this is a personal judgement, I think he's a person who has genuine leadership qualities. Not just a bloke who knows to place deep square leg a bit finer or a bit squarer, I'm not talking about that, I'm talking about a person who has leadership qualities in the broader sense. It's unusual to find someone like that'.

I told John Faulkner that I agreed with him, but had a reservation because of the issue of obscene sledging while Waugh was captain and found it hard to reconcile those qualities. 'I think he wanted to win so badly that he probably got carried away with the mental building up of the team and wanting to dominate—the mental disintegration thing,' I said. 'Australia went out and attacked other teams. I think Cricket Australia stopped them doing that last year, but I just find it hard to reconcile that with the qualities you talk about.'

Faulkner replied, 'Yeah, well I'd also say that a person with leadership qualities has a toughness and ruthlessness, you see, it's just part of the makeup. I've never seen a good leader who is weak . . . I think you've got to accept that with these leadership qualities comes a pretty hard edge.'

During the 1993–94 season, Steve Waugh spoke about the baggy green cap: 'It's always been special for me. There's something special about putting that cap on. You feel the difference when you put it on—for me, anyway. The other blokes might think I'm talking rubbish, but that's how I feel. The cap is one of the few sporting symbols recognised worldwide. Not many teams have something special like us.'

He went on to say, 'There's no way you'll catch me wearing a white hat.' Yet strangely, Mark Waugh wore a white hat most of the time. Mark wore his white hat with his collar turned up; Steve wore his baggy green cap and his collar turned down. Was Mark's easy grace a factor in Steve's urgent need to come out on top all the time? Or was it vice versa? Did Steve's need to dominate breed in Mark a need to show it didn't matter? Or both of the above? Or neither?

During 2003, Waugh and his management established a charitable foundation to raise funds in Australia and India for Udayan through an art union publicised on Cricket Australia's Internet site. First prize, if the winner was Australian, was a seven-day holiday in India, including seats at the final of the one-day series in November 2003. If the winner was from India, the prize was seven days in Australia, watching the first Test against India in Brisbane. Steve Waugh's manager, Robert Joske, told me the art union 'Wasn't all that successful as a concept . . . we're talking thousands of dollars, not tens of thousands of dollars. I'd probably try it again but I need to do it with some significant marketing dollars behind it, not just marketed on the net. It needs to be marketed wider than that . . . to make it work properly I probably have to find a print partner, a newspaper partner in India and in Australia.'

I spoke to Shamlu Dudeja again in February 2004.

'As the head of the Calcutta Foundation I had worked with Steve to build what is called Nivedita House, the home for 80 girls on the premises of Udayan. Now that project is over. After that, Calcutta Foundation, by its own, went ahead and raised funds with the Japanese government and we built a primary school at Udayan.

'Steve still loves the project and so do we and when he comes here he brings medicines and so on, but the people who are actually the administrators feel that they do not want more children there, so Steve and I are looking at the possibility of building a similar home for 200 girls, more in collaboration with some other people who are already hands-on in looking after girl children.

'The position has not been finalised yet. I'm hoping that the new home will be in Calcutta because if it is, my involvement will be greater, but if it's in Chennai or somewhere else, then obviously I will not be so involved. And I've been literally sort of waiting, biting my nails. It's been two years since Nivedita House began, and Calcutta Foundation has been doing a lot of work on its own, but the involvement of Steve in any active project has not been there for the past two years.

'So I'm very very hopeful that the new home will be in Calcutta so that I can get a better chance to be hands-on myself, you know, but I think it depends largely on Steve's sponsors . . . if the people who are giving him money choose another venue, maybe Steve will have not much option.

'I just don't know at the moment. I don't think they know at the moment what's happening, so we'll just have to wait.'

On Australia Day, 26 January 2004, Prime Minister John Howard announced that the National Australia Day Council had chosen Steve Waugh as Australian of the Year. Waugh could not be in Canberra for the announcement—he was in Perth playing for NSW in the Pura Cup match against Western Australia.

Australian of the Year award winners are 'invited to use the prestige and increased public profile to highlight and promote their causes and issues through-out the year'. The Council told me that, apart from his support for the Udayan home in India, in Australia Waugh is a patron of Camp Quality, which provides educational and recreational programs for children with cancer, and the Conductive Education Unit for the Spastic Centre of NSW. Due to privacy regulations, the Council could not tell me

Australian of the Year: Steve Waugh talks to Kerry O'Brien of the ABC's '7.30 Report', January 2004. *(Australian Broadcasting Corporation Content Sales)*

who Waugh's nominators were, although they did say he received more than one nomination.

In a recorded video, Waugh said, 'In accepting, I hope the award will help the focus on me to be about more than just cricket. If it is meant as a recognition in some way of the other work I've done in the community in Australia and in India, then I'm grateful indeed. Times like these also offer the chance to encourage in others my belief in doing things with passion, accepting the importance of competition and keeping firm in our desire to improve and succeed'.

Sponsors of the awards included the Commonwealth Bank, the Federal Government, Channel 10, News Limited, Qantas and Holiday Inn. On Australia day, News Limited papers carried a prominent advertisement for the Commonwealth Bank, featuring a smiling Steve Waugh and the caption 'A Leader by Example'. According to Sydney's *Daily Telegraph*, Waugh 'dedicated his Australian of the Year Award to his other passion—community work'.

At the press conference at the Sydney Cricket Ground in November 2003, when Steve Waugh announced his retirement from Test cricket, he said that one of the reasons he was going was that Rosalie had said she would like him to be at home more often. Lynette said, 'Now he can stay at home and I'm going to go out.' Perhaps Lynette and Rosalie would have to wait another year.

NSW did not reach the Pura Cup Final. As the season wound down, the twins ended their careers playing together, as they had so often in the past. Their last first-class match was another Pura Cup encounter with Queensland, played at the SCG in March 2004, spoiled by rain and lost outright after some speculative declarations.

Steve Waugh's last first class innings ended on 9, when he edged medium-pacer Joe Dawes to Martin Love at slip, giving him a career first-class average of 51.95. Mark, who replaced him at the wicket, ripped 72 from 49 balls, for an average of 52.04, a mere .09 of a per cent higher than his brother.

The Waugh twins were looking a little past their use-by date, but they had certainly paid their dues.

ACKNOWLEDGEMENTS

At Allen & Unwin, my thanks to Patrick Gallagher for commissioning the book and for his support, and to Emma Cotter for her counsel and commitment. Emma was helpful in getting the book finished not too long after the contracted date; at a meeting with her and Patrick, after an extended period of research, I said, 'Well, all I have to do now is write it' and Emma said, 'Jack, you've been saying that for two months now.'

Glenn Gibson in Melbourne was most generous with his time and resources in giving me video highlights of Steve Waugh's career.

My thanks to the many people who agreed to speak to me, including Brian Freedman, Ian Chappell, Mike Coward, Neil D'Costa, Shamlu Dudeja, John Faulkner, Angus Fontaine, Peter Horwitz, James Knight, John Laurie, Rob Laurie, Tim May, Bob Simpson, Graeme Smith, Mick Stephenson, Johnny Warren, and several first class umpires.

Peter Roebuck was a source of useful information and advice, not always on cricket: 'If you have to use a lot of adjectives and adverbs, you must be using the wrong nouns and verbs' and 'If you write something and you look at it and you think it's really clever or smart, just cross it out, cross it out'.

Fergus Stothart went to great trouble to reproduce clean images of newspaper clippings, posters, score-sheets, old photos and a variety of other sources for use in the book.

Andrew Walpole at the English Cricket Board, Dale Levin at TWI and Cyrus Irani at the ABC were helpful and cooperative in allowing me to use images from video coverage as illustrations in the book. I also made use of the extensive cricket archive at Getty Images.

Thanks to Greg Ferris of MSV Media Services for help in taking images from video coverage and presenting them as stills.

I made extensive use of the Cricinfo website, with its comprehensive, informative and well-presented statistics, and the websites of Cricket Australia and Cricket NSW were sources of much information. When at a loss for detail, I often turned to Google with success.

Extracts from David Boon's *Under the Southern Cross*, Ian Healy's *Hands and Heals*, James Knight's *Mark Waugh: The Biography* and Steve Waugh's *Tour Diaries* were used with the permission of HarperCollins; extracts from C.L.R. James' *Beyond a Boundary* with the permission of The Random House Group; and from Michael Atherton's; *Opening Up* with the permission of Hodder & Stoughton. Lothian Books gave permission to use extracts from Graham Halbish's *Run Out*.

I am grateful to Kate Bermingham for the loan of her scrapbooks, which covered the years 1986 to 1994 and were a valuable source of press clippings, photos and other interesting odds and ends.

BIBLIOGRAPHY

Atherton, Mike, *Opening Up*, Coronet, London, 2003.

Austin, David, Cash, Damien, Holmesby, Russell, Hutchinson, Garrie and Ross, John, *200 Seasons of Australian Cricket*, Pan Macmillan, Sydney, 1997.

Benaud, John, *Matters of Choice*, Swan Publishing, Dalkeith WA, 1997.

Boon, David, *Under the Southern Cross*, Harper Sports, Sydney, 1996.

Coward, Mike, *Cricket Beyond the Bazaar*, Allen & Unwin, Sydney, 1990.

Coward, Mike, *Caribbean Odyssey*, Simon & Schuster, Sydney, 1991.

Fishman, Roland, *Calypso Cricket*, Margaret Gee, Sydney, 1991.

Gately, Mark, *Waugh Declared*, Ironbark, Sydney, 1992.

Halbish, Graham, *Run Out*, Lothian, Melbourne, 2003.

Harte, Chris, *The History of the Sheffield Shield*, Allen & Unwin, Sydney, 1987.

Healy, Ian, *Hands and Heals*, Harper Sports, Sydney, 2000.

James, C.L.R., *Beyond a Boundary*, Stanley Paul, London, 1963.

Knight, James, *Mark Waugh: The Biography*, Harper Sports, Sydney, 2002.

Meher-Homji, Kersi, *The Waugh Twins*, Kangaroo Press, Sydney, 1998.

Piesse, Ken, *The Taylor Years*, Viking, Melbourne, 1999.

Richards, Viv, *Sir Vivian*, Penguin, Melbourne, 2000.

Stephenson, Mick, *Bankstown Cricket Club 50 Not Out*, Bankstown Cricket Club, Sydney, 2001.

Warne, Shane, *Shane Warne—My Own Story*, Swan Publishing, Dalbeith WA, 1997.

Waugh, Steve, *Steve Waugh's Ashes Diary*, Ironbark, Sydney, 1993.

Waugh, Steve, *Steve Waugh's South African Tour Diary*, Ironbark, Sydney, 1994.

Waugh, Steve, *Steve Waugh's West Indies Tour Diary*, Harper Sports, Sydney, 1995.

Waugh, Steve, *Steve Waugh's World Cup Diary*, Harper Sports, Sydney, 1996.

Waugh, Steve, *Steve Waugh's 1997 Ashes Diary*, Harper Sports, Sydney, 1997.

Waugh, Steve, *No Regrets*, Harper Sports, Sydney, 1999.

Waugh, Steve, *Never Satisfied*, Harper Sports, Sydney, 2000.

Waugh, Steve, *Ashes Diary 2001*, Harper Sports, Sydney, 2001.

Waugh, Steve, *Captain's Diary 2002*, Harper Sports, Sydney, 2002.

Waugh, Steve, *Never Say Die*, Harper Sports, Sydney, 2003.

INDEX

TEST CAREER

To end of 2003–04 season

Source: Cricinfo

Name	Mat	I	NO	Runs	HS	Ave	100	50	Ct	St	Team
AR Border	156	265	44	11174	205	50.56	27	63	156	–	AUS
SR Waugh	168	260	46	10927	200	51.06	32	50	112	–	AUS
SM Gavaskar	125	214	16	10122	236*	51.12	34	45	108	–	IND
SR Tendulkar	111	180	18	9265	241*	57.19	32	37	71	–	IND
BC Lara	104	184	5	9188	375	51.32	24	43	137	–	WI
GA Gooch	118	215	6	8900	333	42.58	20	46	103	–	ENG
Javed Miandad	124	189	21	8832	280*	52.57	23	43	93	1	PAK
IVA Richards	121	182	12	8540	291	50.23	24	45	122	–	WI
AJ Stewart	133	235	21	8463	190	39.54	15	45	263	14	ENG
DI Gower	117	204	18	8231	215	44.25	18	39	74	–	ENG
G Boycott	108	193	23	8114	246*	47.72	22	42	33	–	ENG
GS Sobers	93	160	21	8032	365*	57.78	26	30	109	–	WI
ME Waugh	128	209	17	8029	153*	41.81	20	47	181	–	AUS
MA Atherton	115	212	7	7728	185*	37.69	16	46	83	–	ENG
MC Cowdrey	114	188	15	7624	182	44.06	22	38	120	–	ENG
CG Greenidge	108	185	16	7558	226	44.72	19	34	96	–	WI
MA Taylor	104	186	13	7525	334*	43.49	19	40	157	–	AUS
CH Lloyd	110	175	14	7515	242*	46.67	19	39	90	–	WI
DL Haynes	116	202	25	7487	184	42.29	18	39	65	–	WI
DC Boon	107	190	20	7422	200	43.65	21	32	99	–	AUS
WR Hammond	85	140	16	7249	336*	58.45	22	24	110	–	ENG
G Kirsten	100	174	15	7212	275	45.35	21	33	83	–	RSA
GS Chappell	87	151	19	7110	247*	53.86	24	31	122	–	AUS
DG Bradman	52	80	10	6996	334	99.94	29	13	32	–	AUS
L Hutton	79	138	15	6971	364	56.67	19	33	57	–	ENG

	O	M	R	W	Ave	BBI	5	10	SR	Econ
Bowling	1300.5	332	3445	92	37.44	5–28	3	0	84.8	2.64